CRIMINAL LAW AND CULTURAL DIVERSITY

Criminal Law and Cultural Diversity

EDITED BY
WILL KYMLICKA, CLAES LERNESTEDT,
AND MATT MATRAVERS

OXFORD
UNIVERSITY PRESS

Great Clarendon Street, Oxford, OX2 6DP,
United Kingdom

Oxford University Press is a department of the University of Oxford.
It furthers the University's objective of excellence in research, scholarship,
and education by publishing worldwide. Oxford is a registered trade mark of
Oxford University Press in the UK and in certain other countries

© The several contributors 2014

The moral rights of the authors have been asserted

First Edition published in 2014

Impression: 2

All rights reserved. No part of this publication may be reproduced, stored in
a retrieval system, or transmitted, in any form or by any means, without the
prior permission in writing of Oxford University Press, or as expressly permitted
by law, by licence or under terms agreed with the appropriate reprographics
rights organization. Enquiries concerning reproduction outside the scope of the
above should be sent to the Rights Department, Oxford University Press, at the
address above

You must not circulate this work in any other form
and you must impose this same condition on any acquirer

Published in the United States of America by Oxford University Press
198 Madison Avenue, New York, NY 10016, United States of America

British Library Cataloguing in Publication Data

Data available

Library of Congress Control Number: 2013954062

ISBN 978–0–19–967659–0

Printed and bound by
Clays Ltd, St Ives plc

Links to third party websites are provided by Oxford in good faith and
for information only. Oxford disclaims any responsibility for the materials
contained in any third party website referenced in this work.

Acknowledgments

Special thanks to Jeremy Waldron, who helped convene the workshop at which most of these papers were originally presented, co-sponsored by Columbia University Law School and the Forum for Philosophy and Public Policy at Queen's University in Kingston Canada. We have commissioned a few additional chapters to broaden the focus of the volume. The chapters have been extensively revised and we are grateful to all the authors for their enthusiasm for the project. We would also like to thank Kyle Johannsen for help compiling the manuscript, and Dominic Byatt at Oxford University Press for his support.

Contents

Table of Cases	ix
Notes on Contributors	xi
1. Introduction: Criminal Law and Cultural Diversity *Will Kymlicka, Claes Lernestedt, and Matt Matravers*	1
2. Criminal Law and "Culture" *Claes Lernestedt*	15
3. Community, Culture, and Criminalization *Nicola Lacey*	47
4. Between Denial and Recognition: Criminal Law and Cultural Diversity *Kimmo Nuotio*	67
5. Responsibility, Morality, and Culture *Matt Matravers*	89
6. Cultural Defense and the Criminal Law *Bhikhu Parekh*	104
7. Family Matters: Is There Room for "Culture" in the Courtroom? *Ayelet Shachar*	119
8. The Cultural Defense: Reflections in Light of the Model Penal Code and the Religious Freedom Restoration Act *Kent Greenawalt*	153
9. What Do We Have to Fear from the Cultural Defense? *Alison Dundes Renteln*	177
Index	205

Table of Cases

CANADA

Algonquins of Pikakanagan First Nation v. Children Aid Society of Toronto [2004], (Ontario Superior Court of Justice, Docket: 04-FA-12584)\   131 n28

Basi v. Dhaliwal [1992] B.C.J. No. 1814 (Vancouver Registry No. 91-2065)\   146–9

Halpern v. Canada [2003] O.J. No. 2268 (Ontario Court of Appeals)\   146

Hassan v. Hassan [1976] Carswell Ont 189, 28 R.F.L. 121 (Ontario High Court of Justice, Docket: Toronto)\   144–6, 148, 149

Hyde v. Hyde and Woodmansee [1866], L.R. 1 P.&D. 130 (Ontario Superior Court of Justice\   145–6

J.S.B v. D.L.S [2004] O.J. No. 16, Court File No. 03–66 (Ontario Superior Court of Justice, Docket: Cornwall)\   141–3, 149–50

Multani v. Commission scolaire Marguerite-Bourgeoys [2006] SCC 6 (Supreme Court of Canada)\   190

Pejo C. (Applicant) and Paulo Cesar C.-G. (Respondent) [2004] (Ontario Superior Court of Justice, Docket: Kitchener A 15/03)\   122 n8, 135–7, 139–40, 149

Reference re Same-Sex Marriage [2004] 3 S.C.R. 698 (Supreme Court of Canada)\   146 n55

Van de Perre v. Edwards [2001] S.C.R. 1014 (Supreme Court of Canada)\   135, 137–9, 143, 149–50

FINLAND

Supreme Court of Finland, Decision 2008: 93\   84 n5

SWEDEN

Svea hovrätt, 2000-06-09, B 3101-00   15–18

UNITED KINGDOM

A-G for Jersey v. Holley [2005] UKPC 23\   60 n3
DPP v. Morgan [1976] AC 182\   28 n3
R v. Brown [1994] 1 AC 212\   50 n1
R v. Morgan Smith [2001], 1 AC 146\   60 n3

UNITED STATES

Adoptive Parents v. Baby Girl, 389 S.C. 625 (2013) (U.S. Supreme Court)\	131 n28
Ake v. Oklahoma, 470 U.S. 68 (1985)\	179 n4
*Cheema v. Thompson*1994 U.S. App. LEXIS 24160 (unpublished decision) (1994) \	189–90
Cheema v. Thompson, 67 F.3d 883 (1995); 1994 U.S. App. LEXIS 24160 (1994)\	189–90
City of Borne v. Flores, 521 U.S. 507 (1997)\	174 n61
Employment Division v. Smith, 494 U.S. 872 (1990)\	173 n57, 174 nn58–9
Gonzales v. O Centro EspíritaBeneficenteUniãodo Vegetal, 546 U.S. 418 (2006)\	173 n52
Kwai Fan Mak v. Blodgett, 754 F.Supp. 1490 (W.D.Wash. 1991); 970 F.2d 614 (1992). cert. denied 507 U.S. 951 (1993)\	179 n3
Lambert v. California, 355 U.S. 225 (1957) (U.S. Supreme Court)\	168 n45
Mississippi Band of Choctaw Indians v. Holyfield, 490 US 30 (1989) (U.S. Supreme Court)\	131
People v. Chen 37 Cal. App. 3d 1046 (1974)\	196–8
People v. Wu 235 Cal. App. 3d 614, 286 Cal. Rptr 868 (1991)\	196–7
People v. Wu Order of depublication (Jan. 23, 1992).\	197 n29
Sanderson v. Tryon, 739 P.2d 623 (Utah 1987)\	140–1 n45
Sherbert v. Verner, 374 U.S. 398 (1963)\	173 nn54–5
State v.Kargar, 679 A.2d 81 (Me. 1996)\	28, 29, 38, 160–1, 167, 168, 172
U.S. v. Bauer, 84 F.3d 1549 (9th Cir. 1996)\	179 n5
Wisconsin v. Yoder, 406 U.S. 205 (1972)\	173 n56

Notes on Contributors

Kent Greenawalt is University Professor of Law at Columbia University. His publications include *Conflicts of Law and Morality* (OUP, 1987); *Religious Convictions and Political Choice* (OUP, 1988); *Speech, Crime, and the Uses of Language* (OUP, 1989); *Law and Objectivity* (OUP, 1992); *Fighting Words* (Princeton, 1995); *Private Consciences and Public Reasons* (OUP, 1995); *Statutory Interpretation: Twenty Questions* (Turning Point, 1999); *Does God Belong in Public Schools?* (Princeton, 2005); *Religion and the Constitution I: Free Exercise and Fairness* (Princeton, 2006); *Religion and the Constitution II: Establishment and Fairness* (Princeton, 2008); *Legal Interpretation: Perspectives from Other Disciplines and Private Texts* (OUP, 2010); and *Statutory and Common Law Interpretation* (OUP, 2012).

Will Kymlicka is Canada Research Chair in Political Philosophy at Queen's University, Kingston, Canada. He is the author of *Liberalism, Community, and Culture* (Clarendon, 1989); *Multicultural Citizenship* (OUP, 1995); *Finding Our Way* (OUP, 1998); *Politics in the Vernacular* (OUP, 2001); *Contemporary Political Philosophy* (OUP, 2nd edn. 2002); *Multicultural Odysseys* (2007); and most recently co-author (with Sue Donaldson) of *Zoopolis: A Political Theory of Animal Rights* (OUP, 2011).

Nicola Lacey is School Professor of Law, Gender, and Social Policy at the London School of Economics. Her publications include *State Punishment* (Routledge, 1988); *The Politics of Community* (with Elizabeth Frazer, University of Toronto Press, 1993); *Unspeakable Subjects* (Hart, 1998); *Regulating Law* (ed. with Christine Parker, Colin Scott, and John Braithwaite, OUP, 2004); *A Life of H. L. A Hart: The Nightmare and the Noble Dream* (OUP, 2004); *Women, Crime, and Character* (OUP, 2008); *The Prisoner's Dilemma* (Cambridge, 2008); and *Reconstructing Criminal Law* (with Celia Wells and Oliver Quick, 3rd edn. Cambridge, 2003).

Claes Lernestedt is Professor of Criminal Law at the University of Uppsala, Sweden. His publications include *Swedish Values?* (ed. with Peter Hallberg, Carlsson, 2002); *Criminalization* (Iustus, 2003); *The Principle of Equality before the Law* (NoK, 2005); *The Cathedral* (with Petter Asp and Magnus Ulväng, Iustus, 2009); *There and Back Again: On Individual and Structure in Criminal Law* (Iustus, 2010); *The Crime Victim and Criminal Politics* (ed. with Henrik Tham, Norstedts, 2011); and *Criminal Law's Map and Landscape* (Norstedts, 2013) (all titles in Swedish).

Notes on Contributors

Matt Matravers is Director of the Morrell Centre for Toleration at the University of York, UK. Among his publications are *Punishment and Political Theory* (ed. Hart, 1999); *Justice and Punishment* (OUP, 2000); *Scanlon and Contractualism* (ed. Frank Cass, 2004); *Managing Modernity* (ed. Routledge, 2005); *Responsibility and Justice* (Polity Press, 2007); *Democracy, Equality and Justice* (ed. Routledge, 2010); and *Toleration Re-Examined* (ed. Routledge, 2011).

Kimmo Nuotio is Professor of Criminal Law at the University of Helsinki. His publications include *Criminal Law Theory in Transition* (ed. with Raimo Lahti, Finnish Lawyers Publishing, 1992); *Teko, Vaara, Seuraus* (Act, Danger, Harm; Finnish Lawyers' Association, 1998); *Europe in Search of 'Meaning and Purpose'* (ed. Forum Iuris, 2004); and *Nordic Law: Between Tradition and Dynamism* (ed. with J. Husa and H. Pihlajamäki, Intersentia 2007).

Bhikhu Parekh is Professor Emeritus at the Centre for the Study of Democracy at the University of Westminster, and a member of the House of Lords. He was chair of the Runnymede Commission on the Future of Multi-Ethnic Britain, whose report was published in 2000. His publications include *Rethinking Multiculturalism: Cultural Diversity and Political Theory* (Harvard, 2000); *Europe and the Muslim Question: Does Intercultural Dialogue Make Sense?* (Amsterdam University Press, 2007); and *A New Politics of Identity: Political Principles for an Interdependent World* (Palgrave Macmillan, 2008).

Alison Dundes Renteln is Professor of Political Science, Anthropology, Law, and Public Policy at the University of Southern California. Her publications include *International Human Rights: Universalism versus Relativism* (Sage, 1990, 2013); *Folk Law: Essays on the Theory and Practice of Lex Non Scripta* (ed. with Alan Dundes, Garland, 1994); *The Cultural Defense* (OUP, 2004); *Multicultural Jurisprudence* (ed. with Marie-Claire Foblets, Hart, 2009); and *Cultural Law* (co-authored with James Nafziger and Robert Paterson, Cambridge, 2010).

Ayelet Shachar is Professor of Law, Political Science and Global Affairs at the University of Toronto. Her publications, including *Multicultural Jurisdictions: Cultural Differences and Women's Rights* (Cambridge, 2001); and *The Birthright Lottery: Citizenship and Global Inequality* (Harvard, 2009), have proven influential in public policy and legislative debates. Her work was cited, most recently, by England's Archbishop of Canterbury and the Supreme Court of Canada.

1

Introduction: Criminal Law and Cultural Diversity

Will Kymlicka, Claes Lernestedt, and Matt Matravers

Much has been written about the challenges that ethnic and religious diversity raise for modern nation-states, including issues of religious education, language rights, family law, and the accommodation of cultural practices in dress codes, public holidays, and so on. But there is one particularly important domain of public life where the challenge of cultural diversity has been under-explored: namely, the criminal law.[1] In writings on criminal law issues, hardly any attention has been paid to the challenge of multiculturalism and the extent to which criminal law rules are "cultured" to the advantage of the majority population has barely been touched upon.[2]

Yet, the criminal law is thought of as society's most powerful tool for regulating behavior, and just for that reason we apply particularly strong safeguards to ensure that criminal sanctions are applied in a fair and clear way. If there are good reasons to think that these requirements are not met in the way criminal law currently deals with issues related to "culture" and "cultural differences" then this is surely something that ought to compel the attention of legal theorists and practitioners. This collection aims to begin to redress this neglect.

It is important to distinguish two levels at which cultural diversity and criminal law interact. First, there are questions about *what to criminalize*, including whether cultural minorities should be exempted from criminal laws that

---

[1] This gap is puzzling given that other structural perspectives on the criminal law have been developed, such as gender and class perspectives. See, amongst many others, Lacey 1998; Norrie 2001. It is also surprising given the attention paid in the media to crimes with a supposedly "cultural" dimension (such as "honor killings").

[2] For two recent examples of normative theories regarding personal responsibility in the criminal law with almost no mention of "cultural" aspects, see Tadros 2005; Horder 2004. The result is the same in most textbooks on criminal law: e.g., Ashworth 2009; Simester and Sullivan 2010. The same gap is found in the literature on criminalization: e.g., Joel Feinberg's four-volume work on *The Moral Limits of the Criminal Law* (1984–88), Packer 1968; Schonsheck 1994.

would otherwise prohibit their traditional customs or practices. Second, there are questions about the rules for *ascribing responsibility* and assessing punishment for individuals who have allegedly violated the law, and whether individual members of cultural minorities should be able to invoke what might be labeled "cultural evidence" or a "cultural defense" as a justification, excuse, mitigation, or other means to avoid (full) liability.

These two sets of questions, although connected in several ways, raise quite different issues. Answers to the first question are based fundamentally on forward-looking considerations about the kind of society we want to live in, and the kinds of interactions we wish to permit or prohibit. Answers to the second question, by contrast, have a strong backward-looking element to them; we want our rules for judging responsibility and punishment to track the actual blameworthiness of the specific individual being prosecuted for a specific action in the past.

Questions of criminalization, and of the limits of the criminal law, have seen something of a revival in recent years (Schonsheck 1994; Husak 2008; Duff et al. 2010, 2011; Simester and von Hirsch 2011), but the main discussions of potential exemptions for minorities from criminal law provisions have been in political philosophy (Kymlicka 1995a, 1995b; Barry 2001; Parekh 2006). Although this literature boasts a great deal of disagreement, there is a broad consensus—one shared by politicians and most citizens—that forward-looking considerations (for example, of gender equality; the interests of children; public health and safety) often provide valid reasons for criminalizing behavior that has been traditional in one or more of the subgroups living in a country (including the majority).

There are of course competing values that must be borne in mind, such as religious freedom and tolerance, and one area of profound disagreement amongst both philosophers and the public concerns when exemptions to public regulation should be given to particular groups. For example, while there are valid forward-looking reasons for criminalizing the possession of narcotics, the fact that some indigenous American groups traditionally use peyote in their religious ceremonies may provide a valid reason to exempt them from this particular legal requirement.[3] However, the presence of debates over exemptions does not disprove the point: it is inevitable that the criminal law in modern multiethnic societies, in pursuit of legitimate forward-looking goals, will prohibit some activities that have been a part of the practices of some groups.

Although the essays in this collection touch on these issues, the main focus is on the second set of questions. These concern the legal assessment of individual blameworthiness. When someone commits an act prohibited in a

---

[3] This is acknowledged by the American Indian Religious Freedom Act, Public Law No. 95-341, 92 Stat. 469 (Aug. 11, 1978).

criminal statute, he or she may be punished for it *if and only if* a long list of additional requirements is met. The ground of such requirements is the idea of individual *blameworthiness*, meant to *justify* the infliction of punishment: the specific individual must be deemed to *deserve* punishment.[4]

The importance of blame to our judgments in the criminal law—and not only there—is immediately apparent if one considers our different reactions to some examples. Think of those who commit otherwise blameworthy acts when sleepwalking or hypnotized. In these cases, blame does not attach to the person because the person's actions cannot be traced back in the right kind of way to his or her agency. In other cases, agency is present, but the agent is not blameworthy because his or her action was justified (as in self-defense). In still others, our judgments of blame are mitigated as when we find out that an offender acted out of character having been subject to stress (say, losing his job). In all these cases, our judgments of the blameworthiness of the agent are responsive to what we think the agent deserves, if anything, by way of punishment. In some cases, we may think the agent has a full or partial defense; in others merely a plea for mitigation (or, of course, our judgments of blameworthiness can be exacerbated by so-called "aggravating" factors).

Precisely how defenses (such as justifications and excuses) work is a complicated—and contentious—area in both legal and moral philosophy and it is into this controversial area that the idea of "cultural evidence" or "cultural defenses" enters. This is because according to some scholars, cultural or religious factors are amongst the range of considerations capable of influencing the individual's thoughts and behavior in ways that render the individual less legally blameworthy. For this reason, the argument continues, what might be labeled as "cultural evidence" may be essential in improving our backward-looking judgments of individual blameworthiness and desert; indeed, taking cultural evidence into account might in some cases even be necessary if the practice of punishing individuals is to be legitimate and equitable. According to proponents of the so-called "cultural defense," the use of cultural evidence when judging individual blameworthiness is a natural application or extension of the logic of existing criminal law doctrines regarding defenses, and of the logic of current philosophical theories of responsibility and agency.[5]

---

[4] It is worth noting that this claim applies more widely than merely to what are normally called "retributivist" theories of punishment. For example, sophisticated (indirect, rule, or side-constrained) consequentialists will also endorse the claim that the offender must deserve punishment (in light of his or her offending act) albeit that the ultimate justification of the system of punishment lies in its good consequences.

[5] This naturally raises the question of how we determine what counts as "cultural." In our view, there is little to be gained by trying to come up with a definition of "culture." This has proven to be a hopeless task in many disciplines. Even sophisticated attempts to define the concept of culture quickly prove unwieldy. Speaking of a book by Clyde Kluckhorn, Clifford Geertz noted:

> In some twenty-seven pages of his chapter on the concept, Kluckhorn managed to define culture in turn as: (1) "the total way of life of a people"; (2) "the social legacy the individual

It is this second question that is explored in depth in this volume, since it raises a number of complex questions at the boundaries of criminal law and political philosophy. These questions are neither new to criminal law nor unique to "multiculturalism," but they are becoming increasingly urgent, and remain surprisingly under-studied.[6] In the rest of this Introduction, we provide some context for the discussion and an overview of the contributions made by each of the authors.

Above it was noted that the proponents of a "cultural defense" hold that cultural or religious norms are amongst those factors that influence individuals' thoughts and actions in ways that may render them less blameworthy in the relevant legal sense. It is important that there are two steps in this argument. First, that cultural or religious norms are influential in people's actions. Second, that this influence is, or ought to be, such as to render the person less legally blameworthy. It is important to note the two steps in order to avoid what the legal philosopher Stephen Morse (Morse 2000: 130) calls the "fundamental psycholegal error," which is to presume that "if science or common sense identifies a cause for human action... then the conduct is necessarily excused." That is, unless one is committed to a very odd account of human action, the claim that a person's cultural or religious background will influence

---

acquires from his group"; (3) "a way of thinking, feeling, and believing"; (4) "an abstraction from behavior"; (5) a theory on the part of the anthropologist about the way in which a group of people in fact behave; (6) a "store-house of pooled learning"; (7) "a set of standardized orientations to recurrent problems"; (8) "learned behavior"; (9) a mechanism for the normative regulation of behavior; (10) "a set of techniques for adjusting both to the external environment and to other men"; (11) "a precipitate of history"; and turning, perhaps in desperation, to similes, as a map, as a sieve, as a matrix. (Geertz 1973: 4–5)

There is growing consensus that we should focus less on what culture *is*, and focus instead on what work the concept of culture *does* in particular contexts. In the context of "cultural defenses" in criminal law, we argue, appeals to culture are intended and used primarily to inform our conception of the responsible individual, and to complicate our judgments about blameworthiness and desert. We discuss below several different ways in which cultural factors might be thought to do work in this regard. We can make progress in thinking through these specific ways that appeals to culture work in criminal law without having resolved the perennial debate about what defines "culture" or "a culture."

[6] For a representative sample of works on this topic, see Brelvi 1996–97; Coleman 1996; Lyman 1986; Macklem and Gardner 2001; Maguigan 1995; Okin 1999; Phillips 2003; Renteln 1993; Sing 1998–99; Waldron 2002; Volpp 1994, 1996, 2000; Wanderer and Connors 1999; and above all, the comprehensive overviews in Renteln 2004; and Foblets and Renteln 2009. However, as we discuss below, with a few notable exceptions, this literature tends to either apply traditional criminal law perspectives without attending to the challenges raised by philosophical discussions of multiculturalism, or conversely applies philosophical theories of multiculturalism without attending to the specificities of the criminal law. Anthony Connolly's recent book, *Cultural Difference on Trial: The Nature and Limits of Judicial Understanding* (2010) uses the courtroom to explore a different philosophical issue of cultural difference. He is interested in the very possibility of cross-cultural understanding, using courtroom procedures as a test case. This is an interesting question in the philosophy of mind and language—the framework of his analysis—but does not directly address the issue of the relevance of cultural diversity for how criminal law and political philosophy conceive of responsibility and blameworthiness.

his or her action is obviously right. But, this does not necessarily mean that those actions are any less his or hers; on the orthodox picture of the criminal law, causes are not excuses just like that.

The "cultural defense," then, can enter into this debate in one of two ways. Proponents can try to show that admitting such a defense is consistent with other defenses in the criminal law or a natural extension of the reasoning that underpins those existing defenses. Or, they can argue that the significance of cultural or religious factors in people's lives is such as to force us to rethink the criminal law more radically. In both cases, many orthodox criminal law theorists are skeptical. For some, the "cultural defense"—like proposed defenses based on rotten social background or battered-woman syndrome—commit the error of thinking that causes—and particularly unusual causes—excuse. For others, the allowing of cultural factors into the courts—or what they often describe as "cultural relativism"—would breach principles of equality under the law and undermine the picture and rhetoric of the law as neutral, non-political, "one law for all," etc.; ideas that preserve the self-image and legitimize law.

One task of this volume, therefore, is to encourage criminal law scholars to reflect upon where, and how, information that could be called "cultural" should be deemed relevant, especially in the application of the rules regarding personal responsibility and blameworthiness. Here some of the debates in contemporary political philosophy about the social construction of the individual, the nature of the "self," and the relations between individuals, groups, and society (for example, the liberal/communitarian debate as well as the general debate on "multicultural" questions) can help in opening up the debate.

However, the target of the essays is not just those working in criminal law and legal theory. As noted above, much of the literature on what ought or ought not be criminalized and which groups, if any, ought to be granted exemptions from some of the demands of the law, has been written by political philosophers working on issues of multiculturalism. Many such theorists have looked at debates around cultural defenses as a test case for the "limits" or "paradoxes" of multiculturalism.[7] However, most of these scholars focus primarily on the first societal level mentioned above; i.e., on decisions about what to criminalize, and why it is appropriate for countries to maintain criminal prohibitions on certain conduct even if these prohibitions contradict the cultural practices of minority groups. Less has been written on the second individual level; i.e.,

---

[7] The specificity of the criminal law context is rarely discussed in these philosophical works. In effect, political theorists of multiculturalism, when they discuss the issue at all, simply pick examples of the cultural defense, take them out of their criminal law context, and use them as fodder for more general arguments about cultural relativism, say, or the conflict between multiculturalism and gender equality. The discussion of cultural defenses in Okin 1999 is a paradigm instance of this.

about how the courts should assess personal blameworthiness. In our view, political philosophers need to contemplate the individual level more carefully, examining the extent to which "culture" should be seen as having the possibility of affecting a specific person's behavior, perception, etc., to such an extent that he or she should be deemed less blameworthy. Moreover, this needs to be done with knowledge of the basic structures of the criminal law, in relation to the other factors that are accepted as reducing blameworthiness. Some philosophers seem prepared to sacrifice fundamental criminal law principles in cultural cases, eliminating scope for defendants to raise issues of desert and blameworthiness. Exposure to general debates within the criminal law would help ensure that the philosophical literature on these topics is cognizant of the special issues raised when applying criminal law at the individual level.

In short, criminal law scholars working in this area could benefit from exposure to philosophical debates about the relationship between culture, agency, and responsibility, and conversely philosophers could benefit from exposure to criminal law doctrines regarding blame, excuses, defenses, and so on. At the heart of these debates is the political, philosophical, and legal construction of the responsible, blameworthy individual, especially concerning that part of the individual that could be referred to as his or her "culture." It is in order to make progress on these issues that we have brought together both groups of scholars in a common dialogue.[8]

As noted above, we start from the premise that once we properly distinguish forward-looking issues of criminalization from (primarily) backward-looking issues of assessing blameworthiness, there is a prima facie case for allowing various kinds of cultural evidence, or if you prefer, for allowing various kinds of "cultural defenses." Both the logic of existing criminal law doctrines of defenses, and the logic of current philosophical theories of responsibility and agency, push us in this direction. But this is just the starting point of our project, and the chapters in this volume offer a number of caveats and complications. In particular, some of our authors question whether rules of responsibility should be seen as entirely or primarily backward-looking, while others question whether (or how) cultural evidence really serves the goal of backward-looking judgments of individual blameworthiness.

To take the first issue, some authors argue that rules of responsibility should not be purely "backward-looking," but are inevitably (and appropriately) designed in light of the broader forward-looking goals of the criminal law as a whole. There are several ways in which forward-looking considerations may

[8] Our main goal is to discuss how these issues *ought* to be resolved, and not simply to catalogue how they actually *have* been tackled in various countries. Nevertheless, we have deliberately included participants from different countries and legal traditions, since different legal systems have different views—and different procedures—regarding the assessment of guilt and desert. We hope to learn from these national and tradition-related specificities, while simultaneously seeking a level of generality that can inform debates across a broad range of contexts.

shape our rules of responsibility: (a) the system of criminal law can only function if it has a level of public legitimacy, and this requires that assessments of individual guilt/punishment, as much as decisions about what to criminalize in the first place, be in line with "common sense"; (b) just as it appropriate for the state to use the power of criminalization to change traditional assumptions and behavior (e.g., by prohibiting marital rape), so it is appropriate for the state to use control over the rules of responsibility to change traditional assumptions about what counts as a "reasonable" effort to comply with the law (e.g., by stipulating that it is not enough that a man believed that a woman consented to sex—he actually has to try to find out); (c) the criminal law is intended to provide a "third force" standing above all of the subgroups in a society as the basis for mutual confidence when interacting with strangers, and this function is jeopardized if people believe that some of the strangers with whom they interact will not in fact be held accountable for prima facie violations of criminal prohibitions.

It is often assumed that once we incorporate these forward-looking considerations, the scope for cultural evidence/defense is likely to diminish, as compared to a purely backward-looking theory of responsibility. But in principle one could imagine forward-looking arguments *in favor* of broadening the scope for cultural evidence. For example, one could argue that it will increase the sense of legitimacy of the criminal law within minority communities, and hence help stabilize the system generally, or that it will provide an avenue for beneficial forms of cross-cultural learning and understanding, reducing overall levels of prejudice and distrust in society.

Assuming that such forward-looking considerations are indeed appropriate to take into account when designing rules of responsibility—and assuming we have some way of predicting the impact of different rules on these forward-looking goals—they raise the obvious question: how do we balance or integrate these forward-looking justifications with backward-looking considerations of individual blameworthiness? Which forms of cultural evidence/defense are most likely to be subversive of these legitimate forward-looking goals, and why? Is there some bedrock judgment of backward-looking blameworthiness—some (perhaps minimal) notion of a "fair opportunity to comply"—that cannot be sacrificed in the name of forward-looking goals?

Regarding the second issue, our authors explore a number of different ways in which cultural evidence might be relevant for backward-looking judgments of responsibility. The starting assumption, as we noted above, is that introducing cultural evidence can improve our judgments about an individual defendant's blameworthiness, and might indeed be necessary to give credibility to the idea of punishing according to blameworthiness. But how exactly do the facts of cultural socialization relate to judgments of individual responsibility? One story, implicit in much of the existing literature, goes like this: someone who is deeply "embedded" in a minority culture is likely to feel certain "cultural imperatives" to act in a certain way, reducing their capacity to control their behavior so as to comply with the law of the larger society, and the existence of this imperative justifies, excuses, or mitigates the crime. An equally common response to this story is to say that it overstates the way in which people are "embedded" in cultures, and underestimates the way in which so-called "imperatives" are continuously being challenged from within and without the group. For such critics, the facts of cultural socialization do not compromise the basic capacity of individuals to understand themselves as making choices for which they can rightly be held responsible, and hence do not disprove that someone had a "fair opportunity to comply" with the law.

This is the familiar pattern of debate found in much of the existing literature. But the chapters in our volume reveal a wealth of examples that do not fit this familiar pattern, including:

(1) Ignorance of the law: newcomers may not realize that X is criminalized in their new country, or may not realize that a particular action would be interpreted as a case of X, since it has a different meaning to them.

(2) Mistake of fact: other kinds of mistaken (or alternative) perceptions of reality due to the fact that behavior or situation X has a different social meaning for someone from a minority culture than it has for someone from the majority culture.

(3) Duress: a woman from a traditional culture may not feel able to question her husband's or father's command to engage in a criminal activity, due to a fear of ostracism or violence.

(4) Provocation: a culturally specific insult provokes someone to commit a criminal activity, emotionally overriding their rational self-control.

(5) Conscientious objection: despite having full rational self-control, and full knowledge of the law, and not being subject to duress, an individual belonging to a certain group nonetheless consciously and deliberately acts in a way prescribed by the group's cultural tradition although prohibited by the criminal law, on the grounds that they believe themselves to be duty-bound to follow the authority of their cultural tradition (or, without feeling strongly "duty-bound" by it, they see strong and good reasons for following what is considered a valuable tradition).

Many of the real-world cases of a "cultural defense" fall into one or more of these categories, none of which exactly fits the familiar "cultural imperative" story. (In fact, the cultural imperative story seems to be a conflation of the third or fourth with the fifth: the third and fourth involve reduced capacity to override an inherited cultural script, without necessarily any endorsement of the normative authority of that script; the fifth involves a conscientious endorsement of the cultural script as a normative imperative, but not necessarily any reduced capacity.)

Once we recognize the breadth of cases we are dealing with—and no doubt there are yet further types of cases that can and should be distinguished—it seems unlikely that we will find any simple generalization about the connection between cultural socialization and judgments of individual responsibility. Rather than very general debates about whether people are culturally "embedded" or subject to cultural "imperatives," we instead face more discrete debates about how facts of culture-related ignorance, mistake, duress, provocation, conscience, and so on bear on judgments of responsibility and blameworthiness. We need to ask, in each of these cases, how we decide whether individuals had a "fair opportunity to comply," and how these cases relate to cases of ignorance, mistake, duress, provocation, or conscience that are not defined as "cultural"—i.e., that are not the result of being socialized in a distinct ethnocultural group. For which of these cases is there something special about "culture" as a source of ignorance, mistake, duress, provocation, and conscience that distinguishes it from other sources, and is a separate formal "cultural defense" needed to capture this special character?

In this respect, talk of "*the* cultural defense" (as opposed to "*a* cultural defense," or simply "cultural evidence") is misleading, suggesting as it does that we already have some clear and well-defined idea of what such a defense is, which one must either reject or accept. Instead, there are a range of ways in which cultural evidence might be invoked as part of a defense, each involving different putative links between facts of enculturation and judgments of responsibility and blameworthiness.

OUTLINE OF THE VOLUME

This is the complex territory that we aim to map and evaluate in the volume, bringing together scholars of both criminal law and political philosophy (as well as scholars from both the Anglo-American and continental legal traditions). Each of the chapters addresses a different dimension of the issue, and from a range of perspectives, with varying degrees of sympathy or skepticism regarding cultural defenses. But the volume is united by the three core issues outlined above: (i) the distinction between societal decisions about criminalization and individual assessments of blameworthiness; (ii) the mix of forward- and backward-looking goals in the rules of responsibility; and (iii) the diverse ways cultural socialization can be invoked to inform judgments of individual responsibility.

Chapter 2, by Claes Lernestedt, focuses on the second and third issues. He starts from the idea that both forward- and backward-looking considerations operate within the criminal law, and that while none should fully trump the other, backward-looking considerations must have considerable weight in the rules for ascribing responsibility. Lernestedt then situates "cultural defense" and "cultural evidence" within this general criminal law framework. In some situations, Lernestedt argues, cultural evidence is required in order for defendants to be treated equally before the law in its most narrow, demanding sense, whereas in other situations the taking into account of cultural factors amounts to preferential treatment. Thus, once we situate issues of cultural evidence within this larger criminal law framework, it becomes clear that the common "either–or" approach to cultural evidence is unsustainable, and that we need more refined criteria or principles for evaluating what effects "cultural" evidence should have. Lernestedt argues that a separate, formal "cultural defense" is a bad idea: this could easily convey the impression that the "cultural" is something additional or "extra." Lernestedt suggests instead that, at least as a long-term goal, "cultural" considerations would not be considered as a separate or exceptional issue, but would be naturally integrated into criminal law's image of the responsible person.

Nicola Lacey also argues that the criminal law combines forward- and backward-looking considerations, but she is less optimistic about combining these without remainder. Lacey considers the argument that the inclusion of cultural evidence in determining blameworthiness is a natural extension of how the criminal law already treats other mitigating factors that affect a person's ability to comply with the law. Lacey explores this claim in depth, focusing in particular on how cultural influences compare with other kinds of influences such as being raised in a broken family or in a poor neighborhood where violence and criminality are common. She argues that while one can indeed make a good philosophical argument why, for example, the victims of poor upbringing should be seen as less blameworthy, there are also good reasons why the criminal law system does not, and should not, view poor upbringing as a mitigating factor. For Lacey, the ends of the criminal law—in particular, the goal of steering the population's behavior—override philosophical arguments about individual blameworthiness and thus there may be only limited room for cultural defenses. Moreover, Lacey argues, the criminal law is "in the business of applying standards" and these standards are, in liberal democracies, general.

The theme of general standards that bind persons as legal citizens is picked up by Kimmo Nuotio. Nuotio locates his argument more on the terrain of political philosophy. For Nuotio, philosophers such as Taylor, Habermas, and Rawls have developed broad theories of how the law in general can operate in a pluralistic society. However, these multicultural theories need to be refined or adapted to the particular aims, demands, and restrictions of criminal law. Modern criminal law requires strong presuppositions of legal personhood; that is, it treats people as responsible and rational individual agents. These presuppositions differ from those of traditional communities, but are now essentially irreversible. The legitimacy of modern law requires people to think of themselves as "citizens" bound together in a political project, and not just as individuals who belong to pre-political cultural groups. Like Lacey, then, Nuotio concludes that issues of legal responsibility cannot be reduced to "mere moral blameworthiness," and that the state has a legitimate interest in preserving the conditions that sustain the mutual recognition of people as *citizens*.

Matt Matravers, too, focuses on the practice of holding citizens responsible, but argues that the conception of responsibility at play in the context of criminal law is different from our everyday conceptions. He argues that responsibility in the criminal law context is best understood in terms of a doctrine of *answerability*, in which both the defendant and the society can be held to account. For someone to be held answerable for a committed act certain conditions must be met. Specifically, the person must be capable of responding to, and acting on, reasons. Equally, certain conditions must be fulfilled for a specific society to have a right to hold him or her answerable. Specifically, the society must have (moral) standing. Matravers considers both of these sets of conditions and the ways in which many accounts of the cultural defense interact with them. He argues that these accounts identify real issues that need to be addressed, but that the significant influence of culture on individuals in most cases neither undermines the responsibility of the agent nor the standing of the state to hold that agent to account for his or her (criminal) actions.

If Lacey, Nuotio, and Matravers can be thought of as skeptical about the reach of the cultural defense each sees the importance of cultural evidence. This is something shared with Bhikhu Parekh and Ayelet Shachar.

For Parekh, issues of a cultural defense must be situated within a broader theory about how conflicts of value between minorities and the majority society should be dealt with. Parekh highlights the significance of cultural meanings across the criminal law: in defining its scope; the definition of crimes; the gradations of crime seriousness and penalty severity; the determination of individual responsibility; the range of mitigating factors and defenses accepted; and in its administration. Given this, he thinks that "there is on balance a good case for finding a place" for a partial cultural defense. However, such a defense would need to be constrained and, as noted above, understood in the context of conflicts of value between majorities and minorities. Such disputes, Parekh argues, must be addressed through extensive discussion and argument, rather than the unilateral or coercive imposition of one side's values on the other. Given this, creating legal space for a cultural defense can serve both forward- and backward-looking goals. That is, the use of a cultural defense would help track and assess personal blameworthiness more correctly, but Parekh insists it would also provide a useful forum for intercultural, future-oriented learning.

If we are to use the cultural defense, or admit cultural evidence in the court, we must know *how* to do so. Critics of the cultural defense often argue that attempting to assess the significance (or even the content) of someone's "culture" is beyond the capacity of courts, and will inevitably lead to arbitrary results. Shachar argues that we can shed light on this concern by examining a closely related field of law: namely, family law. As she shows, there has been considerable experience in the use of "cultural" evidence in family law court cases, including in assessments of the behavior of parents. Shachar advocates what she calls a "culture-demystifying" approach that permits the court to treat cultural factors as one of many relevant elements in its adjudications. This she contrasts with two "absolutist" alternatives: a "culture-blindness" approach that permits no formal place for cultural considerations, and a "culture-override" approach in which culture is treated as determinative. Shachar's preferred demystifying approach might be thought too ad hoc or to allow too much discretion to courts. However, through a close examination of cases, Shachar identifies a number of safeguards and principles that emerge from the family law context that might be applicable to the context of criminal law.

These practical, legal questions are picked up by Kent Greenawalt. Greenawalt notes that decisions about whether to accept cultural evidence have, to date, primarily been left to the discretion of individual judges, resulting in considerable unevenness, if not arbitrariness, across cases. On the legislative level, such issues have rarely been touched upon. In his chapter, Greenawalt examines the most ambitious attempt in the United States to draft a systematic criminal code: the influential Model Penal Code, and its commentaries. Greenawalt examines what mention is made of, and what room might exist for, cultural factors within the Code. In general, his analysis is that the Code pays little attention to cultural factors. However, Greenawalt's argument is that there is room for such factors; the question is how best to accommodate them. Greenawalt considers both the idea of a general privilege for cultural practice along the lines of the Religious Freedom Restoration Act and the clarification and expansion of existing defenses. His conclusion is that the latter offers "the more promising strategy" as it does not require—as would a general cultural defense—judges to decide between those cultural factors that count and those that do not and those that are "really" part of the culture (or the defendant's cultural identity) and those that are not.

In the concluding chapter, Alison Dundes Renteln asks why legal and political theorists have been so cautious about (what she refers to as) the cultural defense. She notes that critics of the cultural defense have often argued that while it might help improve our backward-looking judgments of personal responsibility, it would have serious if not catastrophic consequences for the future operation of the legal system. Renteln distinguishes a number of different versions of this argument—identifying a set of perverse effects that the cultural defense might generate, from concerns about reducing the deterrent effect of criminalization on potential transgressors in minority communities to reducing the sense of legitimacy of the legal system as a whole amongst members of the dominant group. In response to each of these concerns, Renteln examines what evidence, if any, exists to support these speculations, and concludes that fear of the consequences is largely overblown. In the absence of credible evidence for forward-looking harms, she argues, there are "compelling principled grounds" for the adoption of a cultural defense for its backward-looking benefits. Such a policy could then be reviewed if its implementation gave grounds for belief that it had demonstrable ill-effects on the behavior of individuals.

Together these essays explore why cultural diversity raises distinctive challenges in the criminal law context, not found in other domains of the multiculturalism debate, while also exploring how this particular context raises fundamental issues of agency and responsibility that are at the heart of broader debates in political philosophy. Much of course remains to be done in this area. What these essays demonstrate is that progress on these issues will require political philosophers to better understand the specificity of criminal law, and for criminal law scholars to better understand philosophical debates on culture and agency.

REFERENCES

Ashworth, Andrew. 2009. *Principles of Criminal Law* (New York: Oxford University Press).

Barry, Brian. 2001. *Culture and Equality: An Egalitarian Critique of Multiculturalism* (Cambridge, MA: Polity Press).

Brelvi, Farah Sultana. 1996–97. "'News of the Weird': Specious Normativity and the Problem of the Cultural Defense," *Columbia Human Rights Law Review* 28: 657–683.

Coleman, Doriane Lambelet. 1996. "Individualizing Justice through Multiculturalism: The Liberal's Dilemma," *Columbia Law Review* 96: 1093–1167.

Connolly, Anthony. 2010. *Cultural Difference on Trial: The Nature and Limits of Judicial Understanding* (Burlington: Ashgate Publishing).

Duff, R. A., Lindsay Farmer, S. E. Marshall, Massimo Renzo, and Victor Tadros, eds. 2010. *The Boundaries of the Criminal Law* (Oxford: Oxford University Press).

Duff, R. A., Lindsay Farmer, S. E. Marshall, Massimo Renzo, and Victor Tadros, eds. 2011. *The Structures of the Criminal Law* (Oxford: Oxford University Press).

Feinberg, Joel. 1984–88. *The Moral Limits of the Criminal Law*, 4 vols. (New York: Oxford University Press).

Foblets, Marie-Claire and Alison Dundes Renteln, eds. 2009. *Multicultural Jurisprudence: Comparative Perspectives on the Cultural Defence* (Oxford: Hart Publishing).

Geertz, Clifford. 1973. *The Interpretation of Cultures* (New York: Basic Books).

Horder, Jeremy. 2004. *Excusing Crime* (Oxford: Oxford University Press).

Husak, D. 2008. *Overcriminalization: The Limits of the Criminal Law* (New York: Oxford University Press).

Kymlicka, Will. 1995a. *Multicultural Citizenship: A Liberal Theory of Minority Rights* (Oxford: Oxford University Press).

Kymlicka, Will, ed. 1995b. *The Rights of Minority Cultures* (Oxford: Oxford University Press).

Lacey, Nicola. 1998. *Unspeakable Subjects: Feminist Essays in Legal and Social Theory* (Oxford: Hart Publishing).

Lyman, John C. 1986. "Cultural Defense: Viable Doctrine or Wishful Thinking?," *Criminal Justice Journal* 9: 87–117.

Macklem, Timothy and John Gardner. 2001. "Provocation and Pluralism," *Modern Law Review* 64: 815–830.

Maguigan, Holly. 1995. "Cultural Evidence and Male Violence: Are Feminist and Multiculturalist Reformers on a Collision Course in Criminal Courts?," *New York University Law Review* 70: 36–99.

Morse, S. J. 2000. "Deprivation and Desert," in *From Social Justice to Criminal Justice: Poverty and the Administration of Criminal Law*, ed. W. C. Heffernan and J. Kleinig (Oxford: Oxford University Press), 114–160.

Norrie, Alan. 2001. *Punishment, Responsibility, and Justice* (Oxford: Oxford University Press).

Okin, Susan. 1999. *Is Multiculturalism Bad for Women?* (Princeton: Princeton University Press).

Packer, Herbert. 1968. *The Limits of the Criminal Sanction* (Stanford: Stanford University Press).

Parekh, B. 2006. *Rethinking Multiculturalism* (Basingstoke: Palgrave Macmillan).

Phillips, Anne. 2003. "When Culture Means Gender: Issues of Cultural Defence in the English Courts," *Modern Law Review* 66: 510–531.

Renteln, Alison Dundes. 1993. "A Justification of the Cultural Defense as Partial Excuse," *Southern California Review of Law and Women Studies* 7: 437–526.

Renteln, Alison Dundes. 2004. *The Cultural Defense* (New York: Oxford University Press).

Schonsheck, J. 1994. *On Criminalization: An Essay in the Philosophy of the Criminal Law* (Dordrecht: Kluwer Academic Publishers).

Simester, A. P. and G. R. Sullivan. 2010. *Criminal Law: Theory and Doctrine* (Oxford: Hart Publishing).

Simester, A. P. and A. von Hirsch. 2011. *Crimes, Harms and Wrongs: On the Principles of Criminalisation* (Oxford: Hart Publishing).

Sing, James J. 1998–99. "Culture as Sameness: Toward a Synthetic View of Provocation and Culture in Criminal Law," *Yale Law Review* 108: 1845–1884.

Tadros, Victor. 2005. *Criminal Responsibility* (Oxford: Oxford University Press).

Volpp, Leti. 1994. "(Mis)identifying Culture: Asian Women and the 'Cultural Defense,'" *Harvard Women's Law Journal* 17: 57–101.

Volpp, Leti. 1996. "Talking 'Culture': Gender, Race, Nation, and the Politics of Multiculturalism," *Columbia Law Review* 96: 1573–1617.

Volpp, Leti. 2000. "Blaming Culture for Bad Behavior," *Yale Journal for Law and the Humanities* 12: 89–116.

Waldron, Jeremy. 2002. "One Law For All? The Logic of Cultural Accomodation," *Washington & Lee Law Review* 59: 3–34.

Wanderer, Nancy A. and Catherine R. Connors. 1999. "Kargar and the Existing Framework for a Cultural Defense," *Buffalo Law Review* 47: 829–873.

2

Criminal Law and "Culture"

Claes Lernestedt*

PROLOGUE

In a Swedish court case the adults in a newly arrived Congolese family became convinced that the children were possessed by evil spirits, and that these evil spirits had to be exorcized: if not, the spirits would harm adults as well as children. The adults performed a home-made exorcism with a tragic end: one child was choked to death with a bible.

In the first-instance murder trial the reason for the adults' act was clear, contested by neither prosecutor nor court: the (experienced) pressing need to get rid of the spirits. An anthropologist testified as an expert witness, stating that among people in the place from which the defendants came the belief in evil spirits, and in their power to harm, is firm. How did the actors in the Swedish trial (court, prosecutor, defense attorneys) react "legally" to this reason, this motive?

The reaction was more or less silence. This was wrong: it is clear that the motive—the experienced need to get rid of the harmful spirits—according to general rules in Swedish criminal law could have been, and therefore *ex officio* should have been, interpreted as if the defendants were claiming that a defense was applicable: either self-defense or necessity.

Now you might object that there *are* no evil spirits (at least not in tidy Sweden), and no situation of self-defense, necessity, or whatever the equivalent is called in your jurisdiction. But even if we grant ourselves the right to authoritatively decide that there are no spirits (not in Sweden, at least not in these children, at least not at that particular time, etc.), the defendants still believed them to be there. And according to the general doctrine of "putative justification" (e.g., putative self-defense), a mistaken belief about facts can

---

* For valuable comments I am indebted to Jeremy Waldron and Will Kymlicka.

ground a defense, if the situation as the defendants experienced it would have made a "real" defense applicable.

This, though, was not discussed in court. In the written verdict it seems that no one—not prosecutor, not court, not defense attorneys—even thought about treating the motive as a suggested defense that had to be dealt with "legally": it is as if all actors, except the defendants, were in something like a shared bubble of thought. My guess is, though, that the legal actors *were* aware of something problematic. The court stated:

> The court accepts that the background and reason for the defendants' actions is their belief in witches and evil spirits. The evaluation of their actions... must, though, be done in accordance with the Swedish legal system.

How should we interpret this statement, trying—my guess again—to explain, justify, what I call the legal silence? And how should we explain the silence itself? One possible explanation might be that the court wanted to escape problems of a more technical kind. If it had recognized the defendants' experienced need to get rid of the imagined spirits as something falling under an existing defense, and thus somehow had brought the spirits into the system, then further problems would have surfaced, in the examination of the additional requirements for the defense in question to be successful. Let us see what discussions would have needed to take place.

One issue would be to decide whether the defendants' actions were *proportionate* or not to the threat or attack: how much violence is appropriate to ward off an evil spirit presumably from Congo? This is a kind of judgment for which the Swedish court probably would not want to be asked.

Another issue would concern the *reasonableness* of the defendants' (mistaken) interpretation of the situation. We encounter, then, the familiar problems related to the reasonable person (and his or her relatives in other jurisdictions). My guess is that the average court's view would be (1) there are no evil spirits, and therefore (2) a reasonable person would not mistakenly believe in their existence. Indeed, from a contemporary Swedish perspective a strong enough belief in evil spirits might even qualify as insanity. When discussing the choice of sanction for one of the defendants, a young woman, the court quoted the examining psychiatrist:

> Her culturally acquired ideas are so intense, that they in a Swedish setting appear as expressions of psychological illness, a paranoid psychosis with megalomanic traits, hallucinations and delusions. It can be interpreted as a symbiogenic or expanded psychosis...

For the average Swede it would not be reasonable to think that the case was one of spirit possession, but—we assume for the sake of the argument—for the average person in the place from which the defendants came it would. Here, then, is one aspect of the core of the tension when criminal law is related to "culture": which yardsticks—or as some prefer to put it, whose yardsticks—are we to use? We are on Swedish territory, it is the Swedish legal order that shall judge in the case, but it is the individual defendant that shall be judged, whose individual guilt—individual blameworthiness—is to be evaluated.[1] The problem is obvious, the solution is not.

The defendants were convicted guilty as charged, one for murder, the others for gross assault. One final thing of interest happened when the person convicted of murder, after failure in the district court of appeals, tried to take his case to the Supreme Court. By now the motive, from the side of the defendant, had taken a more "legal" shape, although a rather modest one: it was put forward not as a justification, not as an excuse, but as a mitigating circumstance. The defendant argued, to persuade the Supreme Court to admit the case, that the case was of precedent value: there had hardly in modern times, it was said, been a murder case with circumstances so peculiar to Swedish conditions. The Supreme Court asked the Prosecutor-General's opinion on the precedent value, and the latter let the defendant's own argumentation bounce back at him: since the case was so unique it would lack precedent value.

The Supreme Court did not admit the case, so here this particular story ended. But there are many related ones. This means also that the description of the Congolese case as "unique" is in important senses false: if one had raised one's head above casuistics—something which one may reasonably expect from Supreme Court and Prosecutor-General—it would have been obvious that the case in a transparent way could help shed light on important, and indeed general, aspects of the problem area of criminal law and "culture."

What I find provoking with the case is not necessarily the final outcome but the *road* to it: the defendants were denied access to a general defense to which someone acting under a more "Swedish" mistake of fact (whatever that might be) would have had access. An alternative explanation for the legal silence, competing with the technical ones that I suggested, is the existence of a shared, quite strong but seldom clearly articulated view, encouraging and giving the necessary self-confidence to the abovementioned bubble of thought, a view according to which view *our* legal order is entitled to use solely *our* yardsticks: it need not take into account particularities depending on the defendant (for example) coming from somewhere else. Be that to the disadvantage of the defendant: too bad for him or her, *our* problem it is not.

Such views have various origins, but independent of origin they are acceptable only to a certain extent. And the Congolese case is one of many cases—in

---

[1] Throughout the chapter (individual) "blameworthiness" is used in an unusually broad sense for an Anglo-American criminal law context: it encompasses more or less everything related to defendant and situation that must be examined and evaluated, regarding ascription of responsibility as well as penal value (aggravating and mitigating factors, etc.). "Defense" is used in a corresponding sense: a defense is everything that might extinguish or reduce such blameworthiness.

one of many places—pointing to a need for principled *and* nuanced thinking regarding "cultural" issues in criminal law. The new Romans are Romans too, and this must have consequences for "our" criminal law.

INTRODUCTION

> "Judicial punishment can never be used merely as a means to promote some other good for the criminal himself or for civil society, but instead it must in all cases be imposed on him only on the ground that he has committed a crime; for a human being can never be manipulated merely as a means for the purposes of someone else.... He must first be found to be deserving of punishment before any consideration is given to the utility of this punishment for himself or for his fellow citizens."
>
> Immanuel Kant

The next issue is *which* consequences it must have. My chapter is principally a reaction to the (mainly) North American debate on "cultural defenses" and "cultural evidence" in criminal law. An important starting point if one wants to understand this debate is that there is more than one kind of conflict between "cultures," worldviews, etc., at play. In addition to the primary issues—e.g., the defendant who wants to put forward "cultural" evidence—there are also significant differences in opinion grounded in scholars' belonging to more or less branch-specific scientific "cultures" and ideologies, all with their own presuppositions, starting points, and aims (social sciences, philosophy, criminal law, etc.). Interesting differences furthermore seem to be ascribable to one's belonging to different traditions of thought in criminal law.

Such belongings certainly do not explain all differences in opinion on the primary issues—in the end we are all, researchers and defendants alike, *persons*—but they do contribute to a better understanding on where, why, and how we might differ. My discussions of such matters—not least differences between Anglo-American and German-inspired schools of criminal law thinking—are indeed far too sweeping, but I hope to be justified in (or at least excused for) doing this, because I believe that there are relevant differences to be mentioned. The chapter provides slightly reshaped descriptions of the issues and tensions involved, as well as recommendations on how the criminal law should deal with them. The description is the heavier task of the two: once that is done the possible approaches to the primary questions, as well as the arguments for choosing one approach over the other, are quite clearly visible.

What already from the outset makes some difference, I think, is that my point of departure is the criminal law system *qua* distinct part of the legal system, characterized by specific aims, means, and restrictions, and by a profound tension between forward- and backward-looking considerations. This is the point from where I approach the question of how "cultural" issues should be dealt with in the criminal law: from what should fall out when *general* criminal law thinking is applied to the *particular* issues related to "culture." In the debate so far, many scholars seem to have started elsewhere: by first adopting some rather broad view on how society generally ought to handle cultural differences and multiculturalism, and second, more or less fully applying that view also to criminal law's dealing with "cultural" issues. Things then quite often get formulated as if the most (or even only) relevant question were "how can the criminal law be used to reach those future, general ends regarding multiculturalism?" Markedly less attention is paid to what should be seen as distinct about criminal law, including the need to carefully legitimize its application to individual, concrete persons. What in my opinion is a fundamental question, "how *may* the criminal law be used to reach those general ends?," is too rarely asked.

The chapter focuses mainly on ascription of responsibility and what might be labeled "cultural" evidence or information. My own view, to be explicated below, can be summarized as follows:

(1) A quite strict division must be made between aims and (the aims restricting) justifications.

(2) For the punishment of a concrete individual to be legitimate, considerable weight must be given to the demand for personal blameworthiness in a sufficiently profound sense.

(3) For the same reason, considerable weight must be given to the demand for equal treatment in a narrow sense.

(4) "Cultural" information is often necessary for these demands to be met. Thus, "cultural" information has a natural place in the rules determining personal blameworthiness.

(5) A separate "cultural defense," though, is a bad idea.

In the debate on "cultural defenses" etc., the conclusion under (4) is seldom reached. This is for several reasons. Some important ones, in addition to what has already been mentioned, are the following:

(1) No clear (enough) division is made between aims and (restricting) justifications, or between forward- and backward-looking considerations.

(2) Correspondingly, a clear division is lacking also in the rules for ascription of responsibility. The view is firm that these rules (and the yardsticks which are to be used when applying them) set and should set behavior standards for the future. This gives the yardsticks an ambiguous

role: one of determining blameworthiness in the individual case *and* setting behavior standards for the future.

(3) In this ambiguity, the wish to set (rigid and thus guiding) behavior standards for the future is given considerable weight. As a result, (far too) shallow conceptions of blameworthiness and equality are encouraged. The consequence is that the evaluation of the concrete person does not take into account as much information as would be necessary in order for the punishment to be legitimate.

(4) The debate regarding "cultural" factors in criminal law has been sliced as if such factors were (or purportedly were) the most important ones in each individual case. This has (wrongly) brought the debate to the level of structural argument and group policy. This is a level where rules for ascription of responsibility should only rarely operate.

If we agree in principle that personal blameworthiness needs to occupy a fundamental role in criminal law, and that this demand needs to be met in a way which is decently profound, then we cannot be allowed to neglect the impact of "culture," even when this impact conflicts in a most flagrant way with important forward-looking societal aims regarding how we wish present and future inhabitants—including immigrants, etc.—to behave. There are also other values in criminal law, values which concern how the state, through the criminal law, is allowed to deal with those under its jurisdiction. Personal blameworthiness, sufficiently profound, is a precondition for legitimate punishment.

But the demand for blameworthiness is not the only value to be defended. It is, for example, important to have a well-grounded view about what kind of *equality* to strive for. The criminal law is basic to society in a way at least partly similar to that of a constitution: they both define outer limits, a constitution mainly regarding what the state may not do to the inhabitants, the criminal law mainly regarding what the inhabitants may not do to each other (or to the public or the state, for that matter). Such outer limits should be equal and equally valid for all. These are basic points of departure on which we all probably agree.

Unfortunately, venturing deeper into sub-areas of the criminal law, these points of departure do not give as much help as one would wish for. On one level the message of the criminal law is simple and primitive enough: some things are not to be done, almost no matter what, and many central criminalizations concern "everyone, who…" But within the rules for ascription of responsibility we ourselves have taken things so much further, by abandoning earlier strict liability-oriented approaches for a successively more refined system of distinctions and exceptions. Today we probably would agree that quite a large number of differences (between situations, persons, etc.) should play a role when deciding whom and how much to punish (compare, though, e.g., Wilson 1998; Dershowitz 1994). But—we also agree—only differences that *should* play a role should play a role. And the views on which ones should play a role change with time and place (Lernestedt forthcoming). An inability or unwillingness to appreciate this contingency is, in my opinion, part of the problem in the "cultural defense" debate.

Another central problem with the debate has to do with different opinions, in terms of shallowness and profoundness, on what must follow from respecting the demands for blameworthiness and equality. I endorse, generally, interpretations more profound than most of those visible in the debate. My comparatively "culture"-friendly conclusions, reached through applying what I take to be decent general conceptions of equal treatment and blameworthiness in criminal law to the specific area of (what might be called) "cultural" information, contain very little which should be labeled affirmative action. This might be worth emphasizing already at the outset, since many opponents of "cultural evidence" are content to describe things as if taking such evidence into consideration—no matter what the evidence is to prove or disprove—is affirmative action. I hope to convince the reader that such a view is not acceptable, since it rests on far too shallow interpretations of equality and blameworthiness, interpretations which because of their shallowness need to be rejected.

In the next section, relevant general aspects of the criminal law as points of departure will be discussed. What gets touched upon might seem slightly random, but will be better understood in the section that follows, which deals in detail with the "cultural" issues.

THE CRIMINAL LAW

Justifications and Aims

The criminal law is the state's utmost power tool, capable of causing severe harm. The sanctions are harsh; the system's *modus operandi* is restricting the freedom of individuals: through punishment for a committed crime, through threat of punishment at the earlier stage of criminalization. The core functions of the criminal law are primitive and destructive. Thus, it is not your everyday part of the law. One further significant feature of the criminal law is that it increasingly is thought of as belonging to "us all," to society: a crime is committed not only against the victim (where there is one) but also, or exclusively (depending on how one describes it), against the shared enterprise, the whole community (Marshall and Duff 1998; Duff 2007; compare Lernestedt 2012). Now if the punishment in the individual case is the whole community's harsh opinion of the defendant's act, then it had better be as justified as possible. This calls for various restrictions, regarding contents as well as procedure. The difference between *aims* (what we want to obtain) and *justifications* (whether and how we are allowed to try to reach the aims) is crucial. If we want people to eat less candy, it still might not be seen as justified to criminalize candy-eating.

Criminalization

Something short will be said regarding criminalization, primarily in order to point out some relevant differences in relation to the ascription of responsibility (which will be the main focus of my chapter). Starting with the aim of criminalizing a certain type of behavior, this cannot reasonably be anything else but general prevention: to prevent people from behaving in the described manner. The discussions of justification, as well as the conceptual questions, are rather well known (for ambitious discussions see, e.g., Feinberg 1984, 1985, 1986, 1988; Peršak 2007; Husak 2008; Simester and von Hirsch 2011; Duff et al. 2010, 2011, 2013).

Discussion and decision-making regarding criminalization take place on a rather abstract, societal level. The focus is inevitably forward-looking, with visions about how we wish our inhabitants to behave in the future. Here no real individuals exist: rather there is instead an idea, "the Individual," an often quite one-dimensional paper figure pulled with a string over the stage. Decisions on how the state should "see" this individual are to a large extent influenced by normative ideas about how future society (and the future individual) *should* be. This is natural, because criminalization is about trying to change things. One might as legislator, to a certain extent, be allowed to set the aims higher than what is realistic, to treat things "as if." Another characteristic of criminalization is that it is quite compatible with structural ideas. They could be said to occupy the same level: that of groups, of larger patterns, etc.

Finally it should be added that the messages contained in the rules of specific criminalizations must be seen as addressed at (and sent to) two recipients: the courts, as guidance—"if someone does X, then he or she shall be sentenced to Y"—and the people, as imperatives—"you shall not do X."

Regarding criminalization and "culture" there is a fairly limited number of issues to discuss. I will not touch upon them. The discussion needed is to a large extent one about balancing, in various ways, the majority's and the minority's interests (Parekh 1996). Since the discussion is public and the considerations relatively transparent, the risk is comparatively low for (at least unforeseeable) haphazard discrimination for or against one side or the other.

Personal Blameworthiness

Regarding personal blameworthiness and "culture" things are worse, and I will spend the remainder of the chapter with the issue. The aim of the punishment in the individual case could, in a common way of framing it, be either prevention (individual or general) or retribution. This is one of the possible roles which retributive ideas can have in criminal law: as an *aim*, in the sense that, for example, (1) the former status of victim and defendant, respectively, are symbolically restored (see, e.g., Murphy and Hampton 1988), or (2) the legal order strikes back at the one who challenged the validity of the rules, signaling that the rules are valid (Jakobs 1993: 6ff.). Another even more crucial role of retribution is related to justifying the infliction of punishment on a certain individual: the idea is then that only *deserved* punishment is justified, be the aims ever so desirable. This mode of thinking is related to ideas of proportionality: of fitting the punishment to the blameworthiness shown. In the version of retribution which I endorse here, retributive ideas only set limits: we may punish *only* so much as is deserved.[2]

A decent system of criminal law recognizes an unavoidable and insoluble tension or conflict between (forward-looking) aims and (to a large extent backward-looking) justificatory issues. This tension or conflict, though, has not been clearly enough acknowledged in the "cultural defense" debate. This is surely partly because it has not always been clearly acknowledged in criminal law (and theory) either. In my opinion, at least earlier Anglo-American criminal law theory has tended to lack precise distinctions between aims and justifications: the two words seem overall to be given quite little weight, are sometimes used interchangeably or altogether left out, or get substituted by vaguer expressions like "the *rationales* of punishment." Such vagueness conceals the distinctiveness of the backward-looking justificatory issues.

This, together with the double role of retributive ideas mentioned above (one backward-looking, the other more or less forward-looking), facilitates thinking that deterrence and retribution belong, so to speak, in the same category. This in turn facilitates the claim that the two may be balanced rather freely against each other. In the "cultural defense" debate, particularly opponents of "cultural evidence" tend to see the task as one of finding a proper balance between competing aims (where few limits are set to the balancing), not as one of finding a difficult balance between non-comparable, non-compatible entities: aims and justifications. The justificatory issues cannot, of course, escape *all* balancing (in this sense my characterization is a bit oversimplified). But justificatory issues must always be given greater weight, and must be kept

---

[2] This is what Braithwaite and Pettit (1990: 34ff.) would call *negative* retributivism.

more rigid, when confronted with whatever competing policy considerations—whether "cultural accommodation" or something else—happen to be the flavor of the month.

The justificatory issues to a rather large extent concern the demand for personal blameworthiness (ascription of responsibility, penal value). For the layman, on the one hand, the occurrence of bodily movements fitting the description of a crime is often a kind of end-point: the crime is—in some (very shallow) sense—committed. For the criminal law, on the other hand, this should be only the starting point of a long chain of investigations, aiming to find out whether the person also was liable for the act and blameworthy. Different criminal law systems differ with regard to how "personal," how profound, this demand for personal blameworthiness needs to be for the term "blameworthy" to be proper (and, as a consequence, for the punishment of the individual to be legitimate). I will return to such differences further below.

As already mentioned, though, there are more issues involved than the blameworthiness ones. When deciding on the contents (and application) of the rules with respect to personal blameworthiness, some sort of compromise is to be sought between—as it for our purposes might be pictured—(1) the demand for personal blameworthiness, (2) the demand for equal treatment, and (3) the interest in directing future behavior (through setting behavior standards). What alternative approaches are available, and how profound a judgment should the legal order seek when the defendant is tried?

One extreme would be to try to consider *everything*, including the defendant's complete personal history. It is easy to construct arguments for this view. When the criminal law is applied to a specific person, for example, inequalities have often already been in play. Many of those sentenced to long prison terms have in their pre-trial life suffered unfairness. If life in society is a competition (and who can argue against that?) then one sub-competition is "not to break the criminal law," and there, as little as in other competitions, we are on an equal footing. If luck egalitarianism—with its emphasis on the distinction between chance and choice—would be given any bearing, then such differences surely should influence also the criminal law's judgments of personal blameworthiness. But "tough life" arguments normally have no impact on the issue of blameworthiness: for various reasons, a relatively blind criminal justice has been preferred (and is also, generally speaking, to be preferred). A common view seems to be that chance inequalities which society did not compensate for *before* the criminal law entered the stage, should not be compensated for *in* the criminal law. One reason for this view is surely that if too much were taken into account then in the end hardly anyone would be held responsible for anything. This would mean, among other things, that the system's capacity of directing behavior would decrease.

Furthermore, when looking at the more practical work of the criminal law system, it is easy to imagine that the more information which is to be gathered regarding the defendant, situation, etc., the higher the risk gets that we promote unequal treatment. One problem would be variations in factual resources (between different courts, different parts of the country, etc.). A second problem would be variations in courts' willingness to get the information, even if the factual resources do exist. For good reasons it is also presumed that the more the court "sees," the higher the risk gets that the court's own (irrelevant) worldviews, presuppositions, etc. will influence how the defendant is dealt with. In sum, the "consider everything" ambition has to go, and with it the most profound versions of personal blameworthiness and equality between defendants.

The other extreme would be to consider more or less *nothing* but the outward act, and thus look upon the individual defendant as a physical entity more than as a person. This is the ideal of strict liability, attractive if one sees effectively directing behavior, or equal treatment of a very shallow kind, as the proper guiding light. Such views do exist, and they have—mostly when they come in the shape of criticism—certain points to them. Large parts of what needs to be determined regarding blameworthiness are located on the inside, and Barbara Wootton (1963), for example, has argued that what went on in the individual's head should not matter for conviction. Inner facts would according to Wootton be of interest at a later stage—when the issue is to decide which measures are needed to make the person abstain from future crime—but not at the stage of conviction. Wootton's view differs, though, from how most Western countries today picture an acceptable criminal law system: some sort of blameworthiness demand, profound and "personalized" enough, must exist in order for conviction to be justified. Thus, in sum: effective prevention and standard-setting for the future cannot be permitted to rule alone; neither can the idea of maximally narrow equality in treatment.

With neither extreme possible the task is to find a decent compromise between the interests mentioned (blameworthiness, equality, prevention). We are then forced to let some differences matter (between situations, persons, etc.) and others not. What to pick, and how shallowly or profoundly to go? Here our views will differ, not least depending on the criminal law tradition one is influenced by, with its view of the functions of the rules of personal responsibility, as well as on how much of the "personal" person (and not solely the formal entity) must be taken into account for the adjective "blameworthy," and the following punishment, to be legitimate.

In my opinion, the rules for ascription of responsibility first and foremost are there as tools with whose help we are to decide whether this particular individual *may* be punished at all (and if so, how much), the individual then being used as society's tool for signaling that the imperative is valid. If this is the case, then we may not make the portrait too shallow, and the painter should be given almost no room for approaching this particular person "as if." Another way to put it might be that regarding ascriptions of responsibility the person has to be approached with more ontological, not strategic, ambitions: the over-arching guiding light should be an ambition to reach a "true" measure of the individual's blameworthiness. This cannot be done, though, and there are also some good reasons for not going too far in this direction (see above), but what cannot be fully reached should still sometimes be the stern guiding light. This is one such case.

For such rules of ascription of responsibility where normative yardsticks are to be (constructed and) used, the implications which I would suggest are the following. (1) Respect for the demand for (what might be called) "true" blameworthiness necessitates that the investigation gets profound enough, and thus close enough, to *this* particular defendant (in *this* particular situation, etc.). We might visualize some kind of threshold of minimum information. (2) Respect for the demand for equal treatment, in its most narrow sense, necessitates that such yardsticks are put at equal distance to every defendant: not closer to anyone than to anyone else. This means that the yardsticks must be equipped with a certain degree of flexibility. (3) Forward-looking aspirations (prevention, setting standards, etc.) should be given no or little role. The rules which we are discussing are (said to be) there for the determination of blameworthiness—that is: for the determination of whether this particular individual may be used as society's tool for bringing about future ends—and this in itself should bar giving the rules of ascription of responsibility the same function (beyond the extent to which this might flow as a mere consequence from respecting the justification-related demands). These rules should not be allowed to be about trying to change things: they should, one might put it, take the defendant as the defendant is.

Furthermore, my view is—compare what was said above regarding criminalization—that the messages contained in the rules for ascription of responsibility can only to a rather small extent be seen as addressed and sent to the people: most such rules seem to be "transmitted" almost exclusively to the functionary (compare Dan-Cohen 2002: 37ff.; Fletcher 2000: 457, 492). I doubt that these rules have the capacity, in the way a particular criminalization might have, to set behavior standards and thus function as tools for directing behavior.

Anglo-American criminal law thinking, though, seems to look upon things in a different way. The rules of ascription of responsibility are seen as having the function of setting behavior standards for the future, as being addressed to the population in almost the same way as is criminalization. The view is that these rules *are* transmitted to the people, and also that they *should be*. One important consequence flowing from this—correlating with the lack of a clear distinction between aims and justifications—is that an ambiguous double role is bestowed upon the yardsticks that are to be constructed and used: one of measuring blameworthiness in the individual case (backward-looking) *and* of setting standards in order to direct future behavior (forward-looking). My impression furthermore is that the forward-looking, directing ambitions are given considerable weight. From this it flows that *if* these ambitions are to be met—which makes it necessary that the yardsticks are practically able to direct behavior through sending standards to the people—*then* the yardsticks must be made shallow as well as rigid: if they are made too flexible, they cannot direct or "send" anything at all.

Hence the Anglo-American view that the rules for ascription of responsibility contain and should contain more or less *objective* standards or yardsticks. This means that in determining "personal" blameworthiness the particular individual is measured against the one yardstick (standard), and if she does not pass this test a possible next question, next step—whether it should be demanded of *her* (in her particular situation, with her particular characteristics) that she should pass the test—gets no or little room. The Anglo-American view endorses (and must endorse, if the standard-setting is to work) a more formal, more shallow conception of equality between defendants: the over-arching ideal is that everyone, not only regarding criminalization but also regarding personal blameworthiness, in the end gets measured against the same—"objective"—standard.

To generalize and compare, the demand for personal blameworthiness in Anglo-American law and theory has less of the particular individual in it, and more instead of objective standards, than has the law of the jurisdictions belonging to the German tradition: personal blameworthiness is, so to speak, less "personal" in the Anglo-American view (see e.g. Fletcher 1973–74). If such a view is endorsed as the correct one, then the distinction which I have emphasized between issues of criminalization and ascription of responsibility, respectively, becomes of less significance: both sets of rules contain standards of behavior. The same happens to the distinction between backward- and forward-looking considerations, which gets considerably vaguer.

The one "objective" standard is (at least partly) the reason why the concept of the *reasonable person* is of such importance in Anglo-American criminal law thinking, and of markedly less importance in the German-influenced approach. It also helps us understand differences in views on how to handle the issues of "cultural" (and other) variations between defendants. If no "individual" step follows the step which measures the individual against the primary yardstick (or, put differently, if there is not much flexibility in the yardstick), then the design of the yardstick, valid for all, gets to be of fundamental importance. The stakes get tremendously high: on the one hand, from the point of view of (shallow) equality, for example, anything sounding like double standards is viewed as a threat to the ideal of equal treatment. If, on the other hand, there is such a second step or margin, the stakes get distinctly lower. The yardstick can still play a useful role, I think: it is there for all cases, even if it is not (alone) decisive for the outcome in each individual case. With this latter alternative, one *gains* a possibility of more nuanced judgments of blameworthiness, and one *loses* in the capacity for standard-setting. Whether one loses or gains in equal treatment will be returned to at length later. A closing comment in this part might be, though, that when the shallow conception of equal treatment is put forward as the correct one to use, I doubt that this is because the conception is seen as the correct one in terms of substantial fairness. Instead, it is probably because this shallow conception is seen as making possible the setting (and "sending") of behavior standards.

In most criminal law systems, the factors capable of reducing blameworthiness roughly fall into two broad categories: *personal* and *situational*. The first category concerns whether the person can be (held) answerable at all for anything. Children and the severely mentally disordered are the categories normally discussed. Children are seen as being in a process of socialization, which when done enables an understanding of how life in society works, the (formal and informal) rules of behavior, how to evaluate short- and long-term consequences of one's acts, etc. Prior to this, children are not "full" grown-up persons and citizens. This means, many hold, that children should not bear the full consequences of their actions (see e.g. Maher 2005; Nuotio 2005). Regarding severely mentally disordered persons, the question of what is lacking is more complex. Let us only conclude that both groups are considered to lack something which is deemed necessary for (full) answerability, and that no other groups are discussed as being close to them in this sense.

Let us turn to the situational factors. (1) Regarding the *objective requisites* of the crime, as seen in the statute, there is normally quite little room for flexibility. This means that these requisites seldom would be of direct interest for issues regarding cultural sensibility in the application of the law (but see the *Kargar* case below). (2) If an act is *justified* the act is deemed correct. In the Swedish system this need not mean that the act is deemed the best alternative available in a given situation; a wider margin is used. It is sufficient that the legal order ought to tolerate it. The standards used are largely objective, focused on the outward situation. (3) If an act is not justified but the actor is (fully) *excused*, the act is wrong but the actor is not to blame for having committed it. Regarding many excuses, yardsticks in terms of reasonableness, etc. have to be constructed, something which makes this one area where differences between Anglo-American and German-inspired criminal law thinking frequently show: the former uses more of a one-step model, comparing the defendant to a (double role and) more or less objective yardstick, whereas the latter uses more of a two-step model. (4) If the actor lacked the required *intent, recklessness,* or *carelessness* the act was wrong but the actor is not to blame for it. Regarding intent there is in Swedish law in principle no room for yardsticks at all: either there is intent, or there is not.[3] Regarding recklessness

---

[3] Compare e.g. the English case *D.P.P.* v. *Morgan* (1976) AC 182.

and carelessness, though, yardsticks must be constructed. This generates differences similar to those under (3) above. (5) If the act is wrong and the actor culpable, there might still be *mitigating circumstances*. The defendant is convicted; the moral message is guilt and blameworthiness, although reduced.

Now if an answerable defendant raises various defenses to eliminate or reduce personal blameworthiness, these defenses differ—it might be said—in how intensely they challenge the imperatives laid down in the criminalization: in the figure below, the closer to the core a defense is able to eat its way, the more profoundly is the legal order forced to "accept" what happened, and the more profound would be the legal order's defeat, if its sole aim were described as maximizing the protection of the imperatives through signaling to the population that the imperatives are absolute. One simplified way of putting it is that the closer to the core a defense gets, the less strength has the imperative "you shall not do X."

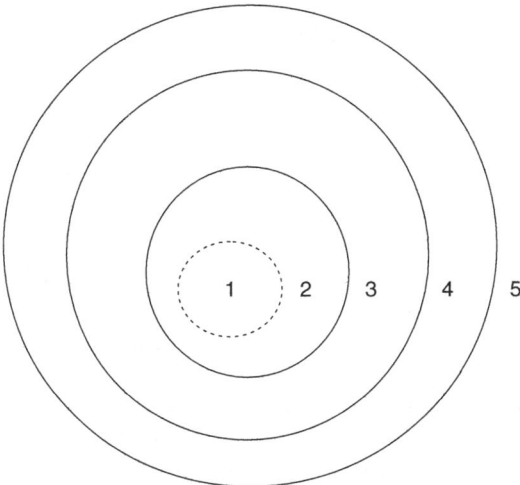

- Under (1) the act in question, even though in *some* objective sense it met the objective requisites of the crime, did not meet them in *another* and competing objective sense. (This is indeed cryptic—normally, if the act does not fit the description of a crime, there is no challenge to the legal order—but see *Kargar* below.)
- Under (2) the objective requisites were met but the act was *justified*.[4]

---

[4] I have used a dashed line here to mark that what gets justified in fact, in some senses, changes the reach of the criminalization. For the purposes of my chapter, though—more specifically for the discussion on what gets "sent" to the population and not—a distinction between the two areas needs to be made.

- Under (3) the act was not justified (and hence wrong) but the actor was *excused*.
- Under (4) the act was wrong and the actor blameworthy, but mitigating circumstances reduced the blameworthiness.

Someone who wants maximal recognition for a "cultural" factor in a particular case prefers that the impact is able to reach all the way to (1). Someone who strives for minimal recognition wants the impact as far from the core as possible, preferably in (5), where there is no impact at all.

CULTURAL EVIDENCE AND CULTURAL DEFENSES

The Situations and the Issues

The debate on "cultural defenses" has so far revolved round a relatively small number of court cases and situational types (see Renteln 2004 for a helpful collection of cases, including those mentioned below). Some examples: a woman of Japanese descent who, due to the shame her husband's infidelity had brought upon the family (not least their children), drowned the two children and tried but failed to commit suicide; a man of Chinese descent who murdered his wife in a rage over her (supposed) infidelity; Sikhs carrying a kirpan in public despite the fact that carrying a knife in public is generally prohibited; the ritual scarring of children's faces; the religiously motivated use of drugs like peyote and marijuana; a man of Afghan descent who kissed the penis of his small child, something which in his culture (under certain circumstances) can lack sexual connotations; a man of Hmong descent, charged with rape, who claimed that when he kidnapped and had (forced) sexual intercourse with a woman (also Hmong), he thought that they had practiced a version of Hmong marriage called "marriage-by-capture," where the woman is supposed to scream and resist (which the victim in the case also did, something that strengthened the defendant's belief that she agreed).

Most defenses raised can be sorted into a few groups: where (what gets defined as) "cultural" factors are claimed to bring about that:

(a) the defendant did not experience the situation the way it really was (or as the legal order experiences it), but the defendant had good reasons, due to his or her "cultural" background, to interpret it the way he or she did;

(b) the defendant neither knew, nor should have known, that the behavior in question was criminalized;

(c) the defendant's volitional ability to do (or want to do) what the law demanded in the situation was somehow impaired;

(d) the defendant's act was justified; and finally

(e) the act did not fit the objective description of a criminal act.

Examples for discussion under (a) are the Congolese case mentioned at the start of the chapter and the "marriage-by-capture" case. Examples under (b), mistake of law, are several, since today's crime catalogs are huge, difficult to grasp and to some extent vary between jurisdictions. Examples for discussion under (c) are the Chinese man, the Japanese woman, and any case where someone has experienced a provocation or an insult. Examples to discuss under (d) are religiously motivated drug use, the Sikhs' kirpan and face scarring.

Among significant sub-questions in the debate are the following: (1) should "cultural" evidence at all be allowed; if yes (2) should there be a separate "cultural defense" or should "cultural" evidence be dealt with under already existing defenses; connectedly (3) are there any "cultural" circumstances that could not be made to fall under existing defenses but nevertheless should have a possible impact (something which might imply that a separate defense in the end is needed); and (4) if "cultural" evidence and defenses should be allowed, how close to the core of the imperatives (see above) should they be allowed to get? I will deal with all of these issues (not, though, in the order stated here) in the sections which follow.

Some Main Positions in the Debate

Some main positions in the debate will now be summarized, to be discussed and criticized further below (I suspect also that the reader will deduce some criticism from what has already been said above.)

One large group of scholars recommend various middle-way compromises of what sometimes seems a rather haphazard kind, being quite reluctant to let the "cultural" move close to the core. The approach is a markedly policy-oriented one, quite similar to the balancing that occurs in discussions regarding criminalization, and seems to have little to do with principled criminal law thinking. I will now, though, focus a bit more on two other lines of thought, which I take to be the most influential so far. They both strongly oppose "cultural" evidence and defenses. They normally disagree on many issues, but here unite in their recommendations. To make the contrast, my descriptions are somewhat taken to the extreme.

The *first* line of thought is one of "blind" justice, represented by the classical, formal-liberal law scholar. The advocate claims that the law's application should be and *is* neutral and equal for all, that criminal law focuses on acts and not persons, etc. It is not accepted that "cultural" differences could be of relevance. In the area of "culture," the advocate of this line of thought sticks to the same canon of views that has been under partly meritorious attack from gender perspectives, for example for having helped in the hiding of structural injustices. To the extent that the gender-based criticism has made any impression, the advocate refuses to apply it to "cultural" issues: law might be "gendered," but "cultured" it is certainly not. The attitude should not surprise: ideals of equality, neutrality, objectivity, etc. are central to the self-confidence of the legal profession. The advocate holds that something "cultural" rambling into the courtroom, disturbing the peacefully neutral proceedings, is contrary to justice. The recommendation, hence, is that there should be no or little room for "cultural" evidence. One frequent argument is that if "culture" is taken into account, some will be measured against different (by which is often meant, more lenient) yardsticks than the rest. This would be unfair to the rest of the population, unable to use such "extra" defenses and "extra" evidence: taking "culture" into account is, more or less, pictured as affirmative action. As I shall argue below, this view presupposes conceptions of blameworthiness and equal treatment that are too shallow.

If the first line of thought is too blind to structure-based differences, the *second* line of thought instead tends to "see" and contextualize too much. It furthermore pays too little attention to criminal law; its particularity and its central distinctions (e.g. between aims and justifications). If a problem with the first line of thought was the inability to accept the relevance of structurally based arguments (at least if what is at issue is "culture"), here the problem is the opposite: there is too much willingness to do so, and no or too little sensitivity to the particularities of the area to which the structural arguments are to be applied. The advocate emphasizes (some version of) a gender perspective and has thick and far-reaching material views regarding what practices and life-styles are free/unfree, normal/abnormal, etc. The recommendation again is that there should be no or little room for "cultural" evidence. The argument seems—roughly—to be as follows: "Cultural" women and children belong in two vulnerable groups whereas "cultural" men belong in (only) one. Thus, in a situation of conflict of interests, the status of women and children must trump. Since in most "cultural defense" cases women and children are victims, and men perpetrators, "cultural" defenses should not be allowed. Among the "rationales" of punishment, the importance of prevention must be upgraded, the importance of retribution (as justifying the punishment of the individual) should be downgraded. Furthermore, if such prevention (by which is meant for the most part, deterrence) is to be more effective—and this is necessary in "cultural" cases—the criminal law cannot be allowed to send the "wrong" signals. Since people cannot understand moral messages that are too nuanced, the interest of sending such messages should be downgraded, the interest of the "right" (forcefully deterrent) messages being received should be upgraded.

I will limit myself to some short comments. A claim that the victim's rights must be protected in "cultural" cases seems in this line of thought to tend to lead to the view that the defendant always should be convicted if the crucial evidence is (labeled) "cultural." This amounts to suggesting a kind of strict liability, limited to a certain species of evidence. In my opinion there should be no room for suggestions going even slightly in such a direction: a demand for intent, for example, cannot be allowed to be balanced away in "cultural" cases but not in others. Furthermore, the rights of the victim generally should be seen as taken care of if the defendant is tried in accordance with the procedural and material rules of the legal order. I doubt that the advocate of this second line of thought is of the opinion that every victim, generally speaking, should have a right that the defendant is convicted. Instead the view might be that this should be so only for cases in which "cultural" evidence plays (could play) a crucial role. In a criminal law setting such a position must be deemed profoundly discriminating.

How We Slice Reality

With the way the problem area has come to be described—with too much focus on the structural perspective in question, and too little on the particulars—the "cultural" aspect is what dominates: in the debate *all* kinds of evidence which can possibly be called "cultural" tends to be lumped together as if it were one. One false expectation which this has produced is that the questions raised should, and can, be answered with reference to one elegant general rule or attitude, no matter what the "cultural" is to prove or disprove in the particular case.

But the fact that "cultural" aspects are a common denominator for disparate cases does not mean that these aspects are also the most important factors in the cases: all cases concern particular persons, facts, and rules, and after the visit to the structural level the criminal law case must be brought back to its particulars. What the "cultural" evidence is to *prove* should then be more important than the fact that it happens to be labeled "cultural." Regarding ascription of responsibility (and otherwise determination of blameworthiness), my general suggestion would be that "cultural" aspects need to be sliced in the same way as the criminal law. Few of the related issues of criminal law responsibility should be sorted in accordance with the structure of a general, group- and policy-oriented debate regarding multiculturalism. For example, as will now be developed, taking "cultural evidence" into account must in some types of cases be seen as a breach of the demand for equal treatment (amounting to affirmative action), whereas in other cases it must be seen as a demand of equal treatment in its most narrow sense. In some cases letting the defendant profit from "cultural" evidence amounts to giving him or her exactly what others have, in other cases it amounts to giving him or her something exclusive.

(a) Let us return to the Hmong man and "marriage-by-capture." In Swedish law, one prerequisite necessary for a rape conviction is that the defendant's intent covers the fact that the sexual intercourse was against the will of the victim. Now if a defendant lacks such intent (the defendant did not understand that this victim did not want it), the defendant cannot be convicted of rape. Consequently, if the Hmong man lacked such intent, *he* cannot be convicted of rape, no matter whether the reason for his lack of intent is deemed a "cultural" one or not, and also no matter (we assume for the sake of the argument) if not one single "Swede" could have misinterpreted the situation that way. To convict the Hmong man of rape under such circumstances would be a grave breach of the principle of equality before the law, in its most narrow and demanding sense. Here, taking "culture" into account is nothing but giving the defendant what other defendants are given.

(b) Slightly different but related lines of argument are valid for the Congolese case. At issue here is putative self-defense, which in Swedish law if further conditions are met brings about a lack of intent. Now if the defendants were convinced that the children were possessed by dangerous and evil spirits, and putative justification exists as a general defense in the jurisdiction in question, then it is obvious that not taking the "cultural" information into account would satisfy neither the demand for (profound enough) blameworthiness nor the demand for equal treatment.

In a next step, once the Congolese have been admitted access to the defense, the differences compared to (a) will show. Here in (b), but not in (a), yardsticks have to be constructed: it must be asked whether the defendants' (mis)interpretation of the situation was *reasonable*. This gives the court room for a normative maneuver which does not exist under (a). We have learned that such room creates difficult questions: how are the *yardsticks* to be constructed? If they are put too close to the particular defendant they lose the character of yardsticks (how about "the reasonable fundamentalist"?) and become pointless. If they are made too distant ("the reasonable Swede") neither the demand for profound enough equal treatment, nor the demand for profound enough blameworthiness, is satisfied. According to the demand for (profound enough) equal treatment, as I have formulated this demand above, the yardsticks may not be put closer to (or farther away from) anyone than to or from anyone else. This, in a case such as the one at hand, rules out the possibility of using "the reasonable Swede" as (a rigid and final) yardstick. The yardsticks must be put closer to the defendants if the demand for equal treatment is to be satisfied. *How* close I leave open (but "the reasonable Congolese with a moderate belief in (evil) spirits" is tempting).

Similar discussions need to be held regarding, for example, what kinds of *provocation* should count as blameworthiness-reducing in the law, what kind of behavior should count as "humiliating" or "insulting," etc. We cannot be allowed to generally exclude the possibility that the likes of the Chinese man, the Japanese woman, the "honor killing" father, etc., in particular cases because of anger could have had such an impaired capacity to conform to the law that their blameworthiness should be deemed reduced (all to the extent that this would be the result for the "Swedish" defendant having acted in a equivalent "Swedish"-evoked situation of anger, etc.). Phrased this way, the issue remains one of taking "culture" into account in order to be able to treat all equally in a rather narrow sense.

Let us pause a little at the ideas behind provocation defenses, as they may well illustrate the tension between backward- and forward-looking considerations. The figure of provocation is ideologically based on either of two basic starting points, (1) a more "personal" and (2) a more "objective" one, each with its own goals. According to (1), what is of primary interest is the mental and physical state in which the defendant was put by the provoking act—a state of anger, etc.—in which we might not be entitled to fully demand that he or she obeyed the prohibition in question, since experience shows that a person having reached a certain inner state has a hard time controlling him- or herself. The reason for having a provocation defense is then to give people provoked into such states the possibility of blameworthiness reduction. The state in itself is what matters. According to (2), what primarily interests us is to set behavior standards regarding what kind of acts one is "allowed" to be (and act as having been) provoked by. Then the interest is more in the provocative behavior than in the state into which the recipient was put. The reason for having the defense is a normative one: to teach people the socially tolerated reasons for being provoked, and perhaps also—at least historically—to teach them which kinds of acts one *should act* as having been provoked by (see Horder 1992 for discussion). I doubt that many countries' provocation regulations contain elements from only one of the two ideologies: a statute based on (1) will have elements of (2) in order to escape full "subjectivism," and vice versa.

Now let us apply the two ideologies to our "cultural" discussion. According to a pure version of (1), if someone is provoked by a certain act and put in the required (physical, mental) state by it, then it should not matter if a member of the majority society would or would not be provoked by the act in question (it actually should not matter if *anyone* else would be provoked by it). No yardsticks need to be introduced. According to a pure version of (2), if the ("subjectively") provoking act fails to match the standard set—that is, the person is feeling provoked for the "wrong" reasons—blameworthiness would not be seen as reduced (see Sing 1998–99 on such matters in "cultural" perspective). In my opinion, a decent regulation of provocation—one which respects the demands of equality and personal blameworthiness as formulated above— must take (for example) "culture" into account when the yardsticks are constructed. The yardsticks must be profound enough, and thus sufficiently close to the defendant (this is the demand for personal blameworthiness), and they must get as close to this particular defendant as they get to other defendants (the demand for equal treatment in narrow sense). Allowing for flexibility in these yardsticks, and this should be emphasized, need not mean leaping into a void of full "subjectivism," and it does not—correctly handled—mean affirmative action.

But here, as in other cases mentioned under (b), the Anglo-American scholar, to the extent that he or she views the yardsticks as also objective standards for guiding behavior, might very well regard taking "culture" into account as giving the defendant something "extra."

(c) Related discussions can be held regarding mistake of law as an excusing condition. A strong presumption that everyone knows the law is practically necessary in order to maintain effectiveness in the criminal law system. It is equally obvious, though, that we are dealing with a fiction: no one knows (the whole of) the criminal law. In my opinion, a rather strict use of the presumption can never the less be justified. One way of doing this is to say that someone living in the territory can be (justifiedly) presumed to have knowledge of the law, because even if he doesn't have it he *should* have it. We might thus be justified in blaming. But then we have good reasons for being potentially more lenient towards (for example) a relative newcomer, not fully integrated with the explicit and tacit rules of the community. As far as a given country's legislation is not fully strict but gives *some* small room for mistake of law as an excusing condition—and this seems to be the case in most jurisdictions—I would be happy to discover that (for example) immigrants are benefiting from such an excuse more than seems to be the case at present. This could still be discussed in terms of equal treatment, if sufficiently profound conceptions of blameworthiness and equal treatment are applied: to let mistake of law excuse in some such cases could be seen as taking into account a relative handicap in the competition "not to break the law."

(d) We now turn to the kirpan-carrying Sikh, the person who on religious grounds wants to use drugs otherwise prohibited, etc. Here it could hardly be argued that a conviction would be against the demands of equal treatment. On the contrary, conviction is rather a demand of equal treatment in the narrow sense, and this is a demand which criminal law normally should endorse. Allowing Sikhs to carry a kirpan is—if we only work with two alternatives for characterizing the outcome—affirmative action. If one is to argue against conviction in such a case, support must be sought in broader ideas of treatment "as equals," with all the vagueness that such ideas carry.

Hence, should all similar "cultural" cases end there, with the conclusion that the rules for ascription of responsibility should not allow (what might be called) affirmative action, whether the countervailing reason is "culture" or something else? No, the cases need not end there, because there is—and needs to be—room also for these kinds of exceptions. The criminal law contains many such already, although not for activities which we would label "cultural."

The cases under (d) are of a different kind than those mentioned under (a)–(c). There is no misunderstanding, no lack of knowledge, no problem with self-control, etc. The cases are (or are close to) what can be labeled conscientious objection. Furthermore, the issue in the examples chosen is more on group-level, regarding groups' shared, group-specific, and conscious behavior in (more or less) everyday life. Thus, the issue is less about *this* particular person, more about his or her group: the individuals are reduced to their being members of a group ("rastafaris," "Sikhs," etc.). What also differs is the strength of the claim from the defendant: it is argued that society should recognize the right to act exactly in this way. The Sikh, for example, is not interested in being *excused* for carrying his kirpan (which would mean that his carrying it is a crime, a wrong), but instead in the carrying being deemed *justified*: accepted or at least tolerated by society. This makes the claim much stronger than those under (a)–(c): here, the challenge goes (close) to the core of the imperative laid down in the criminalization in question. Issues of this kind are regularly dealt with (and should be dealt with) by the legislator, balancing conflicting interests in a discussion regarding (the reach of) a particular criminalization. The issues are also—because they can seldom be seen as matters of equal treatment, but instead of exceptions to it—much more open for discussion than those dealt with under (a)–(c). This, then, is one of the adequate places for arguments from political philosophy in the criminal law.

But what to do when one (d) issue ends up in court? One way of dealing with it is to ask whether the behavior in question can be deemed to fall under the unwritten defense of (what in Sweden is called) "social adequateness." This is a figure the existence of which one must accept in criminal law (although it has many names and is quite vague), if one wants to be able to explain why doctors are not convicted for assault when they are operating, or why soccer and hockey players are not convicted for assault when they (within reasonable limits) tackle or kick each other during an organized game of sport. The reason for such an exemption is, with organized sport as the example, that all things considered the good which comes from people engaging in organized sport is deemed to weigh more than the bad which comes from assaults (within reasonable limits, of course) that take place during such activities.

Now if such activities can be made exceptions to a general rule—the rule which prohibits assault—there is no obvious reason why such a possibility could not be open for activities labeled as "cultural," if the activity in question is deemed valuable enough. Sport, indeed, in the eyes of some qualifies as a strange "cultural" practice, and it is certainly not practiced by all. The crucial question, when we are to decide whether the defense of "social adequateness" should be considered open also for minority practices, is probably *for whom* the activity—all things considered—must be deemed valuable enough; for society at large (and this is what I take to be the traditional view), for society's majority, or for the minority in question?

If then discussions in terms of social adequateness are quite similar to those taking place regarding criminalization, one difference might still be noted between the two: in Swedish law, the court is to take a stand on whether the activity in question *is* accepted in society. This means that the court's room for considerations in terms of what *should be* accepted is in principle smaller than the legislator's.

(e) Finally an issue which takes the intensity of the challenge all the way to the core of the imperative: the criminalization as it reads in the statute. Should "cultural" factors be able to bring about that the objective requisites of a crime, as read in the statute, are not met? The spontaneous answer is no, but consider the *Kargar* case. The defendant had done something—kissed the penis of his small son—which in many countries under almost all circumstances is deemed to be "sexual," of a sexual nature, but for the defendant (and for someone from his "culture") the kissing which had taken place was not of a sexual nature. Instead it was a way of showing love for the child (since the penis is considered a "dirty" part of the body, it is a sign of great love to kiss it).

Now if one would not want the defendant in such a case to be convicted of a sexual crime (a reasonable view, in my opinion), various technical solutions may be possible, depending on the wording of the statute in question, the construction of the concept of crime in the legal system in question, etc. One might, depending on such issues, use a material concept of crime (as in the criminal law of former communist countries in Eastern Europe) and argue that although the requisites were met the legally protected interest was not harmed by this particular act (see e.g. Eser 1966); one might use a *de minimis* rule where such an option is possible; one might conclude that the defendant objectively committed an act of a sexual nature, but that this was not covered by intent; etc (see also Waldron 2002: 5ff.). The last line of thought would probably be seen by some as a good compromise. It would, so to speak, save the wrongness of the act, and thus save the core of the imperative: he did commit an act of a sexual nature, he did commit the crime objectively (and thus the act itself was blameworthy), but he did not intend or understand it, and therefore should not be punished. But for the defendant, and from a "cultural" point of view, such a solution would miss the point in a way similar to the legal order if excusing, not justifying, the Sikh's carrying a kirpan in public: the defendant would not want things pictured as if he did not "understand" that the act "really" was of a sexual nature (as if he was stupid, somehow). Instead, for the defendant, the act was not, even objectively, of a sexual nature. Let us suppose that the statute which is to be applied looks like this:

"Anyone who commits an act of a sexual nature towards a child…"

Who is then to be master of the decision on the sexual nature of the act? Objectively identical bodily movements or behavior can, when just a little contextualized, turn into wholly different activities (see e.g. Waldron 2002: 4). Is there room for different versions of reality in criminal law, actually bringing about (in some relevant sense) parallel realities? And if the legal order of our country has one view of kissing the penis, whereas the defendant in the *Kargar* case has another (which is not only his own, but "culturally" grounded, whatever difference that is meant to make), what room should there be? Is it even legitimate in such a case for the legal order to deem the act as of a sexual kind, if it was not of that kind for the actor? I leave the issue open.

The examples picked under (a)–(e) are meant to show the vast differences between, and the variety of problems raised in, varying issues related to ascription of responsibility and "cultural" information. The examples are also meant to show that all "cultural" issues regarding responsibility *cannot* be dealt with under one general rule, with one general solution or attitude: the particulars are too particular, and indeed too important, in cases with a "cultural" component as well as in all others.

This is one of the reasons why something like a separate "cultural defense" provision is a bad solution: in short, this would encourage a wrong way of slicing the world when "cultural" factors encounter criminal law's rules for the determination of blameworthiness. A separate "cultural defense" would tend to bring the issues up on a group-level where they normally should not be (compare, though, what was said regarding social adequateness). One further and related reason against such a provision is that it would give the opponents of "cultural" evidence prima facie grist to their mill. Its existence could easily (albeit wrongly) be used for arguing that all taking into account of "culture" is something "extra," handled in an "extra" way, where some get what others do not. Moreover, I think that in practice a separate provision would aid those who want to polarize the picture as one of a choice between all or nothing: either we bar "cultural" evidence more or less completely, they might argue, or it will flood and result in a "balkanization" threatening the legal order and society.

One additional reason for rejecting a separate "cultural defense," a reason which lies somewhat outside the scope of this chapter, is my opinion that in relation to criminal law's rules for determining blameworthiness, structural and other group-related perspectives must as much as possible be looked upon as *transient*. What such perspectives bring of knowledge should be worked into the general, multifaceted picture of the person. With the construction of separate defenses, related to particular and structurally defined groups, something risks getting cemented which ultimately should be viewed as a mere transitory (albeit fundamentally important) stage on the road to a more adequate image of the criminal law's person.

Finally, it might be added that with an acceptable profundity in the application of the rules in question (including the figure of social adequateness), I cannot see any direct need for a separate cultural defense.

Personal Particularity and the Twin Risks

To continue the "personal" thread: not only cases, but also *persons*, are particular. The idea that each individual to some extent should have a right to be assessed against his own context is an important part of the motive for allowing "cultural" evidence, and indeed for constructing a general multicultural platform at all. But such a striving for individualization cannot be present only in the defendant's relation to, for example, the Swedish criminal law system. It must to the same extent be present when that system evaluates the relation between the defendant and the "culture" whose supposed patterns he or she claims to be influenced by. It should never be enough nor have any *direct* impact that the defendant, in addition to proving that he or she formally belongs to the "culture" in question, blankly claims that persons from this culture are such and such, do this and that: this would indeed amount to a dangerous essentialization. The value of the kind of "cultural" evidence discussed in this chapter should always stay only indirect, as information in the light of which—among other things—the defendant should be judged.

One line of argumentation which should be mentioned to be fully dismissed is that if the criminal law of the defendant's former country does not criminalize (or punishes more leniently, etc.) the act committed by the defendant, then this fact *in itself* should have an impact on "our" verdict. This would be, somehow, to move the conflict to the level of states, when it should fully stay at the level of personal blameworthiness. We are *here*, it is our legal order that shall judge the defendant as well as construct the rules that are to be used when we judge him. It is the contents and application of these rules, *our* rules, not the formal jurisdictional authority, that needs to be set in question. This also means that the question asked at the start of the chapter—"*whose* yardsticks are we to use?"—is not correctly formulated: the yardsticks should stay ours and no one else's; it is their content which needs scrutiny.

The challenge for the legal order, in sum, is to find a decent road somewhere between on the one hand claiming each person's absolute uniqueness and "atomistic" relation to every (past and present) context, and on the other hand claiming a profound cultural determinism, seeing the individual as wholly captured by his past. The twin risks, each at one end, need to be emphasized: too far-reaching essentialization versus the discrimination which often results if one pretends ("as if") that "cultural" differences of relevance do not exist. If we turn from the defendant to the court, to the Swedish judge for example, of course large parts of his or her (extra-legal) ideas about the world depend on him or her being an individual, the person Ulrika, the person Sven, etc., not reducible to the entity "one Swedish judge." But *something* significant is surely shared. There are obvious risks for, and with, essentializing. But these risks are far from large enough to legitimize pretending that there are no relevant differences to be taken into account. For if we do that we sacrifice the demands of blameworthiness and equality as they should be understood in a decent criminal law.

Harmless and Harmful "Culture"

If the view is accepted in principle that "cultural" evidence must be given potential to influence blameworthiness, then we must be prepared to accept this also in relation to grave crimes. We must accept that the allowing or not allowing of "cultural" evidence cannot depend on what particular crime has been committed. If, for example, A killed B but lacked intent, and this lack of intent was due to "cultural" factors, then A cannot be convicted of intentional killing. Such "generalist" views, though, seem to have had quite low acceptance in the "cultural defense" debate so far. It is as if scholars seem to search for possibilities to restrict the room for maneuver for "cultural" evidence in a way which does not accept the demands of generality. I will now touch upon a few possible reasons for such a view.

The debate manifests, generally, a rather tight relation between on the one hand specific criminalizations, and on the other hand the rules for ascription of responsibility. The worse the category to which a committed crime belongs, the less prone one is to allow "cultural defenses." This attitude probably partly rests on the explicit or tacit view that allowing "cultural" evidence to influence legal judgments is some kind of act of kindness or charity; something that may be granted if we so wish and if we feel that society and legal order can afford it (not too much is lost in terms of "educating" the population), *not* something which might be a demand of even the most narrow conception of equal treatment.

From what has been said so far I hope follows that such views can hardly be defended. General defenses cannot be restricted in their application depending on whether that which grounds them happens to be "cultural" or something else. Their application cannot be made dependent on the severity of the crime in question (to any more extent than this follows generally for a certain defense). The road somewhere between everything and nothing cannot consist in some odd compromise on the theme that "cultural factors can work as a partial excuse, but nothing more." The whole specter of conditions for liability (etc.) must be able to be touched by the "cultural."

But there are, again, probably deeper reasons of criminal law ideology involved. A distinction I have tried to avoid so far can be made between the "special" and the "general" part of criminal law, the former containing the rules regarding specific crimes (criminalizations), the latter containing rules— for example those of personal responsibility—applicable to all or many crimes in the special part (regarding, for example, attempts, complicity, and intent). This distinction is firmly established in German-inspired jurisdictions, where there is a tendency (at least symbolically) to visualize the two parts as being almost separate from each other. In Anglo-American jurisdictions the distinction is more in question and not as established. The rules are seen as forming more of an organic whole (see e.g. Gardner 1998). A starting point in a German-inspired jurisdiction might be to see a rule of the general part as exactly that—*general*—which would mean that (again, only as a starting point) it would be considered an exception if, for example, a certain defense would be applicable only to one certain type of crime, or if a "general" defense were not applicable to certain kinds of crime. In an Anglo-American jurisdiction, by contrast, specific defenses seem to be more tightly tied to particular types of crime. This probably means that restricting the application of a defense, regarding the kinds of crime to which it might be applied, would seem a more natural thing to do.

Regarding the existence and status of a "general part" both camps have points to them. What I here would like to emphasize, though, is that for *some* defenses (and remember that "defense" in this chapter is used in quite a broad sense) there can be no such crime-based restrictions. Lack of intent has already been mentioned, but also such things as putative self-defense (or putative necessity, putative consent, etc.) should be general in this sense. Furthermore, the view that the worse the crime is, the shorter the defenses should reach (and the fewer they should be) is also highly doubtful from another point of view: it means that deterrence and standard-setting are valued the highest. But from the perspective of personal blameworthiness, the worse the crime is, the more severe punishment the defendant risks, the more important is a reasonably "profound" conception of such blameworthiness, a decent (not too shallow) conception of equality, and access to the full range of defenses. A competing opinion would be based on the kind of "charity" thinking mentioned above, and this is not something for a proper criminal law to engage in.

The "Lesser Person" Argument

It is sometimes suggested, by opponents of "cultural" evidence, that letting this kind of evidence influence the judgment of someone's blameworthiness is to treat that person, in our case, for example, an immigrant, as a "lesser person." Respect for him as a "full" person demands that no such considerations be taken. This view is in my opinion wrong, and I shall spend a little time with it.

Let us return to the distinction between (a) personal and (b) situational factors that might eliminate or reduce blameworthiness in criminal law. Those who worry about treating the immigrant who claims "culture" as a lesser person worry that he would belong in category (a), something which would mean—it is said—that he would be put side by side with children and the severely mentally disordered (or even, in some significant sense, be seen as belonging to one or the other of the groups). My reply to this is: *pro primo*, nothing says that it would be impossible to add a third group (or a fourth, or a fifth) under category (a), and such a group need not be associated with children and the mentally disordered to a larger extent than the two are associated with each other (I doubt that the advocate of such "lesser person" arguments would propose that children should be regarded as mentally disordered, or the mentally disordered as children), and *pro segundo*, this does not matter very much, since the reasonable way of looking at (for example) the immigrant is something like a "semi-(a)," a status which makes it likely that he gets into (b)-situations more often than do other people.

Why, and how, a "semi-(a)"? Let us return to children and the concept of socialization. When a child has not yet been socialized, we say that it has not learned how life, society, and life in society works, etc. What one might forget is that for a child there are, roughly speaking, two parallel socialization processes taking place: (1) into the adult world, and (2) into the adult world of *this specific place* (there are significant differences in tacit knowledge between being brought up in, for example, Scotland and Japan, respectively). The child has to cope with both transitions (but experiences them as one); an adult immigrant has to cope with one of them. The situation should still not be classified as an (a)-factor, a personal factor, because the immigrant's process of socialization is far from as fundamental as that of the child. But this process is indeed something that might increase vulnerability and give clear disadvantages in the competition "not to break the law."

CLOSING REMARKS

I have been concerned with the debate regarding "cultural defenses," especially with the views and arguments of the opponents of "cultural" evidence, etc. Among those opponents (and also many proponents), the shared view which was mentioned at the start of the chapter is present. Let us say a little more about it: a deep-rooted attitude, according to which the majority, the ones who were here first (or, more correctly, the ones dominant at the time from which we wish to start counting), own the place, with a strong right to bar influences deemed undesirable. The immigrant is, as other outsiders, supposed to fully adjust, whereas no reciprocal demand should have any bearing on the majority: "boutique multiculturalism" (Fish 1997) is fine, but what is Roman is, in any sense important to the criminal law, settled already. What a Congolese believes and perceives may be of interest in the Congo, perhaps also in some other places (who knows?), but here it is definitely not.

The attitude resembles a village mentality which was deemed self-evidently worth nurturing in small communities in earlier times (see Lenman and Parker 1980; Lacey 2001). This mentality is alive and well also in bigger enterprises (Anderson 1991). The mechanisms seem to be quite the same, although they now are vitalized by a feeling of serious threat. Perhaps massive immigration, so to speak, partly has made the pendulum swing back to a more primitive way of looking at personal responsibility in criminal law, at least regarding immigrants? If not, it is difficult to explain, for example, why one would want to put the newcomer in a worse situation than the domestic, something which indeed amounts to treating the former as a "lesser" person, when arguing for the exclusion of evidence which might get defined as "cultural." What the view does, as I interpret it, is to provide additional self-confidence for the court (etc.) in *not* giving "cultural" information any relevance.

This view should be accepted to some extent, but there must be limits to it. If we accept criminal law as society's *ultima ratio*, there is greater freedom to use other measures than criminal law to enforce various "majority culture" ideals. If the criminal law is thought of as setting outer limits in a way partly similar to a constitution, then it must be quite neutral. The more the majority's "culture" is allowed to trump in criminal law, the "thicker" the criminal law gets. If one wants it more neutral, there are two ways to go: "neither-nor" or "as-well-as." The former would be about removing: if we do not want room for "culture" in court and in the law, we should detect and remove all "culture"-specific rules (and applications) which are majority "thick." This would leave a smaller and in this sense "thinner" criminal law.

The other alternative would be about adding: we might try letting the "thicks" of the majority exist side by side with influences from (for example) minority cultures. This would result in a "thicker" criminal law, but if equally "thick" for each party—not closer to anyone than to anyone else—it would be neutral in function. For reasons given earlier, within the area of criminal law the freedom for "as if" should be bigger regarding criminalization, distinctly smaller—approaching zero—regarding personal blameworthiness. But when the encouraging view—present in many, if not all, jurisdictions—gets to encourage a system in which the rules of personal blameworthiness are seen as (partly, or primarily) setting standards for future behavior, it is easy to see that "cultural" factors will have a hard time getting taken into account in an adequate way.

Scholars engaging in more general multicultural theory—and multicultural theory in other areas of life and law—have done a great deal in enabling developments in the area of criminal law and "culture" (not least through building the platform at all). But they also sometimes seem to come to the aid of the opponents of "cultural defenses." If a scholar wants to defend some new and controversial "multicultural" or "cultural" rights, the scholar would want to present the suggestion in a way that has a good chance of getting approval;

that is, in the most favorable light. With this might follow a tendency to avoid issues which could be even more controversial. Probably there simply has not been time for more interest in "cultural defense" issues yet, since there are many questions to be discussed and solved (and some of them arguably more important), but I do think that the debate on criminal law and "culture" adds an important and distinct dimension to the general multicultural debate. What is at stake is the right to have a "culture," to be "cultured," also when one is bad, under severe pressure, in crisis, when one has done horrendous things which certainly do not at all contribute to a better, richer, pluralistic society. My view here, generally speaking, is that if one does not accept taking the unattractive sides into account, then one is still in some kind of "boutique multiculturalism."

Finally: time often heals. Time often makes whole what were considered fragments. The rules of personal responsibility are contingent, but at each given time we tend to look at them as if they were carved in stone. Long-established exceptions from general rules are quite often not really seen as exceptions at all: we think of them as parts of a coherent whole. My guess (or at least wish) is that in time what we now label "cultural" evidence in criminal law will be seen as a part of that coherent whole, with or without—but preferably without—the particular label.

REFERENCES

Anderson, Benedict. 1991. *Imagined Communities* (New York: Verso).
Braithwaite, John and Philip Pettit. 1990. *Not Just Deserts: A Republican Theory of Punishment* (Oxford: Clarendon Press).
Dan-Cohen, Meir. 2002. *Harmful Thoughts* (Princeton: Princeton University Press).
Dershowitz, Alan M. 1994. *The Abuse Excuse and Other Cop-outs, Sob Stories, and Evasions of Responsibility* (Boston: Little, Brown and Company).
Duff, R. A. 2007. *Answering for Crime: Responsibility and Liability in Criminal Law* (Oxford: Hart Publishing).
Duff, R. A., Lindsay Farmer, S. E. Marshall, Massimo Renzo, and Victor Tadros, eds. 2010. *The Boundaries of the Criminal Law* (New York: Oxford University Press).
Duff, R. A., Lindsay Farmer, S. E. Marshall, Massimo Renzo, and Victor Tadros, eds. 2011. *The Structures of the Criminal Law* (New York: Oxford University Press).
Duff, R. A., Lindsay Farmer, S. E. Marshall, Massimo Renzo, and Victor Tadros, eds. 2013. *The Constitution of the Criminal Law* (Oxford: Oxford University Press).
Eser, Albin. 1966. "The Principle of 'Harm' in the Concept of a Crime," *Duquesne University Law Review* 4: 345–417.
Feinberg, Joel. 1984. *Harm to Others* (New York: Oxford University Press).
Feinberg, Joel. 1985. *Offense to Others* (New York: Oxford University Press).
Feinberg, Joel. 1986. *Harm to Self* (New York: Oxford University Press).
Feinberg, Joel. 1988. *Harmless Wrongdoing* (New York: Oxford University Press).

Fish, Stanley. 1997. "Boutique Multiculturalism, or Why Liberals are Incapable of Thinking about Hate Speech," *Critical Inquiry* 23/2: 378–395.
Fletcher, George. 1973–74. "The Individualization of Excusing Conditions," *Southern California Law Review* 47/4: 1269–1309.
Fletcher, George. 2000. *Rethinking Criminal Law* (New York: Oxford University Press).
Gardner, John. 1998. "On the General Part of Criminal Law," in *Philosophy and the Criminal Law*, ed. Antony Duff (New York: Cambridge University Press), 205–256.
Horder, Jeremy. 1992. *Provocation and Responsibility* (Oxford: Clarendon Press).
Husak, Douglas. 2008. *Overcriminalization: The Limits of the Criminal Law* (New York: Oxford University Press).
Jakobs, Günther. 1993. *Strafrecht. Allgemeiner Teil. Die Grundlagen und die Zurechnungslehre*. 2. Auflage (Berlin: De Gruyter).
Lacey, Nicola. 2001. "In Search of the Responsible Subject," *Modern Law Review* 64/3: 350–371.
Lenman, Bruce and Geoffrey Parker. 1980. "The State, the Community and the Criminal Law in Early Modern Europe," in *Crime and the Law*, ed. V. A. C. Gatrell, Bruce Lenman, and Geoffrey Parker (London: Europa Publications), 11–48.
Lernestedt, Claes. 2012. "Victim and Society: Sharing Wrongs, But in Which Roles?" *Criminal Law and Philosophy*: 1–17.
Lernestedt, Claes. One Size Fits All? On Normative Criminalization Theory. Forthcoming.
Maher, Gerry. 2005. "Age and Criminal Responsibility," *Ohio State Journal of Criminal Law* 2: 493–512.
Marshall, S. E. and R. A. Duff. 1998. "Criminalization and Sharing Wrongs," *Canadian Journal of Law & Jurisprudence* 11/1: 7–22.
Murphy, Jeffrie G. and Jean Hampton. 1988. *Forgiveness and Mercy* (Cambridge: Cambridge University Press).
Nuotio, Kimmo. 2005. "On Becoming a Responsible Person," *Ohio State Journal of Criminal Law* 2: 513–520.
Parekh, Bhikhu. 1996. "Minority Practices and Principles of Toleration," *International Migration Review* 30/113: 251–284.
Peršak, Nina. 2007. *Criminalising Harmful Conduct. The Harm Principle, its Limits and Continental Counterparts* (New York: Springer).
Renteln, Alison Dundes. 2004. *The Cultural Defense* (New York: Oxford University Press).
Sing, James. 1998–99. "Culture as Sameness: Towards a Synthetic View of Provocation and Culture in the Criminal Law," *Yale Law Review* 108/7: 1845–1884.
Simester, A. P. and Andreas von Hirsch. 2011. *Crimes, Harms, and Wrongs: On the Principles of Criminalisation* (Oxford: Hart Publishing).
Waldron, Jeremy. 2002. "One Law for All? The Logic of Cultural Accommodation," *Washington & Lee Law Review* 59/1: 3–34.
Wilson, James Q. 1998. *Moral Judgment: Does the Abuse Excuse Threaten Our Legal System?* (New York: Basic Books).
Wootton, Barbara. 1963. *Crime and the Criminal Law* (London: Stevens & Sons).

3

Community, Culture, and Criminalization

*Nicola Lacey**

"[A] liberal political community [is] structured by the defining values of autonomy, freedom, privacy and pluralism; the role of the criminal law in such a polity [is to define or create] a range of 'public' wrongs that concern the whole community; and the role of the criminal trial [is to be] a process through which members of the community are called to answer for their alleged commissions of such wrongs."

(Duff 2001: 75)

"The reason for admitting a cultural defense lies not so much in a desire to be culturally sensitive, although that is surely a large part of it, but rather in a desire to ensure equal application of the law to all citizens.... [T]he actions of defendants should be judged against behavioural standards that are reasonable for a person of that culture in the context of this culture."

(Renteln 2004: 187–188)

INTRODUCTION

In *Punishment, Communication, and Community* (2001), Duff's central contention may be simply put. It is that punishment is best justified as a political community's attempt to "communicate to offenders the censure they deserve for their crimes" and, "through that communicative process to persuade them

---

* This chapter is reprinted (with minor modifications) from *Crime, Punishment and Responsibility: The Jurisprudence of Antony Duff*, ed. Rowan Cruft, Matthew H. Kramer, and Mark R. Reiff (Oxford University Press, 2011), 292–310.

to repent those crimes, to try to reform themselves, and thus to reconcile themselves with those whom they wronged" (Duff 2001: xvii). In this chapter, my limited ambition is equally simply put. It is to pose the question of whether it is possible to pursue the goal of a criminal law which realizes the values and represents the interests of a "liberal community" in a world of radical value pluralism. I shall examine this question by means of a case study: that of the cultural defense. Over the last twenty years, advocates of the cultural defense have argued that normative considerations of political morality dictate that differences in experience and worldview should modify the way in which criminal law is applied, potentially adjusting the standard applied to individuals. How convincing, I ask, is this argument? Can it be reconciled with Duff's liberal-communitarian vision of criminal justice? And, to the extent that it cannot be so reconciled, does this undermine the case for the cultural defense, or rather necessitate a revision of Duff's argument?

CONTEXTUALIZING CULTURAL DEFENSES

Imagine the following scenario:

The context is England of the late 1950s, not long after the codification of sexual offenses of 1956. The Wolfenden Committee has just published its report, advocating a modest liberalization of criminal law in the area of sexual morality. The second wave of the women's movement is, however, still in the future, and issues about women's and men's sexuality which are to become the popular currency of debate in a decade or so are only just beginning to be voiced beyond the more liberal sectors of society.

In a suburban area in the north of England, a young man is charged with rape. The facts of the case are banal enough. Twenty-one years old, he comes from a stable family and has no criminal record. He lives at home and, like his father, is a semi-skilled manual worker in regular employment. His mother is a housewife. He has been brought up according to a relatively strict moral code; like most of his peers, he has also been brought up to take for granted male ascendancy in matters ranging from intelligence through physical prowess to entitlements to resources. Sexual life is a matter of competition and jesting among his male peers; the jesting is premised on the fact that, while overt expressions of sexual desire among women are disapproved, women's desire for sex is assumed. His accuser is a woman of the same age, with whom he has been going out for six months. The alleged rape took place in a wooded area through which the couple were walking late at night on the way home from an evening out. Sexual intimacies had taken place before, but had always stopped short of intercourse. The young man admits that the young woman said clearly "Please, stop!" and struggled just before the alleged act of rape, inflicting a number of scratches, but attests that the context confirmed his belief that this was a formulaic female demurral and that no serious objection to intercourse was being raised. The young woman claims that she did not consent and unambiguously communicated the fact by the words and gestures already mentioned. The judge leaves the case to the jury on the issues of both consent and the defendant's belief in consent. The jury concludes that, though the young woman was not consenting, the young man genuinely believed her to be. Though the existence or non-existence of reasonable grounds for such a belief are not formally relevant as the law stands at the time, discussions in the jury room make it clear that most members of the jury regard the young man's mistake as not only plausible but reasonable. A woman who goes out with a man for six months, and allows him a certain degree of sexual intimacy, would be unreasonable in thinking that a mere phrase and token physical resistance—made, what is more, rather late in the proceedings—would lead him to think that permission to pursue that intimacy to its natural conclusion had been genuinely withdrawn. As one member of the jury puts it as they return to the court: "After all, everyone knows that women often say 'no' when they really mean 'yes'. So who can blame him, even if he did make a mistake?"

In many jurisdictions over the last twenty years, the question of so-called "cultural defenses" has begun to claim both academic and judicial attention (Volpp 1994; Phillips 2003; Dustin et al. 2004). Most of these analyses focus on cases involving members of minority ethnic or religious communities, and do not address the sort of case which I have sketched above. Yet it is hard to deny that the young man in this—not unrealistic (Temkin 2000)—scenario was acquitted by reason of a genre of cultural defense. The defendant's beliefs about women's sexuality, and about appropriate inferences from behavior, surely count as deriving from his "way of life." Such "ways of life" may affect defendants in a myriad ways potentially reflecting on criminal culpability: shaping their perception of facts; influencing their level of self-control in particular settings; bearing on their awareness of various social and legal norms; underpinning motivations deriving from their attachment to particular norms.

In her comprehensive analysis of cultural defenses, Alison Dundes Renteln (2004) has documented the wide range of ways in which cultural issues potentially bear on the operation of the legal order, mounting a persuasive case both for the relevance of motive to criminal liability and for the relevance of cultural evidence to a proper interpretation of motive, and reminding us that law already operates what might reasonably be called "cultural defenses," but in a covert and partial way. The idea that "horseplay," for example, should feature—along with medical interventions—on a rather short list of exceptions in English criminal law to the general principle that consent is no defense to the infliction of actual bodily harm, discloses a very specific (and strongly gendered) cultural heritage, and one which operates to exclude from the defense forms of physical violence no more potentially harmful yet less resonant with the dominant culture.[1]

Much the same is true of the "I thought that no meant yes" defense in rape cases. Both instances are telling reminders of the fact that it is not only "minority" but "majority" cultural defenses which raise troubling moral questions. Thus the case of "mistaken rape" serves to highlight some of the complexities which any advocate of cultural defenses must confront.[2] First, the example illustrates that "this" culture, in the context of which a person of "that" culture acts, is far from monolithic: value diversity and conflicting ways of life cannot be straightforwardly mapped onto cultural groups identifiable in terms of characteristics such as ethnicity, religion, or an experience of migration. Second, the various attempts to reform the law of rape in both the UK and the US in the last half century suggest that an appeal to the explanatory/excusatory relevance of "culture" in relation to offending behavior is indeterminate in the sense that it implies no general normative conclusion. For criminal law is often in the business of challenging or opposing particular cultural norms; hence— and of key importance to Duff's normative vision of liberal-communitarian criminal law—its room for cultural maneuver may be circumscribed by its fundamentally normative and communicative role.

It therefore appears that the notion of culture is simply not robust enough to do the analytic and ethical work which much of the cultural defense literature sets for it. If criminal law is inevitably in the business of, as Joseph Gusfield put it, expressing "the public worth of one subculture's norms relative to those of others, demonstrating which cultures have legitimacy and public domination" (Gusfield 1968: 58), then an appeal to "culture" per se cuts no normative ice. Cultural factors bearing on a defendant's perception or capacity to conform his or her behavior to criminal law stand on a par with other situational and circumstantial factors—levels of wealth or education for example—and stand to be assessed relative to the evaluative and practical role of the criminal justice system. While Kymlicka (1991) is undoubtedly right that certain kinds of cultural association or membership have a claim on our political and legal attention, cultural arguments bearing on criminal exculpation always call for evaluation in terms of the fundamental values and objects of the criminal process and of, in Duff's terms, liberal political community.

---

[1] For a spectacular example, see *R. v. Brown* [1994] 1 AC 212.

[2] Ripstein (2009: 124–126) has drawn a further and interesting distinction relevant to the scenario under consideration: that between a mistake about consent and a mistake about a person's underlying desires. For Ripstein, the transactional nature of consent implies some sort of socially recognizable act or comportment indicating the making of an arrangement or the making or accepting of an offer. Our example involves both a mistake about the young woman's inner thoughts and, I would argue, a mistake about consent; for the defendant (like the jury) reads the young woman's comportment as conforming with prevailing conventions about "accepting" female communicative behavior in, as it were, sexual transactions.

I shall return below to these questions of conceptual and normative indeterminacy, and relate them to analogous questions about the notion of "community" as a normative foundation of criminal law. But this is not the only line of inquiry which I want to pursue. In addition, I want to focus on the widespread assumption—disclosed in the quotations already given—that cultural defenses speak primarily to what criminal lawyers call the "responsibility requirement" in the construction of liability. Cultural defenses bear, in other words, on the proof of states of mind and attitudes—*mens rea*, mitigation, and excusatory defenses—rather than on the conduct element of offenses or on justificatory defenses.

The assumption of a clear analytic distinction between issues of responsibility and conduct is commonplace in contemporary criminal law scholarship and legislative design both within and beyond the common-law world. As Martin Golding puts it:

> The philosophy of criminal law is concerned with two broad areas of inquiry. First, what harms or states of affair should the law seek to prevent or reduce by means of the criminal sanction and what acts should be designated as crimes?... And second, what should be the criteria of culpability? This latter question concerns the theory of responsibility, and a main issue is the extent to which these criteria should track our ordinary moral views about responsibility and blame. (Golding 2005: 221)

Duff, with his view of defenses as blocking "the presumptive transition from responsibility to liability" (Duff 2007: 263), partially redraws this line. But he is sympathetic to two views which have shaped the debate about cultural defenses: first, that there is a division between criminal conduct and criminal responsibility; and second, that there should be a strong continuity between moral and legal standards of responsibility/culpability.

In this chapter, I will question these assumptions about the intimacy of the relationship between legal and moral responsibility (Cane 2004) and about the bearing of defenses on an assessment of responsibility which can be neatly separated from an evaluation of conduct and detached from a consideration of the overall rationale of criminal law. First, I shall suggest that a proper appreciation of the specificities of criminal law as a social institution should make us cautious about assuming any simple continuity between legal and moral ideas of responsibility, and that these institutional specificities moreover pose some difficult questions about the feasibility of any expansion of cultural defenses. Second, I shall suggest that the questions raised by cultural (and other) defenses cannot be zoned exclusively into the responsibility limb of criminal law, but bear also on the standards of conduct which criminal law purports to uphold: judgments of culpability inevitably evaluate conduct.

The implication, third, is that cultural defenses—like all criminal defenses—raise questions going to the core of the social practice of criminalization. The debate about what criteria we should use in shaping that practice—whether those criteria bear primarily on the delineation of criminal conduct, the attribution of responsibility, or the design of defenses—must therefore lie at the heart of the project. This argument will bring us back to the issue of the normative and conceptual indeterminacy of cultural defenses. For it implies, fourth and finally, that the challenge facing the advocate of extended cultural defenses is analytically indistinguishable from that of how criminal law should respond to the problem of any situational differences—class background, poverty, age, gender—between defendants which may bear on their offending behavior, in terms not only of their evaluation of the legal norm which they are accused of breaching but also of the degree of self-control required to meet it. This, I shall suggest, significantly complicates the idea of (even liberal) community in criminal law theory, and brings us face to face with what is perhaps the most intractable normative question confronting criminal law: how, in Duff's terms, to manage and justify the differential impact of criminal law on the "structurally socially excluded." For, following Duff's lead, I shall argue that the questions raised by cultural defenses should not be understood in exclusively ideal-world terms. Rather, we should be deeply interested in the complex question of the balance which a criminal law system needs to strike, under conditions of both moral diversity and structural inequality, between enunciating clear general standards and making context-specific adjustments for particularly situated defendants.

RESPONSIBILITY AND THE GOALS OF CRIMINALIZATION

In addressing these related questions, I set out from a simple set of hypotheses which provide a framework for the investigation and a means of exploring the linkages between particular conceptions of responsibility and the substantive role of criminal law in modern social governance. Ideas of individual responsibility for crime develop, I suggest, as responses to structural problems of coordination and legitimation faced by systems of criminal law (Lacey 2001a, 2001b, 2008). The content and emphasis of these problems can be expected to change according to the environment in which the system operates: important factors include the distribution of political interests and economic power; the prevailing cultural and intellectual environment; the organization and relative status of relevant professional groups; the array and vigor of alternative means of social ordering; and the prevailing balance between criminal law's quasi-moral and its regulatory, instrumental aspects. The practical orientation of responsibility in criminal law, decisively shaped by the institutional context of the criminal process, suggests that the relationship between moral-philosophical and legal conceptions of responsibility is more oblique than is generally assumed in criminal law theory. The criteria of criminal responsibility inevitably track the various aims and social functions of the criminal process. The requirement of proof of responsibility legitimates state criminalization, in the context of liberal expectations about individual freedom and the proper limits of state power.

In terms of this approach to the practical and normative role of criminal responsibility, the questions raised by cultural defenses might be stated in this way: First, would the admission of cultural evidence in the process of responsibility-attribution foster the legitimacy of criminal law? Second, could evidence of cultural predisposition be adduced in a form appropriate for use in a criminal trial; i.e., in such a way as to allow for legal scrutiny of its adequacy and interpretation of its relevance?

Conceptions of Criminal Responsibility: Capacity, Character, and Outcome

To assess the argument that cultural defenses bear exclusively on the attribution of criminal responsibility, we need to examine the various conceptions of responsibility (Lacey 2007) which circulate in legal discourse, and their respective implications for cultural defenses. One important way of thinking about responsibility in contemporary criminal law doctrine turns on human capacity. On this view, the foundation of not only a person's status as a responsible agent answerable to the normative demands of the criminal law but also of an attribution of responsibility for specific actions lies in human capacities of cognition—knowledge of circumstances, assessment of consequences—and volition—powers of self-control. The crucial factor is the way in which these human capacities are engaged in advertent conduct: to put it crudely, responsible conduct is conduct which the agent chooses. This notion of capacity-based responsibility naturally issues in a focus on so-called subjective principles of *mens rea*: intention, recklessness, or foresight of relevant consequences, knowledge, and so on.

Note that this psychological conception of responsibility provides a legitimating principle which is relatively independent of any evaluation of the relevant conduct (Norrie, 2001; Lacey 2001a). The proof of intention or subjective recklessness being a question of fact, the emphasis is on proof of the requisite mental state, which remains analytically separate from the conduct element of the offense. This feature may be useful in a system which criminalizes a huge range of conduct, much of it beyond the terrain of "real" or "quasi-moral" crime, and in which moral pluralism, value conflict, or social injustice raise awkward questions of fairness. For a factual view of *mens rea* might be thought to foster legitimation not only by purporting to respect autonomy but also by keeping these awkward questions out of the courtroom, or at least by displacing them onto the circumscribed terrain of the defenses or the sentencing stage, where they may be less disturbing to the image of criminal law's universalism and neutrality.

On this choice-based view of criminal responsibility, evidence about cultural predispositions would in principle be relevant wherever they bore on a defendant's basic capacity to choose by affecting her levels of awareness, knowledge, or self-control. But, as with any determining influences, whether of disposition or environment, what is less clear is the point at which such factors should be regarded as sufficiently strong to displace altogether or to moderate formally the degree of choice/capacity and hence of criminal responsibility. And this is, inevitably, an evaluative question. Like other defenses, cultural defenses reveal that the "factualization" of responsibility is an illusion, albeit a convenient one in terms of the legitimation of criminal law in a world of substantial inequality and value diversity.

There is, however, an alternative understanding of capacity-based principles of attribution. If the basic moral intuition is that it is only legitimate to hold people responsible for things which they had the capacity to avoid doing, we can realize this intuition by asking whether the defendant had a fair opportunity to conform his or her behavior to the criminal law standard (Hart 1968). This second approach has the implication that not only subjective mental states but also "objective" standards like negligence, practical indifference, or the imposition of reasonableness constraints in the specification of defenses may be accommodated. It therefore offers an account more likely to be able to rationalize the actual shape of criminal law.

The fair opportunity theory makes apparent what the choice theory obscures: namely that a criminal trial is in the business of making a potentially controversial normative evaluation of the defendant's conduct. The question to be proven is no longer the relatively neutral, factual and dualistic: "Did D cause P's death? If so, did s/he do so with intent to cause death or grievous bodily harm?"; "Did D have sexual intercourse with P? If so, did he or she do so intentionally and aware that P was not consenting?" It is, rather, "Did D do these things in circumstances in which we would say that he or she had a fair opportunity to confirm his or her behaviour to the law?" The answer to this question may, of course, be provided by proof of intent or subjective recklessness. But it might also be answered in terms of D's indifference or failure to advert to a risk which would have been obvious to a reasonable person, or to which it would be reasonable for us to expect D to advert, such that we would be inclined to say that he or she had a fair opportunity to avoid homicide or rape. So long as we are confident that D has the capacities of a reasonable person, this fair opportunity view is perfectly consistent with the moral intuition underlying the capacity principle of criminal responsibility. The question of fair opportunity brings the conduct element of the offense into clearer perspective, implying a more intimate relationship between the responsibility and conduct aspects of criminal liability. For the nature of the prohibited conduct inevitably bears on our evaluation of the fairness of the defendant's opportunity to avoid it.

The fair opportunity approach leaves a wide scope for the relevance of evidence that cultural background bears directly on the substance of our opportunities to conform our behavior to criminal law. But the key evaluative question remains to be answered: what are the criteria by which we should determine whether a particular background affects the *fairness* of a defendant's opportunity to conform her behavior to the legal standard; and from whose point of view is this to be determined? We shall return to these questions below.

These various ways of conceptualizing responsibility in terms of capacity do not exhaust the field. Recent criminal law theory has been marked by a resurgence of interest in the idea that an attribution of criminal responsibility is not so much a finding of capacity as in some sense an evaluation of character (Bayles 1982; Gardner 1998; Kahan and Nussbaum 1996; Huigens 1995, 2002; Lacey 1988; Michaels 1998; Nourse 2002; Simons 2002; Tadros 2005; Lacey 2011). In its most radical form, as Duff has argued, the character conception is morally unacceptable to the extent that, unless we are held to have capacity for our characters, character responsibility implies holding us accountable for things which we could not, or had no fair opportunity, to avoid—as in the case, discussed below, where objective standards of liability are imposed on defendants who lack normal capacities. And in Duff's view, character responsibility is premised on an inappropriately ambitious vision of the moral role of criminal law (Duff 1992, 2002).

Though character responsibility invariably invites us to condemn not merely the sin but also, in some sense, the sinner, we may usefully identify a spectrum of versions. At its most extreme, character responsibility exhibits what we might call "character essentialism" and "character determinism." In other words, it proceeds from a view of human character or identity as fixed, or at least as relatively stable; it regards character as determining conduct; and it regards bad character as constitutive of criminal responsibility. At the other end of the spectrum, we have character responsibility in the sense of a view of criminal conviction as grounded in the manifestation of a vicious characteristic or character trait, or a disposition hostile to the norms of criminal law—a disposition which might be, as it were, "out of character," and which does not necessarily mark out a stable propensity to express such characteristics. Between these ends of the spectrum, we have intermediate positions in which criminal conduct expressing vicious characteristics gives rise to a (stronger or weaker) presumption of bad character in the sense of propensity.

In relation to cultural defenses, the implications of more radical forms of character responsibility in terms of the potential influence of damaging cultural stereotypes in the assessment of "character" are worryingly clear. And even in its more cautious form—asking whether a defendant's conduct as a moral agent displays the sort of vicious character trait which justifies the criminal law in communicating moral indignation (Tadros 2005)—character responsibility naturally invites an attribution of responsibility within a broader time frame than that implied by the capacity principles, particularly where that broader evidence might bear on the agent's responsibility for her own beliefs, desires, and values. This would be conducive to the accommodation of the sorts of factors which advocates of the cultural defense press on our attention. The criteria on the basis of which legal decision-makers should evaluate whether a cultural explanation displaces an inference of vicious character, like the point of view from which such decisions should be made, remain, however, to be determined.

It has also been argued—notably by Tony Honoré (Honoré 1988)—that being the cause of a particular outcome may under certain circumstances ground an attribution of criminal responsibility. Honoré's argument for "outcome responsibility" is based on the idea that we are truly responsible for the outcomes of our actions even when they are "accidental" in the sense that we could not have done otherwise than we did. For the results of our actions become a part of who we are: even though we are related to unintended outcomes differently than to intended results, they nonetheless engage our agency in some morally relevant way. For example, if a person accidentally injures another person while driving, most of us would find it morally repellent if the person simply shrugged their shoulders and said, "It was really nothing to do with me; it was just an accident." Cases of absolute liability in criminal law are cases of pure outcome-responsibility: instances of strict liability subject to defenses, such as a due diligence defense, might be regarded as hybrids of outcome-responsibility and of capacity-based responsibility of the fair opportunity kind or the cautious genre of character-based responsibility.

Where defenses, due diligence or otherwise, are applicable to strict liability offenses premised on outcome-responsibility, issues of cultural defense are potentially in play on the basis of the arguments from both capacity- or character responsibility. In relation to offenses of absolute outcome-responsibility, the position is at first sight less clear. But what if—as is far from unrealistic—a criminal law system includes offenses of absolute liability the substance of which contradicts some deeply held convictions of certain cultural groups? Suppose that it strictly proscribes possession of a drug, the use of which is regarded as a key ingredient in the religious or cultural rites of a particular group. Defendants of this group are charged with the offense: they testify that they were aware of the prohibition, but regarded themselves as morally obligated to ignore it. Here, the cultural defense shades into conscientious objection. It is difficult to restrict the impact of a culturally explanatory argument to the issue of responsibility as distinct from conduct, for its potentially exculpatory or mitigating force may lie in the idea that members of a particular cultural group—or individuals with a particular set of beliefs—should be regarded as exempt from, or less blameworthy in breaching, a general standard. Cultural predisposition is no less relevant to our evaluation of the substantive norms of criminal law than to its practices of responsibility-attribution. Whether cultural evidence is used as a basis for arguing lack of choice, capacity, or fair opportunity to conform to the law, or that a breach of the law does not disclose vicious character, defendants will often be invoking their dissent or dissociation from the substance of the prohibition as part of the cultural predisposition speaking to the "reality" of choice, to "fairness" or to "viciousness."

Criminal Defenses

Whichever conception of responsibility is in play, then, questions of responsibility-attribution cannot be insulated from an evaluation of conduct. But perhaps it would be easier to delineate an adequately circumscribed conception of the relevance of cultural factors within the framework of the defenses? Criminal law theorists have often distinguished between defenses which are primarily excusatory and those which are justificatory. While excuses bear primarily on the conditions or circumstances under which the defendant has acted, and hence on responsibility, justifications bear on the nature of the defendant's conduct. Justifications justify actions; excuses excuse actors. A justification's normative defense of conduct is precisely what has often made courts so wary of such defenses, which at root pitch the defendant's view of the proper standard of conduct against that of the law. Hence most advocates of cultural defenses are careful to pose them at the level of excuse or mitigation rather than justification: to defendants' levels of responsibility in acting rather than in terms of the normative quality of their conduct.

But the excuse/justification, actor/action distinction turns out, once again, to be a difficult line to hold. First, justificatory and excusatory elements are often blended in actual defense arguments. For example, though the provocation defense has gradually acquired a more excusatory character—a claim of psychological loss of self-control—as the codes of honor in which it originated as a partial justification have been dismantled, elements of justification continue to mark the reasonableness standard which the provocation must also meet (Horder 1992). Thus, second, even where a defense is placed on a firmly excusatory footing, evaluations of reasonableness come into play. A provoked reaction must be that of "a reasonable person"; the duress defense is available only where a person of "reasonable firmness" would have succumbed to the threat, and so on. Even in the case of strongly subjective defenses and principles of responsibility, the aims of the criminal process come into play. For example, though defendants in English law are generally entitled to be judged on the basis of the facts as they believed them to be, a mistake induced by voluntary intoxication will be ignored. There is no such thing as purely factual criminal responsibility or excuse: a normative case for the relevant cultural or other argument will always have to be provided. What we regard as an excuse is itself a function of our evaluation of the conduct in question.

CULTURAL DEFENSES: FACT AND EVALUATION

Let us review the argument so far. To escape the problems of normative and conceptual indeterminacy, it is tempting to conceptualize a cultural defense as bearing on the existence or non-existence of criminal responsibility. The most straightforward argument for this position would seem to be via the capacity conception of responsibility. One of the many conveniences of this approach is that it promises a process of legitimation which apparently separates the question of responsibility from any controversial evaluation by defining it as a question of fact for the jury. In a world in which an attachment to the idea of respect for human agency entails that proof of responsibility is a key guarantee of criminal law's legitimacy, and a world, moreover, of value pluralism and cultural diversity, a factual, psychologized mechanism of responsibility-attribution serves to remove controversial normative questions from the core of criminal law.

On this view, cultural circumstances would be relevant to criminal responsibility where they bear on the capacities of choice and awareness which underpin the attribution of responsibility. This sounds straightforward. But as soon as we consider specific cases—cases such as the one with which this chapter opened—we realize that the idea of the choosing subject of criminal law itself begs a host of evaluative questions about the "normal" conditions of choice: conditions of knowledge, education, mental capacity, and so on (Duff 2007: 37ff.). Whether the circumstances alleged to derogate from those "normal" conditions (if indeed any such culturally neutral notion of "normal conditions" could be had) have to do with poverty, lack of education, mental illness, or enculturation within a particular social group, their bearing on criminal liability can hardly escape being based on an evaluation. And that evaluation will inevitably take place in relation to an appraisal of the overall role and importance of criminal law and of the specific norm of conduct in question. The line between attributions of responsibility and the evaluation of conduct turns out to be hard to hold.

Evaluation is key to the delineation of not only the conduct elements of offenses at the legislative stage but also to the application of principles of *mens rea* and to the moral fine-tuning attempted by the judicial application of criminal defenses and principles of mitigation. In these, motive remains of overt relevance to the process of criminal judgment. If defenses are reasonably regarded as exceptional—as concessions to unusual circumstances or particular human frailties—their implication in all-things-considered evaluation is perhaps less threatening to a system whose legitimacy is thought to depend on its universal reach and political neutrality. But this appearance should not be allowed to disguise the truth that all attributions of responsibility partake in substantive evaluations and can never be based merely on findings of fact. For the application of reasonableness standards to even the excusatory defenses places evaluation at the core of criminal judgment.

With either the fair opportunity version of the capacity conception of responsibility, or the character conception, the attribution of responsibility becomes an overtly evaluative matter: the fairness of a defendant's opportunity to foresee a risk, like the judgment of a defendant's attitude in relation to the relevant norm of criminal law, can hardly be seen as a question of fact. This, on the face of it, seems to open up a more promising terrain for cultural arguments. For if evaluations of fair opportunity, attitude, or disposition are always at some level concerned with what is reasonable, it seems appropriate to move from the usual formulation "would a reasonable defendant have intended, foreseen, known...etc what the defendant did?" to asking rather, "what would it have been reasonable to expect *this* defendant to intend, foresee, know...etc?" Such a reformulation is a desirable first step towards the important goal of ensuring the equal application of the law to all within its purview. But it is only a first step. For all the difficult argument—argument about what it *is* reasonable to ask of *this* defendant—remains to be made.

Cultural or Situational Defenses?

We have seen that the relevance of cultural factors is always subject to assessment in terms of evaluative matters such as the "reality" of the defendant's choice, the "fairness" of his or her opportunity to conform; the "reasonableness" of his or her perceptions. Is there any reason to think that the challenge facing the advocate of extended cultural defenses here is analytically or practically different from that faced by anyone interested in how criminal law should respond to other situational differences between defendants which may bear on their offending behavior? The attitudes engendered by the experience of extreme poverty, of mental disorder, of age, of gender, or of some combination of these situational factors, all seem to claim our attention in relation to the evaluation of the conditions under which choices are made; the fairness of opportunities; the reasonableness of perceptions and conduct. Such factors, indeed, are no strangers to defense arguments in a range of criminal cases. My imagined defendant's attitudes to male and female sexuality would be one example. Another, troubling recent example would be the so-called "homosexual panic" cases, in which defendants have sought to excuse an assault or even a homicide on the basis that they anticipated a sexual assault and over-reacted in panic (both the reaction and the panic being premised on stereotypes of homosexual behavior and on prejudices about homosexuality, as well as on disproportionate views about the appropriateness of a violent response) (Berger 2006: 113). As English courts discovered, to their consternation, in relation to the interpretation of the "objective" limb of the (recently superseded) provocation defense, there is virtually no limit to the sorts of circumstances, experiences, and characteristics which defendants can lead as evidence bearing on their capacity for self-control—and virtually no robust conceptual mechanism for distinguishing among them.[3] Yet if all situational differences potentially claim our normative attention, the practical imperatives of a criminal justice system pose some tricky questions about boundary-drawing, maintaining the robustness of legal prohibitions, and preserving an adequate degree of certainty.

These points bear on the crucially important project of setting out some workable criteria for the application—and limits—of cultural (and other situational) defenses. There is a persuasive prima facie case for cultural evidence being available to judges and juries in a far wider range of cases than it is today (Renteln 2004: 208). Yet it is not clear why there is any reason for distinguishing "cultural" evidence from any other evidence bearing on the specificity of the defendant's circumstances which affected his or her capacities, perceptions or values. So when should judges be moved by such evidence? The obvious normative criteria for selection—drawing on values such as equality, human rights and the prevention of irremediable harm (Renteln 2004: 203, 213–217; Volpp 1994; Phillips 2003)—are highly open-textured. Doubtless a further development of such normative criteria would take us some way to producing a theory of cultural defenses. But is the question here a *purely* normative one? If criminal responsibility were coterminous with moral responsibility, perhaps so. But, as I have already argued, it is not. Rather, criminal law operates in a distinctive social and institutional environment which confronts it with particular questions of legitimation and coordination which it must resolve if it is to fulfill *any* of its various social roles. The question of how far criminal law should modulate its standards to take into account the different situations of defendants cannot, therefore, be understood in exclusively

---

[3] See *R. v. Morgan Smith* [2001], 1 AC 146; *A.-G. for Jersey v. Holley* [2005] UKPC 23; see further Norrie 2002 and, on the continuities between the problems encountered in these cases and the issue of cultural defense, Gardner and Macklem 2001.

ideal-world terms. Rather, we need to attend to the difficult question of the balance which a criminal law system should strike, under conditions of moral diversity and social inequality, between enunciating clear general standards and making context-specific adjustments for particularly situated defendants. This is a normative question; but the practical scope for normative maneuver is set by a complex array of empirical considerations.

Within the framework of this sort of inquiry, there might well turn out to be important differences between cultural background and, say, poverty as potentially exculpating conditions, at the levels of both feasibility and legitimation. There is a resonance here with Duff's argument that punishment as currently practiced is morally problematic in that, particularly in relation to members of what we might call "structurally socially excluded groups"—people who make up a large proportion of those proceeded against in many systems—the broad preconditions for justification do not obtain (Duff 2001). Most importantly, the conditions which could underpin political obligation may not hold; and punishment and sentencing may fail, in both substance and form, to address their subjects as rational, capable agents, in normatively and practically comprehensible language. This, however, is not in Duff's view a cause for skepticism or despair—reactions which are rendered morally problematic in his view by the claims of victims, a significant proportion of whom also come from socially excluded or disadvantaged groups. Rather, Duff concludes that a reconstruction of penal practices along communicative lines could itself contribute to the gradual building of the preconditions for a liberal political community of the kind which he affirms.

Following this line of thought, one might argue for adjustment to criminal law standards for particular cultural groups, on the basis that it would contribute to the important goal of retaining their attachment to the basic legitimacy of the system as a whole. Alternatively, one might take the view that the attempt to calibrate the impact of criminal law according to differences of wealth, level of education, or cultural difference is at once indicated by normative considerations yet entirely unfeasible. But our normative and practical judgments might go entirely the other way. If, for example, we attached a very high importance to the integration of all social groups in relation to certain criminal law norms—norms in relation to the value of life and physical or sexual integrity, for example—we might be more sympathetic to the impact of situational disparities of wealth than we would be to situational disparities deriving from cultural attachments founded in class, ethnic, or other identifications. This last argument might be particularly weighty in relation to serious offenses. Cultural factors which bear on defendants' attachment to substantive criminal law norms may, in other words, be more threatening to the law's aspiration to universality and to respect liberal community than situational factors such as extreme poverty lying beyond the defendant's control.

The Reach of Criminalization and Cultural Defenses?

If I am right that the question of cultural or other situational defenses bears upon the most fundamental questions about the rationale for criminalization, it follows that the substantive reach of criminal law is highly relevant to the feasibility of cultural defenses. Duff has made a resounding case for reviving the idea of crime as a public wrong for which all members of liberal community may reasonably be called to answer, drawing on a "liberal-communitarian" political philosophy. This conception aims to have the best of both liberal and communitarian worlds. It gives a central place to the liberal ideals of individual autonomy and pluralism while also recognizing the place of shared commitments generating a meaningful "we" in whose name the criminal law may and indeed must be enforced. And it understands criminal law, whether statutory or not, as a "common law" declaring rather than creating norms which express the political community's most deeply shared values. Conversely, it aspires to avoid the usual liberal objections to communitarianism (Frazer and Lacey 1993) by emphasizing the political community as a partial community in the sense of being both limited in scope (only the most important shared values justify criminalization) and as constituting only one of the various normative communities within which its people live their lives.

In terms of Duff's account of the liberal-communitarian model, there is however room for elaboration of the precise sense in which political theory must take into account "our" membership of political communities, and in particular the sense in which we must begin with "individuals in community" (Duff 2001: 52), with the political community recognized as a starting point in our moral deliberations. Granted that any moral deliberation assumes a set of values which derive from some normative community or other, the difficulty with punishment appears to be that of identifying a sufficiently rich and shared set of values across the relevant territory and of justifying their imposition on those who—as Duff acknowledges they might—utterly reject them. It is not clear that the liberal will be entirely comfortable with the extent to which Duff's approach aspires to the internalization of the dominant community's values, nor that she will be comforted by the suggestion that the offender be invited to express his or her dissent.

This complexity in Duff's theory relates closely, I would argue, to the difficulties posed by cultural defenses. In a culturally diverse and morally pluralistic society, it is hardly surprising that coordinating on particular substantive values to guide the process of criminal legislation has become difficult. What has made it arguably yet more difficult has been the vast expansion of the terrain of criminal law since the eighteenth century, when Blackstone could confidently assert the notion of crime as public wrong (Farmer 1996; Lacey 2009). We have witnessed the rise and rise of criminal law as a regulatory tool of modern governments (Husak 2008)—a tool which has arguably become more and more attractive as other, informal means of social control are perceived to have weakened.

If I am right that questions about the proper scope of responsibility and defenses cannot be separated from questions about the proper rationale for substantive criminalization, this expansion of criminal law makes the accommodation of unequally situated defendants yet more difficult. For, though the expansion leaves the normative question unaffected, it bears directly on the practical question. The more intense and wide-ranging the criminal regulation, the more likely it is to be culturally specific in its conception or unequal in its impact. Hence the more widespread—and intractable—becomes the question of how to strike an adequate balance between the claims of fairness to individual defendants and the overall social goals of the system.

CONCLUSION

In the United Kingdom, the question of cultural defenses remains a minority scholarly interest, even if cultural evidence is beginning to appear more often before criminal courts (Dustin et al. 2004). Though Antony Duff has not as yet addressed the issue of cultural defenses, I hope to have shown that they raise key questions for the translation of his ideal theory into actuality, and provide a fertile ground for the application of some of his and of other scholarly arguments. Two other influential recent monographs bearing particularly on responsibility and the defenses—Horder's *Excusing Crime* (2004) and Tadros's *Criminal Responsibility* (2005)—accord cultural defenses not even a passing mention, despite advancing theoretical arguments which might be thought sympathetic to the incorporation of exculpatory or mitigating cultural arguments under some circumstances. Yet there is certainly a prima facie case which criminal law theorists will need to address, placing the burden of proof on all of us in future to spell out the implications of our arguments for cultural evidence and its relevance, and indeed for matters such as education and public policy stretching well beyond criminal law.

The implications for criminal law, I have suggested however, should be modest. There is, as it were, no space outside culture: no "view from nowhere" from which the appropriate criteria for the relevance of evidence, or reasonableness, or indeed the definition of criminal wrongs can be determined (Berger 2006: 125). Any test for the relevance of cultural evidence will itself be marked by cultural assumptions. Even the global discourse of human rights is imbued with culturally laden normative assumptions. The same is true, inevitably, for conceptions of "normal conditions of choice," "fairness of opportunity," and "viciousness of disclosed character." And all of these issues raise further questions about the constitution of the "we" in whose name criminal law is enacted and enforced.

We can drive this point home by reflecting on the scenario with which this chapter opened. In 2003, the English legislature introduced a Sexual Offences Act which provides that a defendant's belief in the victim's consent to sexual intercourse must now, in England and Wales, be based on reasonable grounds. In the Home Office report which preceded the legislation, it was further suggested that rape defendants should be subject to a "positive consent" standard: in other words, a mistake made in the absence of any positive effort to establish consent would be defined, as a matter of law, as unreasonable. I am not here concerned with whether these (actual or proposed) reforms were sensible or justified. What I want to point out is that such shifting of the legislative goalposts is a clear example of criminal law's intervention in social culture. Such reforms of the law of rape are both responding to cultural changes—towards a stronger attachment to the notion of a woman's right to sexual integrity and a different view of the possible damage which unwanted sex may cause, among other things—and seeking to consolidate or even further those changes. The cultural norm that women are presumptively available for sex even if they express dissent has, in other words, been culturally disqualified by the law. To allow a cultural defense of the kind pleaded by my imaginary defendant would, quite simply, undermine the very purpose of the legislative change.

Criminal law is, inevitably, in the business of evaluation. It is also, inevitably, in the business of applying standards. In liberal democratic modern societies, criminal law's legitimacy depends strongly on the idea that these standards are of general application, and that everyone should be held to the same standard. Criminal law is, intrinsically, a system which announces standards of behavior, and applies them notwithstanding particular instances of dissent from their normative recommendations. This constrains, though it does not remove, the space for cultural (or other) defenses; for criminal law's cultural assumptions are by no means beyond critique. To fulfill any social role at all, criminal law must constantly assure the conditions of its own legitimacy, as well as arrangements under which the evidence on which its judgments are based can be properly coordinated. What is at stake, in a culturally diverse society, is a matter of finding the optimal normative balance between fine-tuning criminal law to meet the fairness claims of differently situated subjects and sustaining the generality and certainty which are the system's conditions of existence and efficacy. There can be no doubt that this task would be considerably easier if the scope of criminal law was less extensive than it has become in countries such as the US and the UK (Husak 2008). But even on the basis of the more parsimonious criminal system which many of us would like to see, stark cultural conflicts—conflicts which, I have argued, sit on a par with diversities premised on ways of life related to age, gender, socio-economic group—will be likely to arise, even in relation to serious offenses. Though some of these cases can be disposed of by a better informed and more even-handed application of existing doctrines such as mistake of fact, many cannot. For they raise questions about the substance of criminal law's prohibitions.

The debate over the cultural defense should therefore take its place within a renewed debate about the proper—and feasible—scope and role of criminal law. Working out—as a matter of social science as much as legal philosophy—the appropriate balance between fairness to variously situated defendants and the goals of contemporary criminal law remains one of its most urgent challenges.

REFERENCES

Bayles, Michael J. 1982. "Character, Purpose and Criminal Responsibility," *Law and Philosophy* 1/1: 5–20.

Berger, Benjamin J. 2006. "Emotions and the Veil of Voluntarism: The Loss of Judgment in Canadian Criminal Defences," *McGill Law Journal* 51: 99–128.

Cane, Peter. 2004. *Responsibility in Law and Morals* (Oxford: Hart Publishing).

Duff, R. A. 1992. "Choice, Character and Criminal Liability," *Law and Philosophy* 12/4: 345–383.

Duff, R. A. 2001. *Punishment, Communication, and Community* (Oxford: Oxford University Press).

Duff, R. A. 2002. "Virtue, Vice and Criminal Liability: Do We Want an Aristotelian Criminal Law?," *Buffalo Criminal Law Review* 6/1: 147–184.

Duff, R. A. 2007. *Answering for Crime: Responsibility and Liability in the Criminal Law* (Oxford: Hart Publishing).

Dustin, Moira, Anne Phillips, and Oonagh Reitman. 2004. "Women and Cultural Diversity: A Digest of Cases," <http://webdb.lse.ac.uk/gender>.

Farmer, Lindsay. 1996. *Criminal Law, Tradition and Legal Order* (Cambridge: Cambridge University Press).

Frazer, Elizabeth and Nicola Lacey. 1993. *The Politics of Community: A Feminist Analysis of the Liberal-Communitarian Debate* (New York: Harvester Wheatsheaf).

Gardner, John. 1998. "The Gist of Excuses," *Buffalo Criminal Law Review* 1/2: 575–598, reprinted in Gardner 2007: 121–140.

Gardner, John. 2007. *Offences and Defences* (Oxford: Oxford University Press).

Gardner, John and Timothy Macklem. 2001. "Provocation and Pluralism," *Modern Law Review* 64/6: 815–830, reprinted in Gardner 2007: 155–176.

Golding, Martin P. 2005. "Responsibility," in *The Blackwell Guide to the Philosophy of Law and Legal Theory*, ed. Golding and W. A. Edmundson (Oxford: Blackwell), 221–235.

Gusfield, Joseph A. 1968. "On Legislating Morals: The Symbolic Process of Designating Deviance," *California Law Review* 56/1: 54–73.

Hart, H. L. A. 1968. *Punishment and Responsibility*, (Oxford: Clarendon Press); 2nd edition, ed. John Gardner (Oxford: Clarendon Press 2008).

Honoré, Tony. 1988. "Responsibility and Luck: The Moral Basis of Strict Liability," *Law Quarterly Review* 104/4: 530–553, reprinted in Honoré 1999: 14–40.
Honoré, Tony. 1999. *Responsibility and Fault* (Oxford: Hart Publishing).
Horder, Jeremy. 1992. *Provocation and Responsibility* (Oxford: Clarendon Press).
Horder, Jeremy. 2004. *Excusing Crime* (Oxford: Oxford University Press).
Huigens, Kyron. 1995. "Virtue and Inculpation," *Harvard Law Review* 108: 1423–1480.
Huigens, Kyron. 2002. "Homicide in Aretaic Terms," *Buffalo Criminal Law Review* 6/1: 97–146.
Husak, Douglas. 2008. *Overcriminalization: The Limits of the Criminal Law* (New York: Oxford University Press).
Kahan, Dan M. and Martha C. Nussbaum. 1996. "Two Conceptions of Emotion in Criminal Law," *Columbia Law Review* 96/2: 269–374.
Kymlicka, Will. 1991. *Liberalism, Community, and Culture* (Oxford: Clarendon Press).
Lacey, Nicola. 1988. *State Punishment* (London: Routledge).
Lacey, Nicola. 2001a. "In Search of the Responsible Subject," *Modern Law Review* 64: 350–371.
Lacey, Nicola. 2001b. "Responsibility and Modernity in Criminal Law," *Journal of Political Philosophy* 9: 249–277.
Lacey, Nicola. 2007. "Space, Time and Function: Intersecting Principles of Responsibility Across the Terrain of Criminal Justice," *Criminal Law and Philosophy* 1: 233–250.
Lacey, Nicola. 2008. *Women, Crime and Character: From Moll Flanders to Tess of the d'Urbervilles* (Oxford: Oxford University Press).
Lacey, Nicola. 2009. "Historicising Criminalization: Conceptual and Empirical Issues," *Modern Law Review* 72/6: 936–961.
Lacey, Nicola (2011). "The Resurgence of Character: Responsibility in the Context of Criminalization," in *Philosophical Foundations of Criminal Law*, ed. R. A. Duff and S. Green (Oxford: Oxford University Press), 151–178.
Michaels, Alan C. 1998. "Acceptance: The Missing Mental State," *Southern California Law Review* 71: 953–1035.
Norrie, Alan. 2001. *Crime, Reason and History*, 2nd edition (London: Butterworths).
Norrie, Alan. 2002. "From Criminal Law to Legal Theory: The Mysterious Case of the Reasonable Glue-Sniffer," *Modern Law Review* 65/4: 538–555.
Nourse, V. F. 2002. "Hearts and Minds," *Buffalo Criminal Law Review* 6/1: 361–388.
Phillips, Anne. 2003. "When Culture Means Gender: Issues of Cultural Defence in the English Courts," *Modern Law Review* 66/4: 510–531.
Renteln, Alison Dundes. 2004. *The Cultural Defence* (New York: Oxford University Press).
Ripstein, Arthur. 2009. *Force and Freedom: Kant's Legal and Political Philosophy* (Cambridge, MA: Harvard University Press).
Simons, Kenneth W. 2002. "Does Punishment for 'Culpable Indifference' Simply Punish for Bad Character?," *Buffalo Criminal Law Review* 6/1: 219–315.
Tadros, Victor. 2005. *Criminal Responsibility* (Oxford: Oxford University Press).
Temkin, Jennifer. 2000. "Prosecuting and Defending Rape: Perspectives from the Bar," *Journal of Law and Society* 27/2: 219–248.
Volpp, Leti. 1994. "(Mis)identifying Culture: Asian Women and the 'Cultural Defense,'" *Harvard Women's Law Journal* 17: 57–101.

4

Between Denial and Recognition: Criminal Law and Cultural Diversity

Kimmo Nuotio*

THE CHALLENGE OF MULTICULTURALISM

The fact of multiculturalism challenges the liberalist presuppositions of modern law, especially liberal individualism, and forces us to recognize the importance of cultures and communities for our ethical and moral thinking in a sense which is relevant for the law as well. I would also claim that multiculturalism pushes thinking on criminal justice issues towards political theory, because it makes it much more important than before to theorize about the premises of the authority of law.

As a very fine-tuned and in many respects strongly value-based and value-oriented field of law, criminal law provides a good context for such reflections. Due to the flexibility of criminal law, cultural issues may be taken into account in various ways, should this turn out to be necessary. Criminal law is also a cultural phenomenon itself, representing the values of the community. Western criminal justice is individualistic in many ways, as it aims at allocating blame and responsibility to individuals for their wrongful actions. At the same time, it is the part of law through which the political community largely defines itself by deciding about issues of right and wrong. Criminal law is marked by an ethical we-perspective. In a broader view, this means that the community forming the polity defines itself by adopting a certain culture of

---

* This chapter was presented at the Institute of Law, Chinese Academy of Social Science in Beijing, as well as the conference on Cultural Diversity and Criminal Law at Columbia University. I would like to thank the audiences in both conferences, and the editors, for their helpful comments.

control, that of criminal justice. Such a culture consists broadly of legal and ideological principles on crime and punishment. This culture also consists of principles of legislative ethics (last resort), views on how the threat of punishment is meant to work, defense rights, etc.

In the following I wish to defend the following three presuppositions and look at the implications these might have when theorizing about cultural factors in criminal law be it at the level of legislative practices or at the level of deciding criminal cases:

(1) The modern law informed by liberal individualism requires strong presuppositions of legal personhood—i.e., it treats people as responsible and rational individual agents. These presuppositions differ from those of traditional communities, but are now essentially irreversible.

(2) The modern law requires people to think of themselves as "citizens" bound together in a political project, and not just as individuals who belong to pre-political groups. This means that issues of responsibility cannot be reduced to "mere moral blameworthiness," and that the state has a legitimate interest in preserving the conditions that sustain the mutual recognition of people as citizens.

(3) Cultural sensitivity deserves attention. Cultural grounds have a role to play in criminal proceedings, but these should find a role in the frame of the ordinary criminal law doctrines.

CRIMINAL LAW, CRIMINAL JUSTICE

Cultural issues have not traditionally been regarded as very relevant to criminal law and criminal justice. One of the reasons is, surely, that the traditional philosophical presuppositions concerning the structures and elements of penal liability are "modern" products that build on rationalistic criteria. The concept of personhood, for instance, is not much connected with things such as what people in general are like in legal analysis, what their beliefs are, etc. The law has rather operated with formal ideas. This is especially true with categories of penal liability.

The legal system treats individuals as responsible legal subjects, and with this construction it presses reality into categories. The philosophy of the Enlightenment had put the human being into the center of legal thinking, as human reason was the ultimate source of all law. Law understood as a form of organizing freedom in a society simply presupposed that people possessed certain general capabilities and could form a joint political body. Human beings were rather regarded as responsible moral and political and legal agents than as individuals determined and conditioned by their environment. Criminal law is more about actions than persons. What people think and believe is, however, not unimportant when determining issues of criminal liability. The history of legal thinking owes more to moral and political theory than to sociology and other forms of knowledge seeking to establish causal links and laws.

Without engaging more with debates on the philosophy of punishment, we should note that the strong dominance of liberal individualism and the ideologies of just desert have further contributed to the non-observance of cultural aspects (see the discussion about liberal individualism in Norrie 1991). The utilitarian emphasis on prevention instead of or in addition to retribution would raise further interesting issues, which cannot be discussed here. Again if we connect cultural perspectives to communitarianism, restorative justice would be more the line to proceed. Different approaches would raise different issues as regards cultural questions.

One way to approach the issue of cultural sensitivity of criminal justice would be to ask whether in fact modern law has failed to see the fact that people are not as free as presupposed by legal thought, that is, that law fails to recognize that culture determines or influences people's actions in ways which could render such laws both inefficient and unjust. Ethnic and religious minorities, for instance, may sometimes be regarded as local communities that are closer to pre-modern law and pre-modern communities than a state-law paradigm dares to see. A better option could then be to leave the law to such communities themselves, letting them handle the conflicts internally. From a radical cultural and communitarian perspective, modern law might be simply wrong.

This observation could have significance if we think about practices such as victim–offender mediation, or other restorative practices that are not directly instances of legal application. We face the challenge of legal pluralism. The problem is, of course, that modern law finds it hard to establish closed regimes that would not need to share the normal commitments to *ordre public*.

In this chapter I rather wish to discuss issues of cultural sensitivity from a traditional legal perspective, building on the deep-rooted traditions of liberal individualism and looking at the tensions caused by cultural challenges in this setting. Since states have gained the monopoly of violence, criminal law is mainly state law. Here I thus work on the premises of state centrism which has been openly criticized by Alison Dundes Renteln (Renteln 2004: 18).

As such, criminal law has a defensive nature as it is intended to preserve values and rights. Criminal law is in any case able to express values and interests, which makes it interesting from a cultural point of view. Criminal law resembles constitutional law in this ability to express the basic values of society. In contrast to constitutional law, criminal law is more clearly a particular order as it defines the limits of rights.

Criminal law is value-laden, but in a liberal Western society it does not seriously impose "internal values" on the communities that are bound by it.

It requires conformity, but nothing more. Some practices may be challenged and prohibited, but it does not generally demand that we internalize certain motives and reasons for action. The legal community is much weaker than cultural communities typically are. The law deals with externalities, not with the attitudes, thoughts, and minds of people. The question of criminal law's relationship with social values has of course close connections with issues of criminal law moralism, such as whether criminal justice can be seen as a means of enforcing morality. The cultural view could easily mean falling back to moralist positions.

Too little work has been done on the principles of criminalization generally, and specifically on the principles of criminalization in a multicultural setting. This is a level on which multiculturalism brings in new types of issues. We could, perhaps, basically agree on some general principles, such as the harm principle, but in culturally sensitive issues the harm to be prevented is often immaterial rather than material in nature and the potential harm as well as the potential burdens of criminalization are perhaps not evenly distributed in the community.[1]

We have usually considered that the issue of humiliation and the degrading aspects of penal justice deal with matters of penal sanctions only. We are not used to the idea that some criminalizations could have effects that are in a negative sense relevant for those whose interests are involved.

Already a criminalization may sometimes have problematic effects, something similar to the humiliating effects of certain penal sanctions, on the lives of people. We are speaking of a phenomenon which resembles the problem of enforcing morality through criminal justice, but which is actually a mirror image of it; a censure of traditional morality by means of an interventionist criminalization. Borrowing the term used by Andrew von Hirsch and Uma Narayan, we could talk about an *acceptable penal content* (Hirsch 1993: 84). Is there anything in penal norms that is not acceptable to some, for cultural reasons? Are there restrictions to the way that criminal justice should infringe on sensitive cultural issues? Should repressive law leave such areas for other, perhaps smoother and more flexible kinds of law? It may indeed be the case that this option should be considered when there is fundamental insecurity about the underlying evaluations (cf. the useful analysis in Ivison 1999).

Criminalizations may differ in various respects. One traditional conceptual distinction has been drawn between offenses *mala in se* and offenses *mala prohibita*. Offenses that are wrong in themselves are usually violations of both someone else's rights and a shared moral conviction. *Mala prohibita*, in turn, entails regulatory offenses that are wrong simply because they have been included in the law-books. It is clear that these two groups of criminalizations

---

[1] Jonathan Schonsheck has discussed the hidden "racism" of a drugs crime regulation. See Schonsheck 1994.

(I am not claiming that such a clear-cut categorization is always possible) present different problems for multicultural societies. As far as the first group is concerned, the problem is that we might have several views on what the fundamental moral rules are, and these might clash even with the rights-based view that individual rights enjoy a special position as protected legal interests. The whole basis of the justification of criminal law which in some sense enforces a common morality needs to be rethought. When no consensus concerning substantial values can be reached, criminal law becomes more political. As an institution it needs to stand alone, without a strong consensus backing it up. This might entail that issues of criminal law become more political than before, because they might seem more open to different legislative options.

We should not, however, accept such a relativist argument unquestioningly. It might turn out that the core area of criminal law, that of core criminalizations, represents some deeper values that could not and should not be relativized so easily. This could be part of the constitutionality of the *Rechtsstaat*, which always recognizes a set of fundamental rights as limiting the use of legislative authority but which from time to time obliges the state to safeguard certain fundamental rights against possible violations by enacting criminalizations. The criminalization of torture is one example. The prohibition of torture counts as central to the legitimacy of all state law. *Mala in se* covers the part of criminal law which is closer to the universal morals than the particular ethics of the community in question. This is why honor killings have to be understood as killings, anyway.

The other part, criminalizations *mala prohibita*, are closer to the particular conception of the good of the society. From the point of view of cultural issues, this area may be problematic because it is so openly interventionist. The interventionist welfare state with its safety regulations and programs readily clashes with culture-based norms and requires adaptation on the part of cultural groups. The obligation to wear a safety helmet instead of a turban is an example of this. Such an obligation is based on the idea that a safety helmet provides safety in the case of a crash and as this sort of paternalistic safety measure has been generally accepted, the legislature has produced a rule making this a general obligation. The issue of a cultural objection to such a general rule had probably most often not been raised at all when the justification for introducing such a rule was discussed.

Many of these issues could be discussed from the point of view of fundamental rights. If doubts arise, such discussions could basically be raised during the legislative procedure. After the legislative measures have been taken, the constitutional provisions on fundamental rights could play a role in adjusting the general norms in the courts as well. There might be legal grounds for cultural exemptions from general rules.

Although cultural issues such as particular minority rights could emerge during the legislative process, it is not quite obvious how much they could and should be taken into account at that stage. It is far from clear how far exceptions from the general legal obligations could be included in the texts of laws, without sacrificing the basic virtues of legislation.

The laws are expected to be general, and exceptions to legal obligations should be made on principled grounds and be based on fair criteria. They should be granted to other similar groups as well. If the sacramental use of the peyote drug is allowed for Native Americans, other groups might wish to enjoy a similar advantage. It might turn out that the real reason behind granting this exemption is not the preservation of and respect for Native American culture and tradition, but something more familiar: the religious rights of each people.

It might also be difficult to address the question of exceptions to general rules at the level of legislation. For obvious reasons, we do not prefer to write down exemption clauses in the legal provisions themselves. The second way of handling the problem could be to try to anchor the cultural adaptations of law in the human rights and fundamental rights law or simply find a proper place for them on the level of ordinary legal doctrine. Cultural considerations that can be backed up with genuine legal arguments probably have a much better prospect of having an impact on the politics of the general rules to be adopted.

Questions concerning cultural adaptations of general legal rules could also arise in the ordinary context of legal proceedings. The defendants of a criminal case might challenge the charges by referring to generally accepted long-term custom, cultural rights, or something similar, and oppose the application of a penal norm to the action in question. Non-applicability would normally mean creating an exemption from the general rule. The application of a rule would thus be contested on the grounds that the consequences of blind following of the rule in question would be detrimental to valuable interests that either can or cannot be backed up by ordinary legal arguments.

The courts most often do not have to openly take a stand on the constitutionality of a specific law, but can restrict themselves to the particular application of rules in a case. This gives room for the emergence of a broad set of techniques of legal argument. Even after non-application in a given case, the law itself maintains its validity. Legal decision-making knows of many lines of argument about how this can be done, but for systematic reasons, the exceptions to the rules need to be systematic and based on reasons. Like cases have to be treated alike.

Challenges on cultural grounds in criminal cases could have a multifaceted nature. They could be supported by internally legal grounds, such as minority rights and human and fundamental rights. At the same time, they could be of a political and moral nature, exposing the political and moral conflict below the calm surface of the law.

Criminal law relates also to the civic role of people, which brings this tension into the groups nurturing their internal traditions and values. Criminal law, if and when it preserves its mundane and secular role, lists the civic obligations of the people, and it creates the presumption of the duty to live accordingly. This presumption is certainly not unproblematic, but it seems to arise directly from the role of criminal law as central state law, or statutory law.

CULTURAL DEFENSE AS A HARD CASE

One might think that there is a link between generally discriminatory practices and the effort to introduce cultural defenses, which could do practically the same job as civil rights, correcting past injustices, and addressing equality concerns. This sense of inequality, of discrimination, could explain the legal fight because if the ordinary liberalist and retributive penal practices result in such a state of affairs, is it not a general problem of how the criminal justice system encounters ethnic and cultural minorities that are often also marginalized otherwise? On this reading, the matter is actually highly political, the cultural defense being needed in order to respond to certain oppressive features of the modern formalist culture of criminal justice. Without such a general context of social justice, the argument for the cultural defense seems much weaker. The introduction of cultural defenses could reflect the acknowledgment that criminal justice has treated minority groups badly and still does, and these injustices need to be corrected by introducing a balancing principle along the lines of a sort of reverse discrimination, now in this case internal to the criminal justice system. This line of thinking would certainly call for criticism because of the problems with formal equality before the law.

The generality of laws necessitates that the courts have to actively continue the work of reconstructing the legal system as a system of rights. This task, which we might speak about as upholding the "integrity of law," presupposes many techniques judges use to try to resolve hard legal cases. Judicial review of the cases necessarily lets the judges decide. As judges are not political but (at least ideally) legal actors, they might not recognize all the political and moral conflicts which form part of the setting, unless the courts are turned into policy-makers. Such a role would be highly problematic also due to the lack of political legitimacy of courts.

Bringing in cultural sensitivity could challenge the legal way of thinking very profoundly. It might challenge the rationality of law in general. It might also challenge the nature of rights, because the fundamental rights or human rights could prove underdeveloped as they apply to cultural issues. We might observe lacunae in human rights in issues that are constitutive for traditional communities such as customs.

We might also note that the tension between culture and tradition and the normative requirements of the law is somehow reproduced in the field of human rights. Human rights are, just as criminal laws are, normatively critical, being means of censorship in relation to tradition and existing culture. I believe that no positive law can permanently resolve the underlying problems, because the cultural criticism, the cultural challenge to criminal justice, presents a proposal for a reversed censorship, which is based on the view that criminal laws should not intrude on cultural issues. This is a battle between two perspectives, two sources of criticism. We are caught in a dilemma: criminal law is primary vis-à-vis culture, but criminal law is still entirely dependent on culture. It is only by way of cultural embeddedness and rootedness that criminal law can defend itself.

We started our observations by noting that the cultural issues could be important because the community might be defined by its culture, and the identity of the members of the community could thus be culturally conditioned in the sense that requires the accommodation of criminal justice. In some sense we could say that what really clash are the actual culture and the normative legal culture. If the normative legal culture is based on the assumption that law represents, as the Kantians would say, a sphere distinguished from tradition, a realm that assures freedom for the individuals, it may face a difficulty in accommodating itself to the cultural challenge. For culture to become relevant for law would require that the cultural conflict be brought into the realm of law as a conflict or tension *within* the legal culture.

One problem that we also must consider is that even taking cultural context into account in criminal law might itself become a denunciatory practice, a denial of recognition. This view indicates that culture is like nature in that it influences and even determines the actions of the individual, thus limiting individual responsibility on factual grounds. Culture would then be regarded as a kind of force that actually diminishes responsibility for one's action in declaring it traditional and customary instead of highlighting its individuality. It is therefore crucially important to think carefully about how and why culture matters. It might be that both culture and law have the potential to work towards non-recognition or misrecognition. Culture itself is not innocent in this respect.

The criminal liability of individuals requires freedom, not having been forced by external factors to act in a certain way. The mentally ill, for instance, lack freedom, because they cannot set their own preferences or express themselves fully in their actions because of their illness. If we constructed culture as a kind of external determinant of action, we would lessen the responsibility of individuals for their actions.

If culture is like tradition, recognizing the importance of culture could mean abandoning many of the underlying presuppositions of legal and moral personhood. The public autonomy of the individuals that Habermas speaks about requires a mutual recognition structure which is based on abstract normative principles. In this sense tradition cannot be a source, or at least the sole source, of the concept of a citizen or of a legal person. In modern law and its post-conventional morality, this structure is formalistic since everyone is recognized as having rights that are freed from any particular social status structure. Every person is regarded as free to set his or her political preferences, and needs to be taken as such a person.

Laws of traditional communities build on much weaker presuppositions of legal personhood. I feel that this is one field of research that should now be taken up very seriously: the problems of law in a multicultural society that includes many types of groups, including such that base their view of legal subjectivity on non-universalistic viewpoints.

The idea is that in a way modern positive law has transformed its underlying moral principles. At the same time as the positive law has become positive and statutory, it has developed to grant people new types of rights: the political rights to participate and the social welfare rights in addition to the freedom rights. These are all constitutional rights now limiting the possibility of a return to the pre-modern conception. It is difficult to imagine how we could step backwards in our legal development. Following this line of thinking we should say that a return will only be possible by deliberately taking political decisions and abolishing the definitional structures of modern law. The legitimacy of a legal system is dependent on us first recognizing each other as right-holders at a pre-legal stage.

REJECTED IDENTITIES

Cultural conflicts often have to do with the fact that different meanings are associated with actions and events by their various participants. The key question is then whether we must guarantee that the legal imputations always respect such cultural sensitivities. Are we generally entitled to have our own personal worldview respected by the courts when they decide cases in which we are involved? Would other solutions mean that some aspects that are constitutive of our identity will be publicly rejected?

The conflict may often be between the two expressions: that of the action itself, and that of its legal interpretation. Criminal law aims at replacing the meaning and evaluation of the act given by the actor himself or herself, or the community, by a legal assessment of it. This might turn into a conflict of interpretation. Criminal law is a sort of institutionalized denial, taking standpoints and presenting them over the heads of the individuals in question as it communicates and allocates blame. But also the criminal law carries the community and its practices with it. Introducing cultural issues to criminal law could be regarded as a process of becoming conscious of the presence of cultural issues in criminal law. The more we become aware of these, the more we see them.

Criminal law and criminal justice both recognize and consciously refuse to recognize at the same time. They recognize wrongs, they label actions as wrongful, and they deny the worth of wrongful actions. They do not necessarily recognize the interpretation of the perpetrator of his or her act as binding in the last instance. But at the same time criminal law and criminal justice recognize the convicted person as responsible for her actions, as a rational member of the legal community. It determines a specific meaning for certain actions.

The legal responsibility and legal liability structures resemble issues of moral responsibility and liability in an important sense. Responsibility and liability for crimes cannot rest on mere moral blameworthiness. What I would like to stress is that the political person, the citizen, needs to be involved in the picture. The duty to respect the law rests on the civic role of a person as a member of a political community. The modern positive law needs to be understood from this perspective, because it cannot guarantee its legitimacy otherwise. The two concepts of person, that of citizen and that of a legal person, need to be brought into contact with each other (see Günther 2005).

Actions may be wrong, not persons. The legal imputation should never, however, appear as fully accidental and surprising. Legal imputation requires a sociological back-up. People need to understand what has happened and why the legal system intervened. The criminal law provisions defining various offenses are deemed to refer to actions in an understandable way, all of which takes place under the fundamental challenge of legitimacy and justice. Important legal principles, such as the legality principle, highlight the significance of the predictability of penal liability and the preciseness of criminal law.

Criminal laws do not speak directly about identities, as this field of law limits itself to issues concerning actions. But certain actions that are prohibited as criminally wrong might be relevant for the identity of particular persons. Issues related to sexual crimes produce quite strong images of sexual manners and sexual identities. Such issues are being dealt with in modern criminal justice by a more fine-tuned approach than before. The protected interest is sexual autonomy, not public morals.

I have chosen this perspective of recognition of the connections between criminal justice and its cultural significance and meaning. We may loosely connect this with the philosophical discussion concerning different aspects of recognition (see Ricoeur 2005), which has an active and a passive side. We actively give recognition to persons, but we also strive to get recognition from others as persons. Practices and structures of mutual recognition are of particular importance in a multicultural society. The law plays an important role as a structure normatively defining interpersonal relations in various ways. It has ramifications for social practices and various kinds of interpersonal relationships. Without some kind of mutual legal and factual recognition of one another as persons, ordered and peaceful life would certainly not be possible.

We should strive for an understanding of what the consequences of such an understanding are to the general thinking on criminal justice in a multicultural context.

The legal system's formality might prove to be a myth. Of course the justice that criminal justice may deliver is always formal in some sense. Predictability and legal certainty are of high value. Like cases should be treated alike. From this point of view, cultural aspects could be fully excluded from criminal justice as irrelevant. But again, justice also requires that we recognize relevant differences. We should treat different cases differently. This is the point that paves the way for cultural differences in the design of legal institutions.

Charles Taylor has made this point very clearly. In a multicultural society, the recognition struggles involve both of these aspects. People wish to be recognized both as equals and as different (Taylor 1994). Criminal justice should be able to do both as well. Failing to recognize important differences could turn the legal system itself into a problem. Formalism could institutionalize discriminatory practices. This tension between formalism (universality) and concreteness is a fundamental one, if we think about the legal status and legal strategies of those who are different on cultural grounds.

A person whose beliefs are strange to us might be measured with false yardsticks if we do not take this fact into account. A person with irrational beliefs might even be regarded as insane and lacking the capacity to be a responsible person. This possibility of complete denial is surely an extreme example of not recognizing someone as a person. We should become aware that our concept of a person is filled with rationalistic presumptions. It is the law's internal rationality that we are imposing on people and that could, at least in some regards, be the most fundamental problem here. As people's worldviews are sometimes not rational, as they believe in gods and witches, their reasons for action are not always rational either.

The effort of making people responsible for their doings is vulnerable in many ways, even without specific regard to multicultural issues. We might end up labeling people instead of actions as bad and ill-intentioned. We might at the same time destroy conditions relevant for mutual recognition in legal and factual terms. It has been one of the achievements of modern criminal justice theory to restrict penal liability to acts and omissions only. And yet, as things are, even prohibitions of a general nature might have consequences in regard to the constitutive aspects of mutual understanding and recognition.

The multicultural setting renders it more difficult than ever to agree on the substance of prohibitions. Recognition as a (political) person with a status and with rights has a great variety of restrictive consequences as to the possibility of construing the criminal law order.

Criminal law has expressive functions as it communicates blame as well as many other things to the community. Criminal law has to do with actions and omissions, and actions and omissions generally are ways of authentically expressing ourselves. They are central to our identity. It is mainly through this link that the cultural issues challenge fundamental premises of penal responsibility. The issue should thus be raised: should criminalizations be allowed to be contested on the ground that culturally legitimate prescriptions require the opposite? Could a criminalization violate cultural rights and be harmful to cultural identities? How should we analyze such a situation legally, are we dealing with a case of conflicting obligations arising from two distinct sources?

Such conflicts are probably not very common, but are not entirely unknown either. If we do not allow for the production of kosher meat at all, this would hit the Jewish community hard. Still, the production of kosher meat or halal meat might require the acceptance of treating animals badly, if no technical solutions are available.[2] Typically the non-regard for cultural rights could mean a kind of discrimination, seen from another angle. However, cultural groups could often claim to have certain group rights that justify such practices. Such group rights should then have to find their ways into criminal law doctrines. Most of these conflicts are not new, but rather are long-standing debates. Criminal laws have often just silently been adapted to avoid such difficult issues of principle by burying them below the surface. Criminal law is much more flexible than it might seem at first sight.

From the point of view of an individual who faces the question of whether to follow the law or the "inner voice," the inner obligation, the situation would of course be problematic if no correction is possible by means of legal interpretation. The dilemma would be that of Antigone. The legislatures necessarily have to aim at balanced solutions, trying to respect traditions as long as possible, but assessing their worth normatively. The same principle could also be useful as a guideline in deciding cases.

We should, I suggest, distinguish between acts committed *for* cultural reasons and acts committed *in order to* defend a culture. The former may include many types of actions that are traditional, and the actor needs almost by definition to be someone who belongs to the culture. In many cases a criminalization actually aims at changing cultural patterns of behavior. This may be painful, but here criminal laws openly and deliberately clash with tradition.

Acting in defense of cultural values is a broader issue, and we might become sensitive to claims presented by others even though we are not directly involved and even though we do not personally share the same values. The issue might attract our attention as a matter of principle, for instance. The latter case may include actions that are traditional, and not particularly deliberated, but which are now being defended on cultural grounds. We might even consider cases in which such claims may be backed up by rights arguments. Cultural rights could also be defended by others than those directly involved in the practices.

---

[2] In fact the Finnish legislation on protection of animals expressly notices some practices of religious slaughter. See § 33 Animal Protection Act.

In an open society, consciously breaching the law is of course always an option. I would, at any rate, not say that breaching the law for cultural reasons generally equates with civil disobedience, despite obvious similarities. Civil disobedience could usually be termed political action which has expressive functions, since it represents a public denial of the legitimacy of some valid legal rule. Culturally motivated deviance may of course also be politically motivated as well, but need not be. Such action always has the potential of becoming political.

The idea that criminal justice has a connection with the concept of citizenship is important here. Notions of modern criminal justice thinking almost necessarily need to operate with some concept of a deliberative person. Holding a person responsible and liable for crimes rests on the idea that all people have the capacity to deliberate on the nature of the act in question. The same goes for citizenship. The citizen also needs to be regarded as a deliberative person capable of forming political views and participating in the public life of the community. This deliberativeness entails some sort of supposed ability to critically assess traditions and cultures as well. In that sense, I believe that we should not protect cultures and tradition merely because they exist, but because they have survived a kind of internal reform and critique. We should not take culturally committed persons as having a reduced capacity for deliberation and critique. On my account, the person concept serves as a basis for constant review and criticism, and a source of dynamics in the "evolution" of cultures.

THE MORAL MESSAGE OF CRIMINAL LAW

Above I briefly mentioned matters related to the philosophy of punishment. Utilitarian philosophy seeks to justify punishment and criminal laws by resorting to consequential arguments. If we move from straightforward deterrence to so-called positive general prevention, a certain communitarian aspect becomes visible once more as the theory emphasizes the internalizing of moral messages on the part of the members of society (see the discussion in Schünemann et al. 1998). We are all participating in communications concerning right and wrong on the various symbolic aspects of penal liability. This idea rests on the assumption that we all have the ability to develop our moral and ethical ideas in this environment as members of society. What follows is that we are law-abiding not only for the reason that this is better for us, that we do not want to risk getting caught and being punished, but that we are also law-abiding for the sake of sharing most of the morals that criminal justice wants us to share. The fact that we are not killing each other is thus not merely a matter of successful deterrence, but of our own choice, our own concerns. We are thinking rationally, we see the common rules from an abstract perspective; we do not appropriate rights that others cannot have either, and so on. Positive general prevention refers to our duties and obligations as citizens. As members of the political community we have certain loyalty to that community.

The theory of positive general prevention seems to require that the community of people is able to share a substantial understanding and that they see the main rationale behind the rules and standards that have been applied. They can thus see the value of defending the validity of commonly agreed rules. In a multicultural society, these communications might break down into smaller circles that read the messages sent by the criminal justice system very differently. This might exacerbate the conflicts of interpretation between groups and cultural communities when sensitive cases are being handled. Such an effect might diminish the legitimacy of legal decisions, especially in circles that for whatever reason do not accept moral and legal values that the legal system incorporates and expresses. The symbolic functioning of the criminal justice system is not always a success story. The story might well end in a crisis of the perceived legitimacy of the actions of the authorities.[3]

A theory of positive general prevention might also be problematic because if we think that cultural customary law is of equal importance to state law, then we might conclude that the criminal justice system is indeed a hegemonic order, and that the general prevention effect is the clearest example of how the legal system tries to override its competitors. The emphasis in positive general prevention would be a healthy reminder of the fact that the society is not just one body in the same sense as the political body necessarily is. This motivates the view that criminal law ought to remain rather limited and formal as the legal community only shares some fundamental values, not more.

The hegemony that reigns in law is not the mainstream cultural thinking, but rather a sort of artificial culture of law. The values that the legal system expresses are internal to law, and legal. It is the value-hegemony of the legal system that is at stake, and whether this hegemony is legitimate or not is something for political philosophy to scrutinize. Every polity probably needs to be able to decide legitimately on issues that are morally sensitive, and the culture-based values do not present any further difficulty. Of course we need to be able to convince everybody of their duty to obey the law, and we can even allow for protests for political reasons.

We should also note that the traditional communities with strong specific cultural values of their own need a back-up if they wish to represent themselves

---

[3] In David Garland's words, "penality communicates meaning not just about crime and punishment but also about power, authority, legitimacy, normality, morality, personhood, social relations, and a host of other tangential matters. Penal signs and symbols are one part of an authoritative, institutional discourse which seeks to organize our moral and political understanding and to educate our sentiments and sensibilities" (Garland 1989: 252).

as legitimate in their use of power. The environment of such strong elements of culture has changed, and this makes every community open to at least internal criticism. There must be a possibility of cultural development even within the confines of traditional cultures.

CASE LEVEL AND DOCTRINAL TOPOLOGY

Criminal law regarded as an interpreted and systemized product is also a product of legal scholarship. Doctrines have a history of their own, and the elaboration of these doctrines is among the greatest achievements of criminal law scholarship. Therefore it would be very helpful to locate the specific issues and contexts in which the cultural reasoning may find ground for being established. It would be a vast task to go through all possible topics. This is rather the work for ordinary criminal law scholarship. First signs of this scholarship being developed are already visible (Frischknecht 2009; Foblets and Renteln 2009).

The key concept is cultural defense. I take it to mean all possible settings in which cultural factors affect the penal liability of individuals in cases brought before the court. The previous general considerations concerning cultural matters and criminalizations already indicate the direction of the findings. It is on the basis of general presuppositions and ideological choices that we frame the proper scope of cultural defenses. The doctrinal scrutiny in fact ties with case law as it takes for granted the relevant criminalizations and elaborates on the conditions for its application in particular settings. The distinction between *mala in se* and *mala prohibita*, the (abstract) morals and the (particular) ethics, is relevant here. The closer we look at the doctrinal issues, the more we find topics for which cultural matters might become relevant.

We should also become aware of the fact that committing offenses differ from typical political choices. People commit crimes in stress and panic, in conditions which calm deliberation seldom is part of. Still, this being so, people deserve that their motives and intentions will matter, as the just assessment of these actions needs proper attention to them. A presentation of all the relevant legal doctrines would require a comprehensive doctrinal scrutiny. My modest aim is to map certain issues which either do not easily adjust to cultural considerations or which do so.

In continental (read: German) scholarship the elements of penal liability have been presented in the form of a concept of an offense. In details the various textbooks follow different models, but some general lines of thought can be referred to. One first relevant distinction is the one between fulfilling the definitional elements of an offense, and that of the unlawfulness of the act. The first one refers to crime definitions of the statutory law, that is, the offense as described in the norm formulation, whereas the second one refers to (defense) grounds which would exclude penal liability for acts committed in special cases (Eser 1987).

When we are dealing with killings motivated by cultural grounds, that is, when certain traditional forms of behavior are (partly) responsible for what has happened, there is very little to be done at this level. The law seeks to establish and defend the inviolability of certain key rights and values, and the protection of human life against willful killing is one such case. Prohibition of willful killing is close to prohibition of torture in terms of the symbolical dimensions of this prohibition. A universal morality surrounds this prohibition which further strongly underlines the necessity not to allow for any substantial relativism, except for very special occasions.[4] Doctrines of use of force by the authorities, or execution of lawful punishment do not count as such. The same rigidness is manifest in the doctrines concerning defenses. Self-defense and duress require serious and threatening external circumstances, whereas mental grounds could never alone constitute such a defense.

In honor killings the motivation is to defend the honor of the family. It is a matter of the doctrine of defenses how close the analogy to a case of self-defense may be. Honor as such may be covered by the scope of application of the doctrine. Most likely the analogy breaks down when the case is being looked at more closely. Self-defense requires an unlawful attack entailing imminent threat. The actions that have harmed the honor of the family are mostly entirely different from ordinary armed attacks. The situation of a sort of conflict of obligation as experienced by the person herself reveals though that albeit not reaching the level of defense, we face something similar, something analogous.

The principle of culpability is essential for criminal liability. This goes beyond the ordinary requirement of intent or negligence, reaching to matters of blameworthiness. In honor killings the perpetrator aims at killing: so far the intent requirement provides no specific problems. The motivation as such is not that relevant at this level. Doctrines of intent are rather neutral and formalistic as these do not ask for any specific motivation. The requirement of intent is, however, not unimportant as we usually see the requirement referring to some form of understanding and consciousness, which again may be affected by cultural understandings and beliefs.

In continental scholarship the distinction between justification and excuse is crucial and well established. A ground of justification, when applicable, negates the unlawfulness of the act. When we are speaking about culturally motivated actions that constitute a serious crime of violence, a ground of

---

[4] Frischknecht discusses the Kimura-case, in which a Japanese living in California had tried to kill herself and her two children after having learned about the unfaithfulness of her husband. The two children were drowned (Frischknecht 2009: 53–54).

justification will be a very rare case due to reasons briefly indicated above. Anglo-American legal thinking builds on reasonableness, whereas continental legal thinking builds on *richtiges Recht*, the law as Right (Fletcher 1985). Justification renders the act justified, whereas an excuse only renders it understandable. Introducing cultural grounds for justification would have an effect on the way the system of rights functions in criminal law. It would be easier to introduce such grounds as excuses only. However, this solution would also mean that the cultural aspects could significantly influence what we expect of people.

The excuse is more interesting for our concerns, as the grounds of excuse relate to motivation which in the particular circumstances of the case render the action understandable and which thus affect the culpability of the action. Excess in case of self-defense, or blameworthy action under duress might be the most typical examples.

Grounds of excuse may have different legal implications. A full excuse will exempt from penal liability (leaving the action an offense, anyway). A partial excuse will work as a mitigating factor, and can be taken into account in sentencing or it can give reason to drop the case. Such distinctions as the ones between the punishable act and unlawfulness or the one between justification and excuse render it possible to think about at what point a cultural ground of action might become viable and significant.

To add one more obvious topic, mistake of law should be added. A person who for reasons of tradition and culture believes that she is entitled to act as she has been accustomed to may sometimes sincerely believe that this is the case also before the law. Mistake of law may work as an excuse, but not without further qualifications.

I believe we should distinguish between serious crimes of violence and the rather borderline cases which are having a somewhat unclear legal status. If honor killings are the cases for which only very little cultural adaptation is motivated, in some lesser cases more room for such measures will be available.

If we take the example of circumcision of boys, performed in the infancy by a medical expert, we could ask whether this constitutes an offense. Surely only very few jurisdictions have addressed this matter directly in the penal legislation. Instead of a separate crime provision, the general rules protecting bodily integrity are applied. If the circumcision is not motivated by health policy grounds, why is this not an instance of an offense, actually? Can the parents consent on behalf of the child to this operation (which is irreversible)? What difference does it make, whether this practice is cultural practice or also religious practice?[5]

---

[5] The Finnish Supreme Court adopted the position that cultural reasons could lead to non-application of the statutory offense by allowing for cultural reasons and reasons related to a membership in a religion to have a role in the argumentation. This is mixed with a reasoning

Finnish and Swedish legal doctrine recognizes an unwritten ground for exemption from liability, namely the "social adequacy" of the act in question. Cross-checking in ice hockey constitutes an assault, but it is not punishable because such behavior has been socially accepted. This sort of exemption from liability could be seen as based on normative cultural grounds. In our culture, sport counts as valid, and if adults wish to fight following such ceremonial forms, why should it not be allowed?

Serving wine to those under age in a religious ceremony could fall under this exemption as well. Many of these kinds of exemptions go unnoticed because we simply are so accustomed to them. No one ever thought of prosecuting the priests for these breaches. Maybe one valid argument would be to see these as justifying grounds, but as grounds which cannot be further broadened. This could be the case specifically as concerns discriminatory practices. New such exemptions should not be granted, and slowly but steadily such exemptions might disappear. The reasoning could be of a "one-way only" argument. The protected communities might revise their practices, and new exemptions will be excluded.

The notion of social acceptance is an open one, and does not require the acceptance of each and every person. It is a matter of institutional acceptance. The German could speak of "the normative force of the factual." This legal institution of social acceptance might fit cultural issues quite well. It is an expression of customary law of some kind, which Nils Jareborg has called a "security valve" that is needed to get rid of cases that just do not belong to the domain of criminal justice for whatsoever reason (Jareborg 2001: 291).[6]

This unwritten principle could gain importance as we discuss culturally motivated practices from the point of view of the dominant culture in terms of criminal justice. Jeremy Waldron has raised important questions of equality before the law that must also be solved when operating with doctrines that draw on cultural and social realities (Waldron 2002). We would not be willing to compromise the whole system by making cultural exceptions to the rules, but in individual instances this may be acceptable. Social adequacy is an important idea because it basically ascribes importance to customs and practices that are already there. There is a sense of legal pluralism in this that might often go unnoticed.

Social adequacy also means of course that the legislator recognizes certain limits to what it can do. Some living practices should not be touched upon. Should this be done, however, for important reasons, such interventionism

---

based on the best interests of the child. The case concerned a small Muslim boy. Supreme Court of Finland, Decision 2008: 93.

[6] Jareborg places circumcision of boys under this concept: the Supreme Court of Sweden had also followed this line of argument. This is one of the very few occasions on which a cultural argument has been openly raised and even accepted in the Nordic judicature and doctrine.

would need to be backed up with good reason. Sport, for instance, can be regulated and prohibited. To give an example, organizing professional boxing events is not allowed in Sweden.

Studying social adequacy is therefore also important because the reasons why we recognize certain practices as worth preserving differ. Sometimes the reason is plain harmlessness, sometimes respect for tradition, sometimes respect for the autonomy of some aspect of life that already has internal rules (sport, medical ethics, the ethics of the media, etc.). However, the appreciation of a practice always needs the support of normative principles.

What are being called the general doctrines of penal liability in continental Europe, the general definitional elements of a crime, are legal norms and principles of a general nature. It is not quite clear what the exact relationship between such doctrines and rights is. Murder and willful killing are wrongs, but many types of factors may influence the legal evaluation of even prima facie wrongful acts. Do I as a victim, or as a potential victim, or simply as a member of the polity, have the right to demand that no new doctrines be developed to mitigate the liability of the perpetrator of a wrongful deed?

Criminal justice is rights-oriented in many ways, but it is not quite directly so. If an act has been committed in self-defense and is therefore regarded as justified, the rule must apply to others in a similar situation as well. Such a defense expresses a rule. But still, the protection of even absolute liberalist rights-based values such as life by means of criminal law could leave some room for discretionary elements of doctrine. Flexibility increases as we move towards sentencing principles. If some aspect of the act is relevant from the point of view of the definition of its penal value,[7] then it should be taken into account.

Many problems are related to the fundamental ideological choices that criminal law theorizing needs to face. The search for the grammar of criminal law, uniting the various approaches, has proved more difficult than one might suppose (see Fletcher 2007).

Sentencing is yet one more level of decision-making at which cultural settings could be of importance. Cultural grounds could operate as mitigating or aggravating factors in sentencing. In fact, the Finnish Penal Code (Ch. 6 Sect. 5) now recognizes a racist motive as an aggravating factor in sentencing.[8] This reflects the view that national and ethnic groups are in need of protection against hostile actions by others. But in Finnish law this is not symmetrical. If a member of such a group attacks outsiders for related reasons, this has not been regarded as relevant.

---

[7] This concept has been used in the doctrine of the Nordic countries as a guarantee that punishment should not go beyond act-proportionality. The Swedish Penal Code, Ch. 29 "On the Determination of Punishment and Exemption from Sanction," refers expressly to the notion of penal value.
[8] See, generally, Finnish Gov. Bill 44/2002: 192–193.

Recognition of racist motives as legally relevant does not mean recognizing them as worthy of support; quite the contrary. They are recognized because of their dangerousness and blameworthiness. They are recognized in terms of their consequences for the rights of certain protected minorities.

The introduction of hate crime laws in the 1980s and 1990s in the US has been called identity politics (Jacobs and Potter 1998: Ch. 5). The idea gained political support because it was easy to understand the message of such policies. It was a politics of recognition that turned into symbolic criminal-policy action. The other line of identity politics, bringing in a cultural defense, is not likely to be backed up by such political enthusiasm. Recognizing by taking the cultural identity of the perpetrator into account has an abolitionist sense as it mitigates liability.

We could expand the discussion to cover the role of cultural conflicts and cultural matters in issues of criminal procedure as well. The standard way of organizing criminal procedure is rather individualistic: an individual accused is prosecuted before a court following procedures in which the prosecutor and the victim have strictly formulated legal roles. Victim–offender mediation, to take an example, would allow for increased involvement of the community in the proceedings, but this might happen at the cost of procedural justice.

BEYOND CULTURAL DIVERSITY

Criminal law is rough law, repressive law. Criminal investigations and criminal proceedings are far removed from anthropological field research in which sensitive researchers try to approach and understand foreign cultures. Charles Taylor formulates the very sympathetic ethical requirement that we should understand the presence of many differing cultures and actually presume that there might be something valuable for us in each and every one of them. Learning from them changes our personal horizons. Preserving cultures sounds attractive in times when many traditional cultures are dying out.

All this is somehow very correct and fine, at least for anyone who has had an interest in hermeneutic thinking. The problem still is that it is really a demanding requirement to say that the criminal justice system should adapt to such high ethical yardsticks and be able to respond to each and every person appropriately to the circumstances. I have already referred to the necessity of building the legitimacy of criminal justice on its political legitimacy, and here the concept of a citizen is central. What is then the relationship between the generalized concept of a person as a citizen and the fact of cultural diversity? Do they mutually exclude each other? Is the only thinkable ethics the ethics of difference?

It is far from clear that what we have at the bottom line of such an ethical requirement of recognizing diversity is diversity itself. Beyond cultural diversity we might perhaps find true humanity, the uniting feature, the respectable person, individual and group autonomy, and make sure that our hard criminal law does not bring harm to the vulnerable core of humanity present in every human being. If we follow this line of thinking, we would again reduce the significance of the fact of cultural diversity. It might be humanism that directs our attention towards issues of cultural sensitivity in the first place. Cosmopolitanism as a citizen concept referring to the membership of humanity would reflect such an aspiration. I will not build on such strong membership views in this chapter, but limit myself to the state context.[9]

Culture should also not be regarded as something rigid and exclusive, but more like a network. People move between cultural surroundings and influences, and no single culture has the force to dictate the entire field. Cultural differences are also at least partly a product of the exercise of group rights, which moves the debate about the proper context of cultural diversity from communitarian to liberalist concerns (see the discussion in Mona 2006).

Criminal justice as a practice of denial and recognition is deeply tied to the general legal scheme in which people have rights and legitimate expectations that their primary interests are respected. The law's double exercise in denying and recognizing simultaneously builds on the premises of mutual legal recognition; otherwise we would not be included in a web of mutual legal obligations. It is in this context of (normatively) pre-existing recognition structures that the struggles over recognition of new aspects, new interests, and new rights need to take place.

We have many examples of crimes reported that are precisely at the focal point of a cultural conflict. We might even have to think of other ways of ensuring that such facts are being noted during the investigations and proceedings. This is also a matter of recognition and identification. We should become aware of such contexts. In terms of legal theory, we could say that sensitiveness, a context-bound and context-sensitive application of law, requires the use of soft hermeneutic tools. In this respect the lessons of cultural sensitivity could reach far beyond merely general cultural issues, to the routines of ordinary legal adjudication. We should include topics such as pardon and amnesty in our discussions. We should discuss the role of anthropological knowledge in criminal proceedings.

REFERENCES

Eser, Albin. 1987. "Justification and Excuse: A Key Issue in the Concept of Crime," in *Rechtfertigung and Entschuldigung. Rechtsvergleichende Perspektiven I*, ed. Albin Eser and George P. Fletcher (Max-Planck Institut, Band S 7/1, Freiburg i.Br.), 17–65.

---

[9] Interestingly enough, the current discussions concerning the protection of human dignity by means of criminal law render it likely that such a deep value-orientation may in fact easily lead to a new kind of moralism.

Fletcher, George P. 1985. "The Right and the Reasonable," *Harvard Law Review* 98: 949–982.
Fletcher, George P. 2007. *The Grammar of Criminal Law: American, Comparative, and International. Volume One: Foundations* (Oxford: Oxford University Press).
Foblets, Marie-Claire and Alison Dundes Renteln, eds. 2009. *Multicultural Jurisprudence: Comparative Perspectives on the Cultural Defense* (Oxford: Hart Publishing).
Frischknecht, Tom. 2009. *Kultureller Rabatt: Überlegungen zu Strafausschluss und Strafermässigung bei kultureller Differenz* (Bern: Haupt).
Garland, David. 1989. *Punishment and Modern Society* (Oxford: Clarendon Press).
Günther, Klaus. 2005. *Schuld und kommunikative Freiheit. Studien zur personalen Zurechnung strafbaren Unrechts im demokratischen Rechtsstaat* (Frankfurt: Vittorio Klostermann).
Hirsch, Andrew von. 1993. *Censure and Sanctions* (Oxford: Clarendon Press).
Ivison, Duncan. 1999. "Justifying Punishment in Intercultural Contexts," in *Punishment and Political Theory*, ed. Matt Matravers (Oxford: Hart Publishing), 88–107.
Jacobs, James A. and Kimberly Potter. 1998. *Hate Crimes: Criminal Law & Identity Politics* (New York: Oxford University Press).
Jareborg, Nils. 2001. *Allmän kriminalrätt* (Uppsala: Iustus Förlag).
Mona, Martino. 2006. "Der Multikulturalismus als staatstheoretische und kriminalpolitische Herausforderung," *Archiv für Rechts- und Sozialphilosophie, Beiheft* 105: 47–63.
Norrie, Alan. 1991. *Law, Ideology and Punishment: Retrieval and Critique of the Liberal Ideal of Criminal Justice* (Dordrecht: Kluwer Academic Publishers).
Renteln, Alison Dundes. 2004. *The Cultural Defense* (New York: Oxford University Press).
Ricoeur, Paul. 2005. *The Course of Recognition* (Cambridge, MA: Harvard University Press).
Schonsheck, Johathan. 1994. *On Criminalization: An Essay in the Philosophy of the Criminal Law* (Dordrecht: Kluwer Academic Publishers).
Schünemann, Bernd, Andrew von Hirsch, and Nils Jareborg, eds. 1998. *Positive Generalprävention. Kritische Analyse im deutsch-englischen Dialog. Uppsala-Symposium 1996* (Heidelberg: C. F. Müller Verlag).
Taylor, Charles. 1994. "The Politics of Recognition," in *Multiculturalism: Examining the Politics of Recognition*, ed. A. Gutmann (Princeton: Princeton University Press), 25–73.
Waldron, Jeremy. 2002. "One Law for All? The Logic of Cultural Accommodation," *Washington & Lee Law Review* 59: 3–34.

5

Responsibility, Morality, and Culture

*Matt Matravers**

INTRODUCTION

The moment at which the criminal law of a liberal state is brought to bear on a person with a different cultural background from the majority—seemingly in response to actions that implicate that background—can create a certain anxiety in liberals. Two separate worries arise: first, that a liberal state in circumstances of pluralism ought not to criminalize—or ought otherwise to make space for—(at least some) practices that "belong" (in some sense or other) to the various cultures and conceptions of the good of its citizens. Second, that even if it were the case that the action was rightly prohibited by the criminal law, the accused ought to have a (partial) defense given that he was motivated by cultural beliefs. My concern in what follows is mainly with the second of these worries. That is, with the idea that there should be a full or partial cultural defense available to criminal defendants.

Having established a few preliminary assumptions, the strategy of the chapter is to consider an example that combines "rotten social background" and "enculturation" and then an example that is more specifically cultural. Two questions arise from the examples: Is the defendant answerable? If so, to whom is he answerable? Addressing these will, I hope, shed some light at least on what are the core issues at stake.

In making the argument, I depend on wider commitments about the purpose and nature of the systems of criminal law and criminal justice. This is important and any serious reflection on cultural defenses must be embedded in a more general account of criminal justice. This can be quickly demonstrated by comparing two (crude) versions of the purposes of the criminal law and trial.

---

* I am grateful to the participants in the Criminal Law and Cultural Diversity Workshop and in particular to Jeremy Waldron for written comments on the earliest version of this paper. I am also grateful to audiences at Manchester and York for comments on various drafts of the paper.

Consider, briefly, Barbara Wootton's view of an enlightened, post-retributive, age. Wootton thought *mens rea* ought to be irrelevant in the construction of criminal offenses. This was partly for reasons to do with her faith in psychosocial interventions and her belief that it is neither possible nor useful to distinguish between the mentally normal, responsible offender and the mentally disordered who are not responsible. As she put it, "if mental health and ill-health cannot be defined in objective scientific terms that are free of subjective moral judgments, it follows that we have no reliable criterion by which to distinguish the sick from the healthy mind" (Wootton 1959: 227).

For Wootton, the purpose of the criminal law is simply to prevent anti-social behavior, and this is to be achieved by treating offenders, where possible, so as to modify their future behavior. *Mens rea* considerations are thus relevant only "*after* a breach of law has been proved" because of "the light which they throw on the likelihood of his [the offender] offending again, and upon the most hopeful way of dealing with him" (Wootton 1978: 224, emphasis added). For Wootton, then, responsibility is not an important issue. The criminal trial simply establishes who did what.

Where the agent's actual knowledge, intentions, mental states, and so on, do matter for Wootton is in indicating how best to treat him. So, the mental state that differentiates a kleptomaniac (if there is such a state) from an ordinary shoplifter is important not because it changes the culpability of the offender (which is neither here nor there), but because the psychosocial interventions that will best rehabilitate the kleptomaniac will be different from those that will best reform the shoplifter.

If this is one's view of the criminal law then issues of responsibility wither away as a concern. Someone who claimed that his culture was implicated in his criminal behavior would merely be telling us something about what psychosocial intervention is most likely to be successful in changing his future behavior. That his current behavior was motivated by culture, rather than say kleptomania, is itself uninteresting except as an indicator as to how to go about reforming him.

Wootton's conception of the criminal law is not that adopted by liberals. The point here is just to show that discussing the cultural defense requires saying something about the system for which that defense is being proposed. Different conceptions of the criminal law will not only have different accounts of responsibility, but may—as the Wootton example demonstrates—have different places for the very idea of responsibility.

The liberal model of the criminal law that I shall assume here has it that the (ideal) criminal law in its core prohibitions (i) addresses harmful behavior that is wrong and where (ii) that wrong can be understood as public (a wrong done to the society as well as the victim) as well as private (there is a wrong done to some person or persons). Moreover (iii) the wrong and harm are serious. In addition, (iv) a function of the criminal law is to protect society from such wrongful harms, but (v) it is a key feature of the criminal law that it is not just a device for regulating behavior. Rather, it calls the defendant to account; it asks for reasons for the defendant's behavior (and, of course, where the defendant is innocent that demand is unreasonable; where the defendant did perform the act he may offer reasons that excuse or justify him acting as he did). Finally, (vi) the criminal law *blames* culpable offenders and punishes them in proportion to their culpability and the seriousness of their offense.[1]

On the conception of the criminal law being deployed here, responsibility must have a central place. Quite how the law ought to think of responsibility is a part of the argument below. However, again it is necessary to say something at least in broad outline. I take it that the conception of responsibility that goes with this conception of the criminal law involves thinking of people as capable of responding to reasons and of acting in accordance with reasons. Consider an example: someone breaks into a mountain cabin during a snowstorm in order to avoid what she reasonably regards as a good chance of freezing to death. If called to account—asked to provide reasons for her actions—she says that her actions did not manifest a guilty will but that rather she was responding to the conditions. Of course, her actions were caused (both in the sense that they are explained by the conditions and in the sense that they resulted from biological processes in combination with environmental factors), but what matters is that the reasons that governed her actions were good ones (ones that the law recognizes).

Now consider a different agent who breaks into the cabin on a sunny day and then claims, as an excuse, that his character was formed in such a way that he is predisposed to breaking and entering. We would not be impressed. Perhaps he is right, but that is not an excuse recognized in law. The reasons upon which he acted were, say, that he wanted what was inside the cabin and the fact that it belonged to someone else provided, for him, no reason for not breaking and entering. This is just the kind of thing the law condemns. As a participant in the moral and legal community—and as someone capable of acting on, and giving an account of their behavior in terms of, reasons—the agent is properly held to account.[2]

I do not want to say much more about responsibility and reasons-responsiveness, but it is worth pausing to outline the way in which this account of the criminal law and responsibility can be used to differentiate between someone who has a legitimate excuse and someone who is exempt from liability. Excuses show that a generally responsible agent is not responsible for some particular act or state of affairs. Exemptions show that the agent is not properly held responsible at all (cf. Wallace 1994).

---

[1] I do not defend this conception of a liberal criminal law. In contrasting it with Wootton, its source is recognizably in H. L. A. Hart's work (Hart 1968). A more recent defense of the "calling to account" aspect mentioned here, that is sure to become canonical, can be found in Antony Duff's work (see, in particular, Duff 1986, 2001, 2007).

[2] The classic account of this is Hart 1968; the position is recognizably Strawsonian (e.g., Strawson 1962), and receives a sophisticated contemporary treatment in Wallace 1994.

The criminal law, then, holds people to account for the reasons on which they act. This claim is unpacked first by considering the following example taken from Stephen Morse (who in turn attributes it to an audience member at a seminar):

> Imagine an eighteen-year-old male gang member who was brought up in a disorganized, broken family living in a dirty, dangerous, disorganized, deprived community. Assume that the gang member is of average or below-average intelligence and does not have much education, but he is not cognitively disabled. Perhaps he is even functionally illiterate. From his pre-teen days, family, school, and church life had little emotional hold on him, but the gang in his neighborhood recruited him. The gang offered him the sense of identity, belonging, structure, meaning and self-worth that his family and community failed to provide. Starting at an age when he was not a fully responsible moral agent—say, as early as ten or eleven—the gang encouraged him with its emotional leverage and perhaps threats to engage in various forms of antisocial conduct. He complied, and by age eighteen, he is a hard guy whose allegiance is firmly to the gang. Now, the gang asks him to execute a rival gang member. The gang no longer needs to threaten him or in any other way to manipulate him. He is committed to the gang and its projects, and he carries out the request, perhaps even proudly. (Morse 2000: 148).

ANSWERING AND RESPONSIBILITY 1: UNDERSTANDING MORAL REASONS

This example raises questions about the difference a background of both deprivation and enculturation should make. In particular, I want to focus on two questions that it raises: first, "is this person (for the sake of brevity, call him Stan) properly called to answer at all?" (this is a form of the question, is he exempt?). Second, "to whom (if anyone) is Stan answerable?" (this, as we will see is also a question of exemption, although of a different kind).

In the case of the first question, I want to focus on the issue of enculturation. Why might we think Stan exempt from criminal responsibility? To answer this, we need to return to the basis on which people are held responsible in the model of the criminal law briefly described above. To be liable is to be properly the subject of an inquiry into the reasons in accordance with which one acted. So, someone who is seriously deluded, insane, or sleepwalking is exempt because it makes no sense to hold him to account for the reasons he acted (since such a person does not grasp, or is not acting in a way guided by, reasons).

It might be thought that this is clear enough. We can test whether someone has the capacity to be reason-following and if so then (other things equal) they are properly answerable for their actions. Stan, it seems, has the necessary capacity (we assume that he is a successful gang member), so he is properly called to answer for his actions. However, this is far from uncontroversial. The critical issue is what is involved in grasping (understanding) a moral reason.

Consider the following accounts concerned with what it is to grasp a moral reason (the first from R. Jay Wallace and the second from Antony Duff). In both, what is offered is a fairly rich notion of what it is properly to grasp a moral reason (that is, what is required is not merely to recognize that there is a reason, but is that the agent appreciates the force and nature of that reason):

> to grasp the reason expressed in a moral principle is a more complex task than it might first appear to be. The understanding required is a kind of participant understanding that goes well beyond the ability to parrot the moral principle in situations in which it has some relevance. What is needed, rather, is the ability to bring the principle to bear in the full variety of situations to which it applies, anticipating the demands it makes of us in those situations, and knowing when its demands might require adjustment in the light of the claims of other moral principles. This in turn requires, at a minimum, a grasp of the concepts that figure in the moral principle in question. (Wallace 1994: 157)

To understand what it is to hurt someone,

> we must be able to understand what it *is* to hurt someone: and this requires an understanding of the kinds of interests and concern people can have, in the light of which actions will be seen as hurtful. We can hurt someone by physical injury; by injuring or insulting someone he loves; by destroying or denigrating his achievements; by ignoring or frustrating his wishes and ambitions; by denying him responses and relationships which matter to him—gratitude, trust, love, friendship. Unless we can understand the significance of such interests, emotions, and relationships in a man's life, we cannot understand what it is to hurt him, or how it can be wrong. An understanding of the moral aspects of my actions, and of the moral value of others, requires an understanding of that dimension of human life which includes both moral values and those interests and emotions which make our actions morally significant. (Duff 1977: 196–197)

As already noted, Wallace and Duff make the case for a very rich account of what it is to grasp, or have an understanding of, moral reasons. It requires that the person has what Wallace calls a "participant understanding" of morality. However, it is important to note that having the "general ability to grasp and apply moral reasons" does not require that one has participant understanding of *some particular set* of moral reasons. Those who do not share liberal moral principles—"racists, torturers and rapists, for example" (Wallace 1994: 164)—will normally possess the general ability to grasp moral reasons, but they have rejected the liberal understanding of moral reasons. They are, as it were, non-participants in the liberal moral community, but they do not lack the capacity for a participant understanding of morality.

Even if we accept Wallace's and Duff's rich account of what it is to grasp a moral reason, this last consideration seems to place Stan firmly in the category of those who do grasp reasons of the right type, but with the wrong content. Stan participates in a form of life which may repel us, but which is intelligible. He may view conventional morality as weak and slavish, but he is able to relate it to his concerns and his way of living (even if only by rejecting it). It is only if Stan's enculturation is such that he lacks the capacity to understand that there is any moral issue *at all* in killing the rival that he is exempt on this account (this is the conclusion Morse comes to about the case; see Morse 2000: 148).

Of course, even if Stan is properly liable, we may offer up his history in mitigation at sentencing. Moreover, (I assert, but do not argue) a humane system of punishment will concern itself with his welfare and with developing in him the capacity not merely to respond to moral reasons, but to respond to the right moral reasons.

Stan's enculturation is of a particular kind and it might be thought that the example is deliberately designed to put the cultural defense in a bad light. So, consider what may be a more sympathetic example:

> In the late 1990s a family of Iraqi refugees moved to Lincoln, Nebraska. The father feared his two daughters, aged 13 and 14, would be corrupted, so he arranged for their marriage to two "good Muslims," aged 28 and 34. The men consummated the marriage and were charged with sexual assault of a minor. They argued they were following Iraqi custom as sanctioned by their faith and did not know they acted illegally.... The two newly wed men faced sentences on sexual assault charges of up to 50 years in prison. They received 4–6 years and were eligible for parole after 2 years. Charges against the father were dropped but he was banned from seeing his daughters, who have been relocated outside of Lincoln. (Tunick 2004: 395)[3]

Is this case any different from Stan's? On the face of it, no. The father and husbands in this case are not without a participant understanding of

---

[3] I shall take this case as given. However, it is worth noting the messy complications and issues of fact in the case. Waldron summarizes them as follows: "A lawyer for the young brides gave a slightly different spin on the case. She believed that the girls' father and mother arranged their daughters' marriages because the girls were adapting too readily to American ways. Arranging their weddings to Iraqi men was a way of keeping the girls from going astray culturally. (And indeed, Lincoln police said they learned of the marriages when the 15-year-old girl was reported missing by her father. She had run away, police said, to the home of her 20-year-old boyfriend, Mario Rojas, 20, of Lincoln. Rojas was also charged with statutory rape.)... In case readers are left in any doubt about the messiness of cases like this, let me add one last detail. A lawyer for one of the bridegrooms suggested that the older girl might in fact be seventeen rather than fifteen. (There is an exception to the Nebraska statutory rape law in the case of someone married at age 17.) His suspicions were aroused by the fact that the girls' parents and one of the girls all list their birth dates as July 1. The three Iraqi men (father and bridegrooms) were political refugees, who came to Lincoln, Nebraska after long stays in Saudi Arabian refugee camps, joining about 500 other Iraqis. 'It is the habit of refugee camps to routinely assign birth dates.' The lawyer said he was trying to get the girls' birth records, but that the Iraqi government was often 'not helpful' about this sort of thing" (Waldron 2002: 217–218).

morality (indeed, in many respects they might be thought to be particularly "morality-fearing" people). It is just that, like Stan, they are guided by reasons that are substantively wrong. The father, for example, acts on reasons grounded in his belief that teenage girls, on account of their sexuality, need to be introduced to marriage, and the control of just one man, as early as possible, and that this is particularly urgent in the face of the unholy and pornographic temptations of Western society.[4] Thus, as in the case of Stan, we might think that there is good reason for accepting mitigation at the sentencing stage (and, indeed, we might think an ideal system would be more lenient than seems to have been the case).

However, there is something slightly too quick about this. Consider again the Wallace/Duff position: the issue is, what connects the requirement of genuine participant understanding and responsibility (that is, why should people who lack a participant understanding of morality be exempt from responsibility)? Wallace's reply is to appeal to a principle of reasonableness. "It is unreasonable to demand that people do something—in a way that potentially exposes them to the harms of moral sanction," he writes, "if they lack the general power to grasp and comply with the reasons that support the demand" (Wallace 1994: 161). It would be as unreasonable, Wallace thinks, as demanding "that a foreigner...should speak and understand one's language like a native" (Wallace 1994: 161). For Duff, similarly, the agent must, for example, have the capacity to understand *from the inside* what it is to hurt someone.

These arguments give us reason to pause. The husbands and father in the Nebraska case seem like "non-native" speakers of the criminal law who are surely entitled to some consideration. Perhaps more forcefully, we may be troubled by the thought that the father really understood himself as "hurting" his daughters; as denigrating or damaging their interests. Rather, in his own eyes, he is acting precisely to secure their long-term interests.

There is, of course, an immediate response to these kinds of arguments. Remember, in the case of Stan, the conclusion that he was rightly held responsible (even if his enculturation could be used in mitigation) was grounded in the claim that he had a grasp of reasons of the right type, it was just that his reasons had the wrong content. This seems to apply to the current case, too. No one denies that the father understood what it is to hurt others in general, or what it is to be hurt, and so on. Similarly, Wallace's analogy seems peculiarly ill chosen. The "foreigner" does not speak "our" language, but he has a general capacity for language. The husbands and father may not have understood the particular reasons that applied to them in this case, but they did not lack the capacity for reason-governed behavior. Rather, they behaved in accordance with bad reasons, which is precisely what the criminal law punishes.

---

[4] I am grateful to Jeremy Waldron for suggesting this account of the father's reasons.

However, this reply seems to miss something. We pause when confronted by the Nebraska example—as we do in the case of Stan—not because we doubt the characters in the examples had the capacity for reason-governed behavior (after all, if we doubted *that*, the cases would be straightforward), but because we worry that the ways in which they failed to understand the particular reasons that applied to them negate responsibility. That is, the principle of reasonableness might be thought to extend to someone who possesses a general capacity to grasp moral reasons, but whose current set of moral beliefs simply makes him unable to grasp some particular moral reason.

Although this is appealing—and it explains why these examples, unlike "ordinary" criminal cases, make us pause—it is (I think) mistaken. To see this, it is useful to break the argument down into two parts. On the one hand, we can ask whether the accused satisfies the general requirement of being the kind of thing that is properly held accountable. On the other hand (assuming the answer to the first question is affirmative), we can ask whether the accused is properly held accountable for the particular act in question.

We might here usefully deploy Scanlon's distinction between attributive and substantive responsibility. To make an *attributive* judgment is to make a judgment as to whether the person is responsible for a given action in the sense that "it is appropriate to take [that action] as a basis of moral appraisal of the person" (Scanlon 1998: 148). To make a *substantive* judgment about responsibility is to make a judgment about what people are required (or not required) to do. That is, judgments of substantive responsibility are judgments about who should pick up the costs or benefits that result from some action. In the Nebraska case, the issue of attributive responsibility is not in question. The father and husbands are the kinds of beings that are properly held to account, and their actions render them liable to criticism for their faulty moral reasoning. Nevertheless, that leaves the question of substantive responsibility—of whether they ought, or ought not, to be left to bear the (full) consequences of their actions. And here we might think not, given that it is plausible that they meet Scanlon's conditions of not having had "adequate opportunity to avoid being subject to them" (Scanlon 1998: 292).

Scanlon's is a much less rich account of what it is to understand morality than that offered by Wallace and Duff, so it is worth unpacking it a little (since someone might object to the Wallace/Duff account precisely because it sets the bar for moral understanding so high). For Scanlon, then, the first question is whether it is appropriate to take the action as a basis of moral appraisal of the person. As noted above, given that the father and husbands were not hypnotized (or similar), and that they possessed the general capacity to be guided by reasons, it would seem that the answer to this is yes. We can sensibly ask the question, are these people to blame (a question we cannot sensibly ask of a stone, a non-human animal, or of someone who is insane). That is to say, the father and husbands are attributively responsible.

However, we need to be careful. The issue is not just whether the thing in question is the kind of thing that can be properly appraised, it is also whether it is appropriate to take *this action* as the basis for the moral appraisal of the agent. So, for example, we may have a generally responsible agent who suddenly, in response to an adverse reaction to some prescription drug, behaves badly. An hour later, once the effects of the drug have worn off, he is back to his usual self. In such a case, we would not criticize him because the "action is not, in the appropriate sense, attributable to the agent" (Scanlon 1998: 277). We can also worry about the character of the action (and not just about the connection between the action and the agent's judgments). Scanlon offers the following gloss:

> The excusing conditions most often appealed to in everyday life belong to a second category.... Rather than blocking altogether the attribution of an action or attitude to an agent, these conditions alter the character of the action that can be attributed. Ignorance and mistake of fact are typical conditions of this second type. I may think, for example, that your stomping on my foot reflects a lack of concern for my pain and for my right to be free of unwanted touching. But this appraisal of your action must be modified if I learn that you assumed that the toy spider on my boot was real, and having had experience in the tropics, you thought you were saving my life by killing it before it had a chance to bite me. In the light of these further facts, I can still correctly attribute the action to you, but it may no longer indicate a blameworthy attitude on your part... (Scanlon 1998: 279)[5]

This seems to get to the heart of what worries us (if it does) about the Nebraska example. Concentrate on the father: what troubles us surely is the possibility that the father was genuinely acting on the basis of what he believed to be the best interests of his daughters. Far from being the moral equivalent of an accessory to their abuse, or of someone who provides children to pedophile rings, he might have been acting (no matter how wrongly) as a loving father within his (cultural) understanding of what that demands of him. If so, his actions are correctly attributed to him, but his blameworthiness is much more problematic.

One quick way to deal with this is to say that that is precisely why such considerations should be allowed to influence discretionary decisions over, say, prosecution and sentencing, but not decisions of fact (over whether *he did it*). However, that is too quick since the criminal law is often, and properly, concerned with the agent's intention in the construction of criminal offenses (that is, what it is *he did* may include reference to his intentions, recklessness, and so on). Where it is so, then cultural considerations may speak to the agent's state of mind and so to whether he is guilty at all (and not merely to the degree of his culpability).

---

[5] I have discussed Scanlon's account of these excuses in Matravers 2003.

Take a (stylized) example: Bert comes from a society in which it is the norm for women to pretend to resist men's sexual advances, but in which it is established that a woman who allows herself to be alone with a man would welcome such an advance (to be clear, the example is set up to be clear rather than plausible). Finding himself in a different society, alone with a woman, Bert has intercourse with her ignoring her expressed non-consent. If the *mens rea* of rape includes that the alleged offender knows that the alleged victim does not consent to the intercourse or is reckless as to whether that person consents to it, Bert is (at least arguably) innocent of rape.

It is worth making two quick points about this. First, understanding the influence of culture in this way incorporates it in our normal categories of the criminal law. Cultural background may be an important indicator of the agent's likely state of mind, but it does not have a different qualitative status from any other piece of evidence. Second, for a variety of practical reasons, the criminal law might establish "objective" reasonableness tests so that the question becomes "would a reasonable person have known?," or "is this reckless from the perspective of what could be asked of a reasonable person?" For serious criminal wrongs, this seems to me to require a sacrifice of justice to practicability (Renteln 2004 makes an interesting case for more culturally nuanced reasonableness tests), but practicability is not a value that should be dismissed too quickly in a system as cumbersome as the criminal law.

EXCURSUS ON MORAL REASONS AND LIBERALISM

Some of the above depends, of course, on the claim that the law embodies the "right" moral reasons and that Stan and the Iraqi refugees respond to the "wrong" moral reasons. This raises two issues; one about whether such claims can be vindicated and the other about whether, even if they can, such reasons are properly placed at the heart of a liberal regime which presides over a pluralistic society.[6] I do not intend to say much about the first of these. For some, the claim that prohibitions on such things as murder and rape reflect universally valid moral reasons is—or ought to be—uncontroversial and I shall take it for granted here.[7]

---

[6] All this is without prejudice to the possibility that real-world legal systems may need (moral) improvement quite apart from the issue of their capacity to accommodate cultural claims.

[7] As it happens, I believe that claims such as these can only be vindicated as the socially constructed norms that regulate the ethical community of its members conceived of as a cooperative venture for mutual advantage. However, guiding one's behavior in accordance with the regulative priority of moral reasons is not something that is rationally required. That is, (a) morality is best understood as the construction of a particular ethical community (I am not, then,

In the Nebraska case, the law speaks to the wrong done in intentionally having sexual intercourse with someone who has not consented. Of course, it adds to that the (more controversial) claim that a minor cannot consent, and a stipulation of the age at which someone is no longer a minor, but these things, too, it claims as more than simply the outcome of democratic decision-making (rather, they are backed up by moral reasons).

That, of course, raises the second issue of what place such considerations have in a liberal, pluralistic society. One might, for example, think that the liberal state should take as little interest as possible in moral matters, that it should leave (as far as is practicable) crime and punishment to thick moral communities and that it should confine itself to regulating conflict; providing roads, utilities, and other services; and ensuring that members of the thick moral communities within its territories provide a viable "exit" for those who would rather leave the group. More plausibly, one might think that the liberal state should try to minimize the degree to which its legitimacy depends on any thick moral commitments about the good, while maintaining a fairly robust stance on what is right. Where this matters for the discussion here, or so it seems to me, is in issues of criminalization. A liberal state committed to respecting pluralism about the good should be very cautious in its use of its coercive power in general and particularly so in the case of the criminal law, which has a condemnatory aspect.[8] This is not the topic of this chapter although I think it is an issue of the first importance. The governments of the UK and USA, for example, criminalize far too much (see on this Husak 2008). Of course, the cultural defense may be important in matters that are merely "regulative" rather than "criminal,"[9] but a great deal of the heat is taken out of the argument once the aspect of moral condemnation is removed.

---

a universalist), and (b) it is not irrational (although it may be unwise) to reject the regulative priority of moral reasons (although it is not irrational to endorse it either. Indeed, there are very good, but not decisive, reasons to do so) (the defense of this position is in Matravers 2000). It follows from this that someone may reject the moral system and refuse to be any part of it. If he does so, he cannot on my account be punished (which involves moral communication between co-participants) although he can be subject to coercion. If, for example, the Iraqi refugees in Nebraska simply refused to recognize the legitimacy of the moral demands made on them by the court and renounce (or refuse) to recognize themselves as governed by the local norms, then the court can dispose of them as it sees fit (perhaps in accordance with the demands of deterrence). However, that would not be a moral matter.

[8] The position described here is similar to that defended in Brian Barry's *Culture and Equality*. That is to say, the critical issue is whether "there are sound reasons for having the law in the first place" (2001: 333 n.57). The only thing I would add is that "sound reasons" for having a *criminal* law need to address not only its content, but also the fact that it is regulated by the criminal law.

[9] This is one of the things emphasized in Renteln 2004.

ANSWERING AND RESPONSIBILITY 2: ANSWERING TO WHOM

In *Punishment, Communication, and Community*, Antony Duff introduces an important distinction that he uses to discuss the problem of doing penal justice in conditions of social injustice. "A normative theory of punishment," Duff writes, must identify "the conditions given which the punishment of a particular offender or the punishments imposed by a particular system are justified." However, it also needs to do more than this: it needs to identify the *preconditions* of just punishment. That is, the "conditions that must be satisfied before we can engage in this practice [the practice of just punishment] and before we can discuss the legitimacy of particular actions taken or policies pursued within the practice" (2001: 179).

Duff considers a number of preconditions of criminal liability, but the one that is most important here is that those who call the alleged criminal to account must have the *standing* so to do. What motivates his concern for the standing of the court (or, more generally, of those who attempt to call the alleged offender to account) is the thought that if someone or some institution is to call someone else to answer for some action, then he or it should have not merely the institutional, but also the moral, standing to do so (there is a useful example in Duff 2001: 185–186).

There seems to me to be something deeply compelling in all this. The response, "who are *you* to say that?," does, as Duff says, seem to speak to the *preconditions* of answerability. Moreover, if one believes that the proper function of the criminal system (or one of its proper functions) is to hold people answerable, then the question "to whom is the alleged offender answerable?" must be answered and this, in turn, leads to questions about the standing of those identified.

It is important to note that there is a difference between criticizing and calling to account, although at times they may be hard to distinguish. Thus, President Mugabe might criticize the absence of democracy in Florida during the US Presidential election of 2000, and he might make disparaging remarks about a system that allows critical electoral decisions to be made by the brother of one of the candidates. In response, one might think "who is he to criticize" or "it is a bit bloody rich coming from him," but those kinds of thoughts do not seem to negate the criticism.

One of the important purposes of this argument for Duff is in discussing what follows from the severe economic injustice of our societies for our practices of penal justice. If, for example, we assume that Stan's plight is to some degree the consequence of serious social economic injustice then the standing of the court to hold him to account is questionable:

> If, for instance, the police or the courts have not taken criminal attacks on members of this disadvantaged group seriously, this failure undermines their standing

to call members of this group to answer for attacks that they commit, since it shows that the community does not treat the members of the group as fully sharing in those values. Second, the question is whether this person is answerable as a citizen to his fellow citizens: but if their collective treatment of him has effectively excluded him from many of the rights and goods of citizenship, if they have collectively failed to treat him as a citizen, how can they now call him to account as a fellow citizen? (Duff 2001: 187–188)

Of course, Duff would accept that Stan is answerable to someone (paradigmatically, his victim), and that Stan has done something seriously wrong (he is criticizable). The issue is not whether a wrong has been committed, but to whom the perpetrator is answerable for that wrong.

I argue elsewhere that Duff's tying together of the preconditions of criminal liability and the standing of the court is valuable, but problematic when applied to the problem of economic injustice (Matravers 2006). It might be thought, though, that the idea could usefully be deployed in the case of a clash of cultures such as is exhibited in the Iraqi refugee example.

The claim is that a court based in one culture and representing one set of values may lack the moral standing to call to account defendants whose culture and values are very different. Such an argument could take two forms depending on what is asserted by the court.

On some interpretations of liberalism, the court alleges that the defendant has failed to respect others' culture and law, in particular the culture and law of the majority community (assuming that it is the majority community's culture and moral norms that are reflected in the municipal criminal law). If so, the issue of standing would depend on the seriousness with which it could be alleged that the liberal state itself fails to respect the culture of others within its boundaries.

For reasons given above, this does not seem to me to be the right way to think of the criminal law. The criminal court ought not hold the defendant to answer for failing to "do in Rome as the Romans do," but for performing a serious moral wrong. If so, and if the state is not itself seriously unjust, no issue of standing arises.[10] That said, there is more than one way in which the defendant might allege that the state's position undermines its standards.

Consider the following possibility: the father alleges that modern America corrupts young girls by promoting their early sexualization. The father points to Britney Spears and to magazines targeted at 9–11 year olds that instruct their readers in the intricacies of the fellatio. He then asks what standing the court has to make him answer for trying to protect his daughters from corruption by marrying them off to "good Muslims." That is, the father is criticizing

---

[10] Think of the Nuremburg trials: the issue is whether the Allies had the moral standing to call the Nazi leaders to answer for their crimes against humanity not whether the Allies had the standing to demand compliance with the victors' standards of what morality demands.

contemporary US culture and the content of its laws. He is, or may be, offering a suggestion for how these might be reformed. Now, there may be something to this claim (after all, we are not infallible), but it does not undermine the standing of the court to hold the father answerable for his particular offense and issues such as these need to be kept separate from issues of cultural accommodation in the criminal law. Rather, they point away from the criminal trial and to the need to rethink the values and structure of the wider society.

CONCLUSION

If the criminal law expresses important moral injunctions then those who culpably break it perform serious moral wrongs. Issues of cultural pluralism seem to put pressure on both parts of that formula.

In terms of culpability, cultural cases may worry us because someone acting in accordance with his cultural standards may, in virtue of that, be less culpable than someone acting for another reason. However, this is not because of anything particular to culture (there are many things that influence our motives and intentions). In some cases, this will mean that, in the legal sense, the "act" has not been performed at all (in the case of Bert, if he is innocent, then in the law's eyes no rape occurred). In others, it will speak in mitigation at the penalty phase. Although not uncontroversial, these are legal ideas with which we are familiar. The significant influence of culture (usually) does not undermine the responsibility of the alleged offender in any general sense because it does not (usually) undermine the alleged offender's capacity to grasp and follow reasons.

In terms of the criminal law expressing important moral injunctions, cultural pluralism may bother us either because we think it points to a deep relativism that defeats any claim to be able to vindicate those moral claims, or because we think that what follows is that a liberal state ought to respect "difference" and so not attempt to foist its moral values on others (even when it is in the right). In my view, both those positions are mistaken, but the latter points to an important need for caution in the liberal state's use of the criminal law.

REFERENCES

Barry, Brian. 2001. *Culture and Equality: An Egalitarian Critique of Multiculturalism* (Cambridge: Polity Press).
Duff, R. A. 1977. "Psychopathy and Moral Understanding," *American Philosophical Quarterly* 14: 189–200.
Duff, R. A. 1986. *Trials & Punishments* (Cambridge: Cambridge University Press).
Duff, R. A. 2001. *Punishment, Communication, and Community* (New York: Oxford University Press).

Duff, R. A. 2007. *Answering for Crime: Responsibility and Liability in the Criminal Law* (Oxford: Hart Publishing).
Hart, H. L. A. 1968. *Punishment and Responsibility: Essays in the Philosophy of Law* (Oxford: Oxford University Press).
Husak, Douglas. 2008. *Overcriminalization: The Limits of the Criminal Law* (New York: Oxford University Press).
Matravers, Matt. 2000. *Justice and Punishment: The Rationale of Coercion* (Oxford: Oxford University Press).
Matravers, Matt. 2003. "Responsibility and Choice," in *Scanlon and Contractualism*, ed. Matt Matravers (London: Frank Cass), 77–92.
Matravers, Matt. 2006. "'Who's Still Standing?' A Comment on Antony Duff's Preconditions of Criminal Liability," *Journal of Moral Philosophy* 3/3: 320–330.
Morse, S. J. 2000. "Deprivation and Desert," in *From Social Justice to Criminal Justice: Poverty and the Administration of Criminal Law*, ed. W. C. Heffernan and J. Kleinig (New York: Oxford University Press), 114–160.
Renteln, Alison Dundes. 2004. *The Cultural Defense* (New York: Oxford University Press).
Scanlon, T. M. 1998. *What We Owe to Each Other* (Cambridge, MA: Harvard University Press).
Strawson, P. F. 1962. "Freedom and Resentment," *Proceedings of the British Academy* 48: 1–25.
Tunick, M. 2004. "'Can Culture Excuse Crime?': Evaluating the Inability Thesis," *Punishment & Society* 6/4: 395–409.
Waldron, Jeremy. 2002. "Taking Group Rights Carefully," in *Litigating Rights: Perspectives from Domestic and International Law*, ed. Grant Huscroft and Paul Rishworth (Oxford: Hart Publishing), 203–220.
Wallace, R. J. 1994. *Responsibility and the Moral Sentiments* (Cambridge, MA: Harvard University Press).
Wootton, Barbara. 1959. *Social Science and Social Pathology* (London: George Allen & Unwin).
Wootton, Barbara. 1978. *Crime and Penal Policy: Reflections on Fifty Years' Experience* (London: George Allen & Unwin).

6

Cultural Defense and the Criminal Law

*Bhikhu Parekh**

In this chapter I examine the case for cultural defense in the administration of cultural law. I argue that since every system of criminal law is culturally embedded and has a distinct cultural orientation, it should make some space for cultural defense in order to avoid doing injustice to those belonging to different cultures. Cultural defense, however, has its limits, and I end by outlining some of these.

CULTURAL BASIS OF CRIMINAL LAW

It is widely assumed that since criminal law deals with the great evils which all human beings dread and seek to avoid, such as death, bodily harm, imprisonment, rape, and theft, it is subject to little cross-cultural disagreement. Although there is some truth in this view, it is highly exaggerated. No system of law including the criminal law is mandated by human nature and in that sense culture-free or transculturally valid. We need to decide the degrees of gravity of different evils, which of them to criminalize, how to determine the agent's responsibility for his or her actions, the basic purposes of criminal law, and so on. And these decisions are invariably shaped by the beliefs in terms of which we understand and organize our lives. This becomes clear if we examine the six major aspects of criminal law.

First, its scope or content, that is, what areas of human conduct fall within the ambit of criminal law. Views on this vary between societies, and over time in the same society. Atheism was a criminal offense for centuries in many European societies, but it is no longer so today. Homosexuality was not a criminal offense

---

* I am grateful to Professors Will Kymlicka and Jeremy Waldron for their most helpful comments on an earlier draft of this chapter.

in classical Greece, but became one with the rise of Christianity and remained so in the West until recently. It is still a criminal offense in some deeply religious Southern states of the United States and is punishable with death in some Muslim societies. Apostasy is a criminal offense in almost all Muslim countries but nowhere else. In pre-modern China and in some Muslim societies, causing grievous bodily harm to and sometimes even killing an adulterous wife was not or is not a criminal offense; in many others, it is.

Second, definitions of major crimes such as murder, rape, theft, and assault. Child sacrifice in some tribal societies is seen as a form of divine propitiation and is not considered murder; most societies today criminalize it. In many patriarchal and communitarian societies, honor killing is seen as a legitimate act of communal self-defense, a way of affirming its structural norms, and is even admired; other societies find it morally unacceptable and define it as such. In many pre-modern societies, helping oneself with the surplus food of another to relieve one's own or others' distress was not only a case of justified theft but was not considered theft at all. Bourgeois societies absolutize the right to property and privilege entitlement or ownership over others' basic needs.

Third, gradation of the gravity of crimes and different degrees of punishment attached to them. Many traditional societies with their relaxed attitude to sexuality and loosely defined social relations did not view rape as a major offense, or even as an offense at all. Rape was generally not a serious crime in Europe until the nineteenth century, and is not one in some non-Western societies today. It became a serious offense when our ideas on gender relations and the individual's, especially the woman's, relation to her body underwent changes. Matrimonial rape, increasingly seen as a criminal offense in the West, is an alien concept in patriarchal cultures where the woman's body is viewed as her husband's property with which he is free to do what he likes. In some Hindu kingdoms and in classical Rome during certain periods, stealing temple property was a more serious offense than stealing other forms of property, and often invited far greater punishment than causing grievous bodily harm. In almost all hierarchical societies, murder or rape carried more severe punishment if the victim belonged to a higher status group, a practice abolished in modern egalitarian cultures.

Fourth, determination of individual responsibility. Except in such cases as organized conspiracies, modern Western societies take a highly individualized view of responsibility. If an individual intended a particular action, he is causally and legally responsible for it and its foreseeable consequences. In many traditional and some contemporary communitarian societies, his community or family shares responsibility for it and incurs proportionate blame and punishment. Again, societies based on the idea of individual agency determine responsibility on the basis of what they expect a reasonable person to do in a similar situation. The latter in turn is shaped by their beliefs concerning how much self-restraint and willpower individuals can be required to exercise, how detailed a calculation of consequences may rightly be expected of them, and the nature and power of emotions and whether they are amenable to rational control. Some of these beliefs vary from culture to culture.

Fifth, the range of mitigating factors or acceptable defenses, views on which are closely connected with those on individual responsibility. Almost all societies today criminalize rape, but vary in their views on acceptable defenses. In some Muslim societies, the fact that a woman was provocatively dressed and severely strained her attacker's capacity for self-restraint is accepted as a mitigating factor. Just as "fighting words" mitigate the defendant's violent response, a woman's "come and get me" dress or conduct is supposed to provide partial defense for his sexually aggressive behavior. Again, in some societies "heat of passion" is a mitigating factor, but it is either not a factor or is so to a lesser degree in some Buddhist societies where reasonable men and women are expected to keep their passions firmly under control.

Sixth and finally, administration of criminal law. The way in which it is administered is not external but integral to the system of criminal law because the latter's capacity to deliver justice depends on and is as good as those in charge of administering it. The judge and the jury bring with them their own cultural and other biases, and even when they guard against these, some of the biases sometimes persist and shape their decisions. This is one of the main reasons why great care is taken in many societies to ensure that the judges and the jury reflect the diversity of social background and views, and why race or religion related cases are expected to have a racially or religiously mixed jury.

Every system of criminal law then is shaped by a particular way of understanding and organizing human life, and is embedded in and legitimized in terms of the central beliefs of the wider society. Since some evils arise out of the universally shared human impulses and dispositions, and since no society can do without some notion of responsibility, different systems of criminal law do overlap and converge in different areas. Since, however, these evils are defined, graded, and interpreted differently, and ideas on responsibility vary, no two systems are ever identical. The cultural embeddedness of criminal law creates problems in a multicultural society which includes minority groups, be they immigrants, indigenous people, or long marginalized communities, who take different views on some or all aspects of criminal law. They might ask why certain types of conduct are criminalized and not others, why the reasonable person, duress, and provocation are defined in certain ways, why responsibility is determined in a particular manner, and so on, and might plead for the accommodation of their views on these matters. They might contend that the failure to do so not only has a discriminatory effect on them but makes the criminal law an instrument of cultural control, using the violence of the state to mold them in a particular manner and being no different from other forms of forced assimilation.

Such a demand is often rejected on one of two grounds. First, it is argued that the criminal law is concerned with the universally common evils of human life and has nothing to do with cultural biases. This response is incoherent because, as we saw, the legal system is not an embodiment of pure reason but is informed by a particular way of understanding and ordering social relations. Having grown up within it, we often fail to notice its institutionalized biases which outsiders detect more easily. The question therefore is not one of "our reason" as opposed to "their culture" but rather that of our culture against theirs.

Second, it is sometimes argued that we cannot have different systems of law for different cultural groups, that their equal treatment requires uniformity, and that those living in Rome should live like Romans. This argument is not without its merits. Every society has a historically inherited cultural structure, and is based on certain widely shared beliefs and practices. The latter cannot be easily unscrambled without creating a widespread sense of dislocation and discontinuity and depriving its members of a vitally necessary stable frame of reference. Furthermore the majority has a right to its identity just as much as its cultural minorities have, and cannot be expected to disregard and undermine it in order to accommodate them.

In spite of these and other merits, the "when in Rome" argument is flawed and cannot do the work expected of it, especially in a liberal society. It applies to newcomers and not to long settled groups or the original inhabitants. Furthermore, while it makes sense in the administrative and other morally indifferent areas where uniformity is crucial, it has little validity in moral matters. If "Rome" is unjustly constituted, based on morally outrageous practices, or makes morally unacceptable demands as in the case of a racially segregated or totalitarian society, it has no or only a limited claim to compliance. So far as the liberal society is concerned, it values human rights including that to cultural identity. It is also based on respect for persons, and subject to the concomitant obligation both to justify its beliefs and practices and to reconsider them when these are shown to be deeply discriminatory and likely to result in injustice. In short, the cultural structure or identity that the liberal society cherishes requires it to accommodate legitimate cultural differences, and not to press the "when in Rome" argument beyond a point where it becomes offensive and demeaning.

There is then a strong case for cultural accommodation, for recognizing and respecting cultural differences when the latter are morally acceptable.[1] Cultural accommodation can take several forms. It might involve criminalizing activities that might currently not be criminalized (for example, incitement to religious hatred and mocking religions or religious communities), decriminalizing

---

[1] For a fuller discussion, see Parekh 2006: Chaps. 9 and 12.

those that might be currently criminalized (for example, polygamy), exempting minorities from certain laws (for example, those against the use of certain kinds of drugs), disallowing the right to buy or sell property in the territories of indigenous people, and so on. Cultural accommodation might also take the more limited form of taking the individual's cultural background into account in the enforcement of the law. The two forms of accommodation raise different sorts of questions. The former involves issues concerning the nature and limits of cultural rights and is primarily addressed to the legislature. The latter raises the question of cultural defense proper, and primarily concerns the courts. In the rest of this essay I shall concentrate on it.

CULTURAL DEFENSE

Cultural defense comes into play when individuals have violated the law and ask the court to consider culturally relevant information in judging their action, determining their responsibility, and deciding on appropriate punishment. It raises three questions. First, what kind of defense is it? How does it differ from other kinds of defense and does it amount to denying individual agency and responsibility? Second, why should we allow cultural defense? And third, what are its limits? I shall briefly consider each in turn.

Cultural defense is articulated in terms of the beliefs and practices of the community to which the individual claims to belong. It is not an appeal to what Rawls calls a comprehensive philosophical doctrine, or to the agent's deeply held moral beliefs, or to the way he is shaped by his unfortunate socio-economic circumstances, or to the history of oppression, genocide, or racial humiliation to which his community might once have been subjected. All these can be and sometimes are taken into account by the courts and allowed to provide defenses, but they are different from cultural defense, which basically involves an appeal to the beliefs and practices of the individual's cultural community and by which he claims to be bound.

Discussion of cultural defense sometimes goes wrong because it fails to understand the nature of culture and the individual's relation to it. Culture refers to a body of beliefs and practices in terms of which a group of individuals understand and organize their lives. It includes their views on the natural and the human world, their values and ideals, their expectations of each other, their notions of rationality and forms of reasoning, their manner of structuring human relations, the meaning and significance they assign to different human activities, and so on. As thinking beings, human beings act on the basis of how they understand themselves and their situation, and that in turn is shaped by their culture. They do, of course, reflect on their culture, criticize and revise it, add to it elements derived from others, even replace it with another, but they cannot transcend or operate outside the realm of culture altogether. In this basic sense human beings are cultural beings.

While the individual's culture shapes his or her thoughts and disposes them to approach the world in certain ways, it does not and cannot determine them and deprive them of their agency. This is so for several reasons. No culture is a unified and monolithic whole. It includes different bodies of ideas derived from its history. They sometimes point in different directions, requiring its members to reflect on them, examine their underlying reasons, bring them into some kind of harmony, and determine their comparative importance. Furthermore cultural beliefs and practices are necessarily general, and require individuals to understand and interpret them and decide how to apply them to new and unexpected situations. Human beings also enjoy access to other cultures which enable them to see their own from the outside, to appreciate its contingency and weaknesses, and to borrow what they find valuable in others. The presence of other cultures creates an awareness of alternatives, and opens up a space of freedom that militates against cultural determinism.

A cultural community then does not consist of human automata programmed by it to function in predetermined ways. It simply cannot come into being, let alone last, unless its members are able to think for themselves however inadequately, adapt it to new situations, and interpret, evaluate, and when necessary reconsider their inherited beliefs and practices. Their culture inclines or disposes them to think and act along certain lines, shapes their normal and taken-for-granted responses, and makes certain choices difficult and painful, but it does not undermine their agency. It does not "make them do" anything or even dictate what they must do; rather it provides a framework within which they understand their situation and respond to it appropriately. Cultural defense or an appeal to an individual's culture is not intended to absolve the agent of her responsibility for her action. Its purpose rather is to clarify the nature and meaning of her action, explain why she did it, and in some circumstances to provide a defense of it.

A good case for cultural defense can be made on the ground that it improves the quality, indeed, is the very precondition of justice. The court is concerned to do two things, to decide if an action violates the law, and to determine if and to what degree its agent is responsible for it. Unless the court contextualizes both, it risks misunderstanding them and doing the agent injustice. All justice is individualized justice in the sense that it relates to *this* defendant not anyone else, and to *this* action and not one that abstractly or superficially looks like it but is really quite different.

No action carries its meaning on the surface. It needs to be interpreted, and that involves locating it in the agent's system of meaning. A Nigerian woman is found to have scarred her child's cheeks. Is this a case of deliberately causing grievous bodily harm?[2] It could be if that is what she meant to do as a way of punishing him or in a state of anger, but it is not if it is part of a socially obligatory tribal initiation ceremony. In one case the bodily harm is its intended outcome and sole purpose; in the other it is an incidental though not unforeseen outcome resulting from following a cultural practice and lacks the vital element of *mens rea*. In each case her action has a different meaning, and is in an important sense a different act. The court might choose to punish the woman, but it would at least need to acknowledge the difference and give its reasons for treating her on a par with someone who did it with the sole purpose of hurting the child.[3]

The law aims to protect children from sexual abuse or being made objects of sexual gratification. With that objective in mind, it punishes parents for, among other things, fondling, caressing, or making oral contact with their children's genitals. An Afghan refugee kisses the genitals of his eighteen-month-old son as a way of showing his affection, this being a common practice in his society. Should the court punish him and take his child into public care? That would be most unjust and bring the law into disrepute because it is based on a total misunderstanding of both his action and the relevant law. The law cannot and does not aim to ban all parental contacts with children's genitals. Some of these contacts could be accidental or occur in the course of bathing them or dealing with an ailment. The law bans those contacts that are designed to obtain sexual gratification, and that is not the case with the individual in question. If we are in doubt, we can easily resolve it by inquiring if it is a common social practice in his community, checking with his wife what he really did, and so on.

We misunderstand not only an action but also the agent if we fail to take his cultural background into account. A Chinese defendant accused of murder might remain passive and show no sign of remorse when declared guilty. The court might conclude that he is a cold and calculating murderer and sentence him to death. If it had appreciated that it is a deeply ingrained Chinese practice, indeed a moral norm, not to show emotions in public, and had looked for other signs of remorse or accepted the man's word, it would have judged him differently and passed a different sentence.[4]

Law allows the defense of provocation, and here again culture can be relevant. A Mexican owes his fellow countryman a small sum of money. When the latter asks for its return, he shouts *chinga tu madre*, at which point the creditor pulls his gun and shoots him. It makes sense to say that any reasonable person

---

[2] These and following examples are drawn from real cases, but I have decontexualized them to tease out their underlying principles and avoid commenting on the relevant court decisions. For some of these cases, see Renteln 2004: Part II.

[3] Cultural defense by itself is inconclusive because one needs to show not only that a particular belief or practice is prevalent in a community but also that the individual in question shares it.

[4] The district court itself spoke of a "reasonable probability" that the "result would have been different" if this had been pointed out by the defense counsel (cited in Renteln 2004: 41).

should be able to take such a remark in his stride and exercise self-restraint. However, our view of the defendant's action would be different if we appreciated that the remark had the double meaning of having sexual intercourse with one's mother and the Virgin Mary, and that it is regarded by many Mexicans not only as a gross insult but also as a challenge to one's religious commitment and sense of honor. The court needs to ask not how *any* reasonable person but how a reasonable *Mexican* man would respond to this remark, and judge the defendant accordingly. It should certainly punish him, but would be wrong not to take account of the provocative nature of the remark in deciding the sentence.

Culture is also relevant in determining the agent's degree of responsibility for his or her action. An elderly Muslim woman carries drugs on the orders of her father-in-law. She did not ask what she was being asked to carry because that is not allowed in her authoritarian culture and, even if she had, she would have been in no position to disobey him without inviting severe social and even physical sanctions. She clearly carried the drugs, is not an automaton or insane, and is responsible for her action. However, a consideration of her cultural background might show that she had lived all her life in seclusion, was deeply conditioned into doing as told, acted under pressure amounting to duress, and was virtually an instrument of her father-in-law's will. These and related factors diminish her agency and blameworthiness, and it seems unjust not to take them into account in determining her degree of responsibility. She is not the sole agent of her action, he too is implicated, and both deserve punishment, he far more than she. Cultural defense does not deny her responsibility, nor applies a lower standard of it as is sometimes argued, but rather allocates it differently. We admit diminished responsibility in other cases such as the violent attack on her husband by a long humiliated and ill-treated wife, and cannot refuse it in this one simply because the vulnerability and duress are cultural in nature.[5]

Taking the defendant's culture into account thus is necessary to do him justice. It ensures that the court has made a genuine attempt to understand him and his action, taken full account of what the action meant to him and why he did it, and has in general done all that could be expected of it. This not only makes the resulting punishment acceptable to him but legitimizes the wider system in his and his community's eyes. It also ensures that the community concerned does not turn away from the prevailing legal system and find ways of settling disputes behind its back and without its procedural safeguards as

---

[5] Subservient and weak-willed individuals like the drug-carrying Muslim woman are also to be found in the wider society. They too might rightly claim such a defense, but it is not cultural in nature. What distinguishes the Muslim woman is that she was brought up in a certain way, has internalized a certain view of herself, and that an intricate network of sanctions is designed to keep her in her place.

some minority communities alienated from the prevailing system of administration of justice have been known to do.[6]

Since a good case can be made for cultural defense, the question arises why it is often opposed or allowed reluctantly and stealthily (see, for example, Choi 1990; Sheybani 1987; Gallin 1994; Sacks 1996; Goldstein 1994). First, it is sometimes argued that it leads to exemptions and exceptions of all kinds, and undermines the uniformity, clarity, and predictability that we expect in a law. Although the latter are important considerations, they are not the only ones. Furthermore the law is replete with and indeed cannot deliver justice without qualifications, exemptions, excusing conditions, targeted rights, and so on. Emergency services have no speed limits, churches are exempt from taxes, and some commodities do not invite sales taxes. We have gender-specific prohibitions of pornography and health programs, religious institutions are often exempt from sex discrimination laws, extra public subsidies are given to rural but not to urban transport services, Holocaust denial is a crime in most European societies but not the denial of the Armenian massacre or justification of slavery. In almost all these cases we think we have good reasons to compromise the uniformity of the law. The cultural defense is no different. The only relevant question is whether it is justified in principle, and I hope to have shown that it is.

Second, it is argued that cultural defense violates the principle of equality before the law by allowing some individuals defenses not available to others and thereby conferring on them additional rights. The objection is mistaken because, as we saw, such differential defenses are part of every system of law and not unique to cultural defense. More importantly, the objection mistakenly equates equality with uniformity or equal treatment with identical treatment. Since equality requires ignoring irrelevant and taking account of relevant differences, equal treatment sometimes involves different treatment. Furthermore we need to be clear about the level at which equality is sought. A person under threat requires greater protection and allocation of public resources, but he is not being privileged or given more rights. He enjoys the same rights as others, but makes greater demands because of his particular circumstances. This is broadly the case when culture is taken into account. During Prohibition in the United States, Catholics and Jews were allowed the use of wine for religious purposes. This did not mean that they were privileged over the rest. Like the latter, they were subject to the requirements of Prohibition in non-religious areas of life. And the rest of their fellow citizens too would have been exempt from these requirements for religious purposes if their religion had so required.

---

[6] For a case involving the likely minority loss of confidence in the court's capacity to deliver justice, see Renteln 2004: 63.

Third, it is sometimes argued that taking culture into account allows unacceptable minority practices to continue, and harms those adversely affected by them. The argument has considerable merit and is one of the main reasons why cultural defense is often resisted. A Chinese bludgeons his adulterous wife to death because she had dishonored him and his family and challenged his manhood, all of which in his culture deserve death. His action and others like it violate what we believe and can show to be basic human values, and cannot be allowed to claim cultural defense. Not all cultural practices, however, are of this kind. The fact that unacceptable cultural practices cannot offer defense does not mean that no practice can.

The argument we are considering makes two further mistakes. It assumes that cultural defense is conclusive and overrides all other considerations. This is not the case, for it provides only a partial defense, and may be overridden in certain situations. We shall return to this later. It also takes a narrow and one-dimensional view of cultural defense. The defendant's culture is introduced to serve several purposes, such as to understand the nature of his action, to explain his reasons for doing it, to determine his degree of responsibility, to defend his action, and so on. The argument under consideration considers only the last role of culture. Even if we disallowed it, culture would still remain relevant for other purposes.

Fourth, it is sometimes argued that cultural beliefs and practices are contested and that there is no general agreement on their content and authority. This is true of some cultural practices but not all, and in the case of the former, we may disallow cultural defense or give it a limited weight. The important question in these matters is not the level of disagreement in the community, for no community is homogeneous and monolithic and its culture is rarely a unified whole. What the court needs to determine is how the defendant himself understood a particular cultural belief or practice and how it influenced his action. Difficult questions do of course arise. The defendant might be seriously mistaken about his culture, use it as a convenient excuse, or take an excessively conservative view of it.[7] Such questions, however, are not unique to cultural defense. They arise in other areas of life as well, such as claims to conscientious objection, what a right to religion requires in particular situations and whether a Sikh's turban or a Muslim's beard is a religious requirement, and can be dealt with in similar ways.

Fifth, it is sometimes argued that although cultural defense is legitimate, it is best subsumed under other established forms of defense such as diminished responsibility, provocation, absence of *mens rea* and duress, as the courts have

---

[7] A Haitian man claimed cultural defense when charged with abusing his wife. Most of his community protested that his behavior had no cultural sanction and that his claim stigmatized and demeaned them. Allowing cultural defense brings the relevant culture into the public realm, opens it up to wider security, and stimulates a healthy internal and external debate.

sometimes done in jurisdictions that disallow cultural defense. While some forms of cultural defense can be subsumed under existing categories, others cannot be and need to be considered in their own terms. Furthermore there are good reasons to acknowledge cultural defense in its own right. It leads to greater clarity and openness about the nature of the defense, and both the defendant and the prosecution know what sorts of arguments are expected of them. It also allows us to focus attention on our own as well as minority cultural practices, assess their merits and relevance, and to generate pressure for such changes as are necessary. It also has the additional advantage of not so stretching the existing legal categories as to render them vacuous or indeterminate.

There are also other alleged difficulties with the principle of cultural defense, such as who is entitled to invoke it, if it extends to second or third generation immigrants and bicultural children, whether it rests on a dubious notion of collective rights, and whether it stands in the way of social integration. Some of these objections are based on misunderstanding whereas others make valid practical points that can be taken care of. Although cultural defense is sometimes presented as a form of collective right, it is not so; rather it is largely a matter of considering an individual's cultural background in order better to understand him and his action and to do him justice. Unless social integration is confused with total assimilation, cultural defense facilitates it by showing respect for legitimate minority differences, assuring them justice, and securing their trust in their legal system. As for "one law for all," it does not obtain in practice as is evident in the exemptions, exceptions, and differential protection that all laws allow. Furthermore cultural defense does not deny one law for all when the law permits it to all with relevant cultural claims, including subcultural groups within the majority community. Some of the other objections that are largely practical in nature do not admit of easy answers, but they are not intractable. The impressive jurisprudence built up in Britain, Canada, India, the European Court of Justice, and other jurisdictions that implicitly or explicitly accept the principle of cultural defense shows how it can be operationalized without subverting or even weakening the central guiding principles of criminal law.

LIMITS OF CULTURAL DEFENSE

Although cultural defense is not without its problems there is on balance a good case for allowing it in the administration of criminal law. The defense, however, is not unlimited, indiscriminate, and absolute. As I have suggested from time to time, it is subject to important constraints. I shall highlight four of the most important ones.

First, in a multicultural society we interact with people with unfamiliar cultural beliefs and practices, and would not be able to engage in meaningful relations let alone live together peacefully with each other if we constantly feared that our otherwise innocent remarks or gestures might be construed very differently and invite hostility and worse. One might casually remark to a Jehovah's Witness that he once had a blood transfusion. He takes it to mean that he is being accused of moral hypocrisy, turns violent, and claims grave provocation in self-defense. If the Afghan refugee were to kiss my child's genitals, I would be right to suspect the worst and tell him off. He might turn violent, and claim in self-defense that I had implicitly accused him of being a pervert and a child molester and undermined his reputation.

In these and similar cases the individuals involved could not possibly be expected to know the culture of the offended parties and the way in which their remarks were likely to be interpreted. We may therefore rightly require people to show self-restraint and tolerance and explain to those involved why they take strong exception to their remarks, and disallow cultural defense when they act precipitately. Other things being equal, we might also limit cultural defense to cases where those involved belong to the same cultural community and can be presumed to know the cultural import of a remark.

Second, the system of criminal law needs to enjoy widespread support and legitimacy within the wider society, and should not step too far out of line with its norms of justice. Its members should feel confident that the system applies to them all the same laws and standards of responsibility, and that no one convicted of crime will get away or receive an unduly lighter sentence on the basis of a cultural defense. While cultural defense secures the confidence of the minorities, it could risk giving the impression of privileging them if it is applied indiscriminately or in an unprincipled manner. We need to retain the confidence of both the wider society and the minorities. In many cases there should be no conflict because the wider society itself is likely to see the point of allowing cultural defense to its minorities. It would, for example, be most surprising if many members of society did not feel deeply uneasy if the Afghan refugee were to be locked up and his eighteen-month-old child taken into care, or if the Nigerian woman were to be charged with grievous bodily harm and her son with scarred cheeks taken away from her.

Occasions are, of course, likely to arise when the wider society might not be so sympathetic to the way cultural defense is invoked or applied. It might, for example, be outraged if the insulted Mexican man in the case cited earlier were to be exonerated, or the drug-carrying Muslim woman let off with a warning. Balancing different cultural norms and stretching the prevailing normative consensus without provoking an outrage is not easy. When the crime involved is grave and the cultural practice is contested or ambiguous, courts may disallow cultural defense. Although this might result in some injustice, it should be accepted as a legitimate trade-off in the interest of general confidence in the legal system. In other cases the court might admit an unpopular cultural defense if it thinks that the unpopularity is due to strong anti-minority feelings, xenophobia, or widespread misunderstanding of the facts of the case, and hope that the wider society would over time come round to its view. In yet other cases it might admit cultural defense in the first case coming up before it, but make it clear that such actions in future would be met with full legal sanctions. This is how the British and French courts have dealt with female circumcision, polygyny, excessively harsh punishment of children, and other offensive minority practices (Renteln 2004: 52).[8]

Relating the necessarily general law to the concrete circumstances of a unique individual case is not a mechanical and deductive process. It requires taking account of relevant factors concerning the defendant and the wider society, weighing them up, judging them against the letter and the intention of the law, and reaching a decision that is widely perceived to be right or fair. Sometimes courts get this right, on other occasions they do not. In the latter case their decisions provoke a debate among professionals and the general public, which performs the vital function of bringing different notions of justice into a creative interplay and helping unite both the wider society and its cultural minorities around shared norms of justice. In all societies, particularly the multicultural, courts do not simply apply the law as the positivist view maintains, but help evolve nuanced and richer norms of justice and sustain society's confidence in the legal system.

Third, cultural defense is one of several factors to be taken into account by the courts. It is not the only one, nor always the most important, and could be overridden by other considerations. The court may think that the defendant could and should have made a reasonable effort to familiarize himself with the wider culture and comply with the law. The crime involved might be grave, and the court might think that cultural defense does not measure up to its enormity. A compelling public necessity too may override defense as when a crime such as honor killing or forced marriage has reached an epidemic proportion in a particular minority community and requires a robust response (see European Conference Report 2004).

Finally, in many cases of cultural defense the defendant claims to act on certain cultural beliefs. He might say that he killed his newborn child because he thought that his wife was impregnated by an evil spirit, and that he was not killing a human being but an evil spirit that was likely to cause his family and community serious harm. Another man might kill an unusually tall or extremely short woman with an ugly stoop, believing her to be a witch as

---

[8] As the judge remarked in the case of the Nigerian woman discussed earlier. "You and others who come to this country must realize that our laws must be obeyed.... I am prepared to deal with you with the utmost leniency. But let no one else assume that they will be treated with mercy. Others have now been warned" (cited in Renteln 2004: 50).

judged by the criteria of his culture. An orthodox Christian father might kill his daughter because she intends to convert to Islam, arguing that her death would save her from eternal hellfire in the afterlife.

These are all complex cases, and our responses need to be nuanced. In some cases we might take the belief as given, not sit in judgment on it, and only ask if it is widely shared in the defendant's community and could have led him to act in a certain way. If the answer to both yes, we may allow a limited cultural defense, whatever we may think of the belief itself. In other cases we cannot stop there because of the nature of the belief involved, its prevalence, its likely consequences, and so on. We may then need to judge the content of the belief and examine its basis. People entertain and act on all kinds of beliefs, and we cannot accept them all as valid or deserving of respect. We may confidently disregard beliefs and practices which we can show in an open dialogue to violate basic human values, are based on ignorance of facts or poor reasoning, do not stand up to an even moderately critical scrutiny, and disallow defenses based on them.

CONCLUSION

My main concern in this chapter has been to show that a valid case can be made for the principle of cultural defense in the administration of criminal law. Cultural defense is not unlimited and conclusive both because cultural beliefs and practices might be indefensible and because individuals are never so determined by their culture as to lack the capacity for agency. It is a partial defense, its moral and legal weight in the scales of justice depends on the nature of the crime, and it might be overridden under certain circumstances. The fact that it is limited in these and other ways does not, however, negate its importance. Rather it should reduce the opposition to it and render it more acceptable

REFERENCES

Choi, Carolyn. 1990. "Application of Cultural Defence in Criminal proceedings," *UCLA Pacific Basin Law Journal* 8: 80–90.

European Conference Report. 2004. "Honour Related Violence with a Global Perspective: Mitigation and Prevention in Europe" (Kvinnoforum, Stockholm, October 7/8), available at: <http://ec.europa.eu/justice_home/daphnetoolkit/files/projects/2003_048/kvinnoforum_honour_related_violence_conference_report_2004.pdf>.

Gallin, Allice. 1994. "The Cultural Defense: Undermining the Policies against Domestic Violence," *Boston College Law Review* 35/3: 723–746.

Goldstein, Taryn F. 1994. "Cultural Conflicts in Court: Should the American Criminal Justice System Formally Recognize a 'Cultural Defense'?," *Dickinson Law Review* 99/1: 141–168.
Parekh, Bhikhu. 2006. *Rethinking Multiculturalism*, 2nd edition (Basingstoke: Palgrave Macmillan).
Renteln, Alison Dundes. 2004. *The Cultural Defense* (New York: Oxford University Press).
Sacks, Valerie L. 1996. "An Indefensible Defense: On the Misuse of Culture in Criminal Law," *Arizona Journal of International and Comparative Law* 13: 523–551.
Sheybani, Malek-Mithra. 1987. "Cultural Defense: One Person's Culture is Another's Crime," *Loyola of Los Angeles International and Comparative Law Journal* 9/3: 751–784.

7

Family Matters: Is There Room for "Culture" in the Courtroom?

*Ayelet Shachar**

The use of culture in the courtroom has been thoroughly explored in the criminal law context (e.g., Volpp 1994; Lawrence 2001; Phillips 2003). But what about the civil side of the justice system? Is there room for an introduction of the "claims of culture" in adversarial disputes between individual litigants who are parties to a *civil* action?[1] If such claims are deemed admissible, a further set of second-order questions emerge: should cultural factors be taken into account by judges on an ad hoc, case-by-case basis? What weight should be given to considerations of culture in relation to other relevant factors? Should the legislature attempt to pre-define a balancing formula? And how precisely should a judge respond to *competing* claims of culture raised by the different parties? Legal scholars and political philosophers have paid surprisingly little attention to these questions.[2] This chapter begins to amend this lacuna by thinking through the normative and jurisprudential dilemmas raised when we permit cultural factors to enter the courtroom, especially in cases that deal

---

* This chapter was originally prepared for presentation at the Criminal Law and Cultural Diversity Workshop, Columbia Law School. I am grateful for the insightful responses that I received from Will Kymlicka, Jeremy Waldron, Claes Lernestedt, Alison Renteln, Kent Greenawalt, Richard Banks, and the students enrolled in my Multiculturalism and the Law seminar at Harvard Law School. Specials thanks are due to Ran Hirschl for his invaluable comments and suggestions. An earlier and shorter version, entitled "Demystifying Culture," appeared in I·CON, *International Journal of Constitutional Law* (2012), 10/2: 429–448. Copyright Oxford University Press. This study was supported generously by a Connaught Research Fellowship in the Social Sciences and benefited significantly from the dedicated research assistance of Kristel Hammer. All errors are mine.

[1] I use the term "the claims of culture" and interchangeably "cultural factors" throughout this chapter as a generic name for identity-based claims, referring to a wide range of potential sources for such claims, including religion, race, ethnicity, indigenous identity, national origin, and so on.

[2] A notable exception to the criminal-only focus is found in the marvelously comprehensive treatment of the cultural defense by Alison Dundes Renteln (Renteln 2004).

with matters of personal loyalty, betrayal, anger, love, and attachments to children or adults—as they play out in the break-up of family relations where the disagreeing parties invite the court to act as a third-party adjudicator in their dispute.[3]

Analytically, I will distinguish between two different functions of the claims of culture in these disputes: (1) they may serve as a legal *sword*: namely, allowing the party that raises them an advantage that is not equally accessible to the other side, a move that may prove crucial from the perspective of an adversarial litigant locked in a family courtroom showdown;[4] *or* (2) the claims of culture may, under different circumstances, serve as a *shield*: ensuring that the involved party is not deprived of an otherwise universal treatment (or entitlement) because he or she belongs to a family or community that follows a non-mainstream practice or belief system. My inclination is to support the latter while restricting the former, especially in those contexts where the general law is designed to provide remedy or protection to the interests of more vulnerable parties.

With this distinction in mind, I will defend the treatment of culture as a *relevant*—but not as a sole or predeterminative—factor in the judicial decision-making process. This position, I will argue, is both theoretically sound and institutionally feasible, as will be demonstrated on the basis of a comprehensive study of family law cases reported in Canada over a period of twenty-five years (1980–2005).[5] These cases offer a particularly germane prism to explore the relevance and weight that is (and ought to be) given to cultural factors. The reason for this is simple yet powerful: family law stands at the juncture of private and public, contract and status, individualized and societal considerations. The disputes I recount here offer a window into understanding not only the dilemmas facing the specific litigants whose cases are adjudicated, but also provide a revealing account of broader societal visions about gender,

---

[3] The vast majority of family law issues are resolved by *agreement* between the parties, often negotiated with the assistance of their lawyers. The very act of turning to the court (as in the cases addressed here) represents the last stage of an already protracted dispute.

[4] In the criminal and constitutional context the "sword" is not pointed against the other party (as in the civil cases that I analyze here), but rather against the state. It could involve, for example, a request for a judge hearing a constitutional case to permit a conduct that is otherwise impermissible in general law, i.e., an exception or exemption. The claims of culture are also made explicit in the context of a cultural defense in criminal law—the focus of many of the chapters in this collection. When a cultural defense is raised in the criminal context, a judge is asked to consider the cultural background of the accused, or his or her non-mainstream interpretation of the act, seeking to establish (*ex post*) an excuse, justification, mitigation or negation for a particular conduct that, prima facie, breached the criminal code.

[5] This study was conducted by using the Quicklaw database collection of electronic decisions of Canadian courts, copyright of Carswell, a Division of Thomson Canada Ltd. It covers the jurisprudence in the common-law jurisdictions of Canada, to the exclusion of the province of Quebec in which family relations are governed directly by the *Civil Code of Quebec*, Book Two (arts. 400–659), S.Q. 1980, c. 39.

power, and the place of culture and religion in the family, as reflected in and constructed through the law. The content of this societal vision may, and often does, change over time.

To provide just one familiar example: in child custody cases, the "tender years doctrine" that dated back to the nineteenth century automatically presumed that the custody of a young child should be granted to the mother (barring truly extraordinary circumstances), whereas today, such a doctrine is interpreted as impermissible because it violates equal protection and the principle of gender neutrality.[6] As a result, the tender years doctrine is no longer with us; it has been formally replaced in most jurisdictions by the best-interests-of-the-child standard. This in turn means that the requirement to consider "*all* the needs and circumstances of the child"[7] is anything but foreign to modern family law, opening up the possibility for inclusion of the "claims of culture" in the legal analysis. When rendering decisions in custody, access, and adoption cases, judges are required to determine a range of loaded questions: which parent should have custody over a child? What restrictions might apply to the access of the non-custodian parent? These determinations are difficult under any conditions, but become even more complicated by the issue of exercising discretion in view of what are defined as the "relevant" factors. In cases where the parties hold differing cultural or deeply held belief systems, these competing perspectives and visions of the good life inevitably invite the question of *which* factors are relevant for precisely such a consideration. This is a question that has no simple answer. As one scholar aptly observes:

> [n]o aspect of family law is easier to summarize and harder to apply than that governing [the placement] of children. The applicable rule is, quite simply, that courts are to do what is in the best interests of the child. There are no other rules as such; and, because every case must be decided on its own merits and has no precedential value, none can be construed. Best interests of the child; beginning and end. (Fodden 1999: 181)

The best interests standard is, by definition, significantly open-ended (in theory) and highly context-specific (in practice).

Given that there is no predetermined formula for abstractly defining the best interest of a given child, we need to know a great deal about the real (and often limited) alternatives on offer by the competing adults who are willing to serve as the child's custodian parents, for example, before it can be determined what is in the child's best interest. Instead of treating this indeterminacy as a severe fault, the context-specific aspect of the best interests of the child standard can be seen as a latent virtue (Alston 1994). It permits treating culture as

---

[6] For a critical account of the socio-historical context in which the tender years doctrine evolved, see Grossberg 1983.
[7] Children's Law Reform Act, R.S.O. 1990, c. C.12, s. 24(1).

a legitimate consideration, where relevant—but crucially as only one among many other considerations—rather than *the* absolute trump card that one of the parties can raise to end a dispute. Such a qualified admission of the claims of culture into the courtroom is *demystifying*: it asks the court to treat the parents' culture(s) or religion(s) in the same manner as any other factor that might shape a child's environment, by weighing and balancing it with other considerations. On this account, "[c]ulture is," to cite a recent court decision, "but one of [many] factors and does not stand in any higher or lower position than the rest."[8]

The culture-demystifying approach that I will defend here must be distinguished from two "absolutist" alternatives: at the one end of the spectrum, we find the *culture-blindness* approach, which permits *no* formal place for culture or religion in the courtroom. At the other end, we find the opposite alternative: treating culture as a determinative factor that *overrides* other context-specific considerations that shape the life circumstances of a particular child or family, or what we might call the culture-override approach. I will speak briefly about each of these two approaches, before turning to discuss the possibility of allowing *some* room for culture to be introduced as a factor in civil disputes between private parties in family matters.[9] By ensuring that identity-based factors are neither excluded nor privileged, the culture-demystifying approach comes closer to fulfilling the goals of fairness and justice to the specific litigants whose interests are at stake—allowing them to elaborate, if they so wish, on the "sources of the self" that make them who they are, whenever these factors bear relevance on the family dispute at issue.[10] By treating culture as a legitimate consideration—with the key provision that it is only one among many other factors—the culture-demystifying approach aims to alleviate the trepidation from the option of allowing cultural or religious factors to be raised in the courtrooms of diverse socities committed to the separation of state from religion.

The discussion proceeds in four parts. Part 1 briefly highlights pertinent distinctions between the criminal and civil litigation processes, explaining why the claims of culture are likely to operate differently in each context. In part 2, I elucidate the culture-blindness and culture-override alternatives before turning to defend the culture-demystifying approach. In part 3, which comprises the majority of the chapter, I analyze how the culture-demystifying approach operates in practice based on a quantitative and qualitative study of the docket of private family law litigation at all levels (trial, appellate, and supreme

---

[8] *Pejo C. (Applicant) and Paulo Cesar C.-G. (Respondent)* [2004] (Ontario Superior Court of Justice, Docket: Kitchener A 15/03), para. 8.

[9] There are certain circumstances under which a legislative text obliges a judge to refrain from considering cultural factors or, conversely, calls for treating them as overriding. I discuss both scenarios below.

[10] I am here borrowing from the title of an influential book by Charles Taylor (Taylor 1992).

court) that involved a "cultural" element within a period of twenty-five years of Canadian jurisprudence (1980–2005). After presenting the quantitative parameters of this study, I will turn to a qualitative discussion of a number of illustrative cases focusing specifically on civil disputes involving adoption, custody, and access. This is followed by a discussion of the place and weight of culture in decisions concerning spousal obligations after the termination of a "marriage" relationship that, at least formally, does not fit the mold of the standard civil legal definition of this institution. My analysis relies on real-life examples drawn from the jurisprudence, providing a prism through which to explore both the potentially negative and positive effects of the "sword" and "shield" uses of culture in the service of adversarial litigants. Part 4 concludes.

CRIMINAL VS. CIVIL "USES" OF CULTURE

Logic requires that we consider the pertinent distinctions between the criminal and civil sides of the justice system before turning to assess the deployment of cultural claims in either setting. Let us begin with the basics: in the criminal context, the legislature predefines the elements of a prohibited act or omission (*actus reus*), as well as the fault element that attach to that offense (*mens rea*). The power to create offenses punishable by fine, penalty, or imprisonment lies with elected officials, not with private individuals. The state, as a public institution, is responsible for enforcing the criminal code: this requires several distinct steps, such as investigating criminal behavior, deciding to prosecute, bringing the accused to trial, not to mention imprisoning (or otherwise punishing) those convicted and sentenced to incarceration. Given this immense power of the state vis-à-vis the individual, the criminal process has many built-in safety valves, including the imposition of constitutional standards, criminal defenses, and the right to counsel.

In criminal law, the burden of proof ("beyond a reasonable doubt") lies on the prosecution. Even if it proves that the accused committed the prohibited act, the accused may still avoid conviction by raising a relevant defense (such as the established defenses of mistake of fact, intoxication, provocation, self-defense, necessity, and duress). These defenses can operate as mitigating factors or as complete defenses; in the latter case, such defenses may lead to the acquittal of the accused. Clearly, defense lawyers—whose job is to represent *their* clients—are keen to bring forward any plausible defense that may assist their clients' case. The interplay between "offenses" and "defenses" creates an opening for the use of claims of culture by defense lawyers. For instance, they might ask the judge or the jury to consider the cultural socialization that may have affected the individual's responsibility (or his or her perception of the law or the social meaning of their action) as a means of generating a "defense that is sensitive to the particular experiences and frailties of the accused" (Roach 2004: 18). The counter concern, of course, is that if each person in a diverse society may have his or her own perception of the law (or will become a "law unto itself") and attribute a differentiated social meaning of their action, then the criminal justice system will lose its authority and credibility in terms of establishing a unitary and disciplinary system of law and order. These tensions are brought to the fore by the debate over the cultural defense in criminal law, as explored by many of the chapters in this volume. Another entry point for defense lawyers to raise the claims of culture relates to the ability of the accused to act according to a standard of "reasonableness": this in turn requires a more contextualized consideration, especially where a mixture of objective and subjective standards is at issue (for instance, in serious crimes such as murder or attempted murder). Finally, the sentencing hearing permits a great range of information to be introduced concerning this *specific* offender, again opening the door for the claims of culture to find their way into the courtroom.[11]

Compare this to the classic (and often idealized) image of the civil litigation system. Here, society offers *individuals* a forum, or mechanism, for the peaceful resolution of their disputes: turning to the court system, or, in recent years, encouraging them to turn to alternative dispute resolution options, such as mediation and arbitration. Unlike the central role played by the state in pursuing criminal prosecution, the civil litigation process relies on *private* litigants. In principle, any person can commence civil litigation, assuming that they have a good cause of action.[12] Although a presiding judge may join claimants or permit the introduction of third-party litigants, parties to a civil action retain great control over shaping the boundaries of their legal dispute; for instance, they may choose the forum, name their defendants, formulate the pleadings, and so on. Another core feature of a civil action in the common-law world is its assumed *adversarialism*: each party is expected to put forward the strongest legal argument to advance its claim, which is by definition adversarial and partisan. This opens the door to raising the claims of culture, if they advance the claims made by the plaintiff (or the defendant), provided that these claims are relevant to the dispute. Such claims are often inserted into the fact-finding aspect of the dispute; however, they may also be of use in determining the scope of rights or remedies of the involved litigants.

The adversarial process thus relies on a conceptual framework that presupposes significant party autonomy and parity: this helps explain why the sole responsibility for bringing the dispute before the court for adjudication lies

---

[11] In Canada, s. 718.2(e) of the Criminal Code of Canada, R.S.C. 1985, c. C-46, specifically instructs judges to consider "all available sanctions other than imprisonment that are reasonable in the circumstances," stating specifically that "particular attention [must be paid] to the circumstances of Aboriginal offenders."

[12] A "cause of action" simply put, refers to a claim or complaint that is recognized in legislation or case law and for which the legal system can offer a remedy.

with the parties (or their lawyers). All things being equal, the expectation is that once engaged in litigation, these parties will pursue their interests fully, i.e., without compromise and without leaving any potential legal argument unexplored. In describing the received wisdom of the adversarial tradition, Abram Chayes has memorably observed that litigation is here understood as a "contest between two individuals or at least two unitary interests, diametrically opposed, to be decided on a winner-takes-all basis" (Chayes 1979: 1281). While this vision is oversimplified, and as its critics rightly observe, tends to ignore actual power differentials between the parties, it remains valuable in explaining why a winner-take-all contest raises the stakes significantly for those involved; it may, inadvertently, increase a strategic use of the claims of culture if the party raising them has reason to assume that "culture" will help sway the judgment in their favor.

The classic Anglo-American-Canadian image of the adversarial system envisions the government as detached from the mechanism of initiating litigation (although it plays a crucial role in ensuring the backdrop conditions that permit the operation of an independent judiciary (Holmes and Sunstein 1999)). This is quite different from the criminal process, where the state not only defines "public wrongs" (as Blackstone memorably put it) but also *enforces* the provisions of the criminal code against those who are suspected of having breached it.

The civil litigation system, for its part, rests on a market-based assumption that private parties who are motivated by self interest will be more diligent than any other entity (such as a state agency or inquisitorial judge) in finding all the relevant evidence favorable to their case and in critically testing the legal arguments or the evidence presented by the other party. At the base of the adversary proceedings, "we encounter the old laissez-faire notion that each party will (or indeed can) bring out all the evidence favorable to his [or her] own side...to 'out-produce' the presentation made by his [or her] competitors" (Neef and Nagel 1974–75: 162). In such a system, it can be predicted that parties will try to put forward *whatever* legal arguments that they believe will best serve their (inevitably partial) case. If a "claim of culture" might prove useful and relevant to advancing a client's argument, a diligent lawyer will likely bring it before the court.

Typically, the parties to a civil action will gain their day in court if they bring forward a dispute that requires concrete judicial resolution based on a recognizable cause of action and a viable request for remedy. In family law, this may translate into a dispute over who will have custody over a child in this particular family, or whether the spouses owe each other any support obligations after the break-up of their marriage, and so on. Unlike a pure model of private ordering, the state (through its various agencies) takes a great interest in defining and regulating the rights and obligations between family members; this is particularly true after the break down of the relationship. While there is significant room for the parties to define certain civil aspects of their relationship through agreement (for instance, in prenuptial contracts), they remain subject to a web of family legislation and public-policy regulation, which at minimum, defines default rules and basic standards that must be fulfilled.[13] Furthermore, certain aspects of family law are non-negotiable between the parties; a state-defined minimum age of marriage is a classic example. But the parties are free to shape their child-rearing practices, including the inculcation of culture and religion in them, so long as their actions do not breach a standard of care. Identity issues that concern the child's unique sense of self and well-being—nothing less—may become contentious if the family breaks up. In practice, most parties manage to resolve these inevitably charged issues through negotiation, mediation, and mutual agreement.[14] Yet, some hard cases will inevitably reach the family courtroom. The parties—now engaged in an *adversarial* process—will likely raise *any* legal claim that they believe will advance their cause (or respectively weaken the other's side case), *including*, if relevant, the claims of culture. What weight, if any, should such claims have in resolving civil disputes in the family law arena?

AGAINST ABSOLUTES

To address this question, we need to set its parameters. Image a continuum: at one end of this spectrum lies the *culture-blindness* approach, which permits 0 percent weight to be given to "culture" in family disputes between competing stakeholders. At the other end, we find the *culture-override* approach: setting culture at a weight of 100 percent, thereby turning an identity-based factor (such as a parent's or a child's cultural heritage, religion, or race) into an absolute, overriding consideration. I discuss these contrasting alternatives in turn.

Culture-Blindness

It is useful to latch first to a familiar anchor point: that of a culture-blind vision of society. On this account, the best way to respond to the real-world diversity of modern societies is to ensure that no weight is given to sub-national or

---

[13] Criminal restrictions against harming or abusing children, which may lead to the termination of parental rights, apply to separated or divorced parents just as they would apply to parents acting together. Such cases are typically brought by state officials (for instance, a child welfare agency), and go beyond the scope of this chapter.

[14] In Canada, it is estimated that approximately 85 percent of family disputes are resolved without an adversarial process; the parties often turn to lawyers, mediators, and arbitrators to set the precise terms of their post-marriage rights and obligations. In cases involving domestic violence, parties are barred from turning to alternative dispute resolution processes in order to shield vulnerable parties from unfair and undue influence by more powerful and violent spouses.

group-based identity markers in our engagements with those others to whom we are joined through shared citizenship, market interaction, or even intimate relations. More specifically, the state (through its laws, agencies, and officials) must treat individuals equally—irrespective of race, gender, creed, religion, national origin, or any other collective identity-based factor.[15] Furthermore, it cannot support or endorse a particular religion or culture, and instead must follow a model of strict neutrality that is often understood as a cornerstone of the modern (or "unitary") concept of citizenship.[16]

Importantly, the culture-blindness model does not ignore the value that people may attach to religion or other sources of group-based identity. Rather, as Brian Barry observes, it is precisely because "of the important role that religion plays in many people's lives... [that the liberal state] must emphasize the importance of *neutralizing* it as a political force" (Barry 2001: 25). In defense of such unitary (as opposed to "differentiated") citizenship, Barry advocates a strategy of privatizing and depoliticizing identity and difference. This commitment, he argues, is crucial if the liberal state is to make good on its promise to offer a neutral and level ground on which people from different backgrounds and cultures can meet and coexist.

The culture-blindness approach conceptually relies upon, and normatively reaffirms, the classic liberal distinction between the public and private realms, or the so-called separate spheres solution: it relegates "difference" to the private sphere, while treating citizens as unencumbered individuals in the public sphere.[17] This immediately raises the problem of classification: What falls within the private realm, and, no less importantly, what type of regulation ought to be exercised over relations in this realm, and by whom? These questions come to the fore when we think about how the law ought to address claims of culture as they arise in the context of the family, which already sits at the intersection of the public and private spheres (Minow and Shanley 1996; Cott 2000; Shachar 2008).[18] A strict application of the ideal of unitary (or *un*differentiated) citizenship demands that no consideration be given to the claims of culture and identity in responding to legal challenges that arise at the societal or the individualized level.[19] Such blindness, so goes the standard argument, acts as

---

[15] The classic unitary conception of citizenship "emphasizes the individual, and the individual's capacity to transcend group or collective identity, to break the shackles of fixed identity (social station, hierarchy, traditional roles, and so forth)" (Beiner 2003: 30). For a critical account of this standard of unitary citizenship, which focuses on formal equality potentially at the cost of substantive equality, see Young 1989.

[16] An alternative and influential vision of *multicultural* citizenship has been advanced in recent years. See, e.g., Kymlicka 1995.

[17] On the critique of the unencumbered self, see Sandel 1982.

[18] The recent debate in Canada over the use of religious arbitration to resolve family disputes represents the increasingly blurred lines between the public and private justice in family law dispute resolution. See Shachar 2008.

[19] For critical discussion, see Lernestedt's chapter in this volume.

a formal guarantee for equality of status by all citizens: it rejects the notion of granting privilege to some, just as strongly as it militates against granting certain exceptions or accommodation for others. Obviously, this has never been the historical record, but the *ideal* of universal citizenship offers a parsimonious principle, which is captured well in the mantra of "one law for all":[20] no one is above the law, no one is subject to a different set of laws, no one is exempt from the law (Waldron 2002). The law must treat all individuals equally, here understood as ultimately demanding that no weight will be given to sub-state or group-based identity or difference.[21]

In the context of family law jurisprudence, culture-blindness lends support to two interrelated principles: (1) formal equality (no religion or conception of the good is "better" than another, or should be given preference);[22] and (2) neutrality (courts should avoid examining the content of a religious belief or act, given that such an inquiry involves a value judgment about the good in addition to potentially infringing on the semi-sacred separation of state from religion). These principles of formal equality and neutrality bear significant practical and public-policy implications (Lacey 2000; Greenawalt 2005). In the acrimonious American debate over transracial adoptions (Bartholet 1991; Perry 1994; Banks 1998; Fogg-Davis 2001), for example, they informed the introduction of federal legislation, stipulating that federal funds would be denied to any public or private adoption agency that used race as a criterion in making permanent placement decisions.[23]

In cases of custody and access disputes between separated or divorced parents, culture-blindness may be interpreted as demanding that the courts refrain from considering factors such as the parent's religion, or his or her plans for educating the child in light of the role that religion plays in that parent's life (Greenawalt 2005: 972), while a judge is permitted, indeed, *asked* to conduct,

---

[20] The unitary model of citizenship has been challenged, however, by many feminist and multicultural scholars as merely focusing on formal equality, rather than examining substantive inequality. It has further been charged as failing to fully recognize the marginalization that members of many historically disenfranchised groups—women, blacks, indigenous peoples, non-white immigrants, ethnic and religious minorities, gays and lesbians, to mention a few prominent examples—still experience on the basis, at least in part, of their "difference." This difference, it must be noted, is itself defined vis-à-vis a standard of an idealized citizen which members of marginalized communities have never had a chance to define. For a lucid and concise discussion of these claims, see Kymlicka 2002: 327–337.

[21] The exception to this blindness approach is found in affirmative action programs, which can be defended on remedial or compensatory grounds (overcoming past discrimination), or on grounds of diversity as a value in itself (expanding our horizons through exposure to diversity). See SCC 2008.

[22] Constitutionally, in the United States such preference may amount to a violation of the separation of state from religion, amounting to a prohibited "establishment" of the latter by the former.

[23] See the Multiethnic Placement Act of 1994 (MEPA) and the Interethnic Placement Act of 1996 (IEPA). The IEPA explicitly exempts proceedings that involve Native American children whose adoption is subject to the provisions of the Indian Child Welfare Act (ICWA).

a detailed (if not outright intrusive) investigation about the *non*-religious parent's life-style and the environment in which the child will be raised by that parent. As Linda Lacey astutely observes, the blindness approach, which dominates American case law of custody and access (in part due to constitutional constraints set by the establishment clause), holds in essence that a family law judge "may consider *any* imaginable factor *except* religion" (Lacey 2000: 417).[24]

Barring such considerations *altogether*—as a category—represents a major drawback of the "blindness" approach, at least according to its critics. This is due, in part, to the prevalent (though as we shall see, often unfounded) worry that *any* evaluation relating to the parent's or the child's "identity" or "culture" will become an overriding consideration. Add to this the constitutional and institutional concern that any discussion of religion or culture will somehow implicate the judge in a value judgment on the tenets of the faith.[25] This leads to an asymmetrical situation whereby decisions concerning children might hinge on factors such as which parent will send the child to an academically superior school, or whether the child will be exposed to activities that are perceived as advancing his or her emotional and intellectual development; but the judge must absolutely *refrain* from even considering the effects of a parent's religious belief or practice on a child, despite the almost commonsensical recognition that such factors are at least equally as important as any other consideration in determining the specific family arrangements that will best serve the child's interests.

Culture-Override

At the other end of the spectrum is another extreme: the culture-override. Here, the child's or the parents' religious affiliation, national origin, or other identity-based factors are elevated to a paramount, if not absolute, consideration. In its most unrelenting interpretation, this approach subjects individuals to different legal regimes according to their "personal status" (Shachar 2001: 63–87). While we usually associate this type of a regime with antiquated medieval times, or the *millet* system under the Ottoman Empire, it may come as something of a surprise to learn that many civil law countries in continental Europe still use private international law principles to distinguish between the citizen and the immigrant in determining *which* system of family law codes will shape their intimate relations. As Marie-Claire Foblets and Adriaan

---

[24] Obviously any generalization about family law in the United States must be taken with a grain of salt: it is an area governed primarily by state legislation and regulation.

[25] Increasingly, however, courts asked to make decisions in transnational custody disputes as well as domestic cases encounter "unfamiliar ethnic, religious, and legal traditions...and have struggled to understand and accommodate the tremendous cultural and religious diversity of America today within a legal framework established long ago." See Laquer-Estin 2004: 501.

Overbeeke explain, courts and other public officials have favored "the preservation of cultural distinctiveness of immigrants" by following the perception that nationality remains a valuable personal status, and therefore, civil disputes involving family relations (and related matters) ought to be governed by the family codes of the immigrants' country of *origin* rather than their permanent country of residence (Foblets and Overbeeke 2004: 25). Thus, civil courts in Belgium have until recently found themselves compelled to recognize, through private international law, the application of the *lex patriae* (the foreign law governing family relations in the immigrant's country of origin), subject to the public-policy exception, even if the members of that specific family have already settled *permanently* in Belgium. Similar provisions, with some variations, are found in other European civil law countries, such as Germany and the Netherlands.[26]

In subjecting the immigrant to the family law code of her country of origin, her civil status and discursive positioning as a "foreigner" is highlighted and reified. Add to this the fact that a significant percentage of immigrants to Europe in the post-World War II period have arrived from Muslim countries, many of which incorporate *religious* (personal status codes) provisions into their national family law legislation, and it is not surprising that the charged question of *which* family law should apply becomes intertwined with larger debates over citizenship, religious-collective assertions of identity, and gender equality—especially in the current era of tightening family-based immigration regulation in Europe (Shachar 2005; Joppke 2008; Orgad 2010).

Increasingly, litigants, lawyers, academics, and courts are rebelling against this type of culture (or national-origin) override. Instead, parties themselves are given a greater degree of freedom in determining their choice of law: whether to follow the law of the new home country or that of the country of origin. Another way to break the dominance of the culture-override in such situations is to resolve these conflicts-of-law dilemmas by following the "real and substantive connection" criterion, for instance, as established by proof of habitual residence, rather than pure reliance on national origin (Shachar 2011). These developments permit litigants with multiple membership affiliations to participate in the decision as to *which* country's jurisprudence will govern their marital relations and the consequences of their break down (Foblets and Overbeeke 2004: 29–31).

While it is almost tempting to write off the culture-override as an implausible alternative, given that it locks the individual into a semi-essentialized identity, we should avoid making overly hasty judgments. In certain circumstances, it has been applied as a *remedial* policy, designed to protect the survival of certain

---

[26] In the Netherlands, see Article 1(2) and 1(1b) of the Wet Conflictenrecht Echtscheding, Staatsblad, 1981, which now permits the displacement of nationality as the primary (and default) connecting factor if established that a party no longer bears a "true social connection" to the country of origin.

minority communities. A striking example of this pattern at work is found in the United States, in reference to placement decisions concerning Native American children. These decisions are subject to exclusive *tribal* jurisdiction and follow an explicit (pro-tribal) preference approach. The culture-override entrenched in the governing federal legislation, the Indian Child Welfare Act (ICWA), is so strong that it trumps not only the interests of non-members, but also the explicit wishes of member-parents. The effects of this policy preference can be harsh, as demonstrated by the landmark case of *Mississippi Band of Choctaw Indians* v. *Holyfield*,[27] where the U.S. Supreme Court held that the tribe had the upper hand over the expressed wishes of a tribal member (here a Native American mother) who had intentionally given birth outside the territorial jurisdiction of her tribe's reservation and then immediately placed her newborn twin babies with non-native adoptive caregivers.[28]

This remedial policy runs into the familiar tension between measures of collective justice (here intended to protect the survival interest of the community as a whole) and the imposition of heavy costs to the liberty interests of individual parents and children. It also raises the specter of treating children as the "possession" of a tribe or nation, rather than allowing them, or their parents, a degree of freedom to define their own identity, including the option of *not* preserving the communal affiliation. While I do not intend to resolve these tensions here (I have addressed this topic elsewhere), what is most significant here is recognizing that the problem does not lie with the consideration of identity-based criteria per se, which gain added meaning in light of historical injustice claims.[29] Rather, it lies with the *weight* given to this factor: if only members of the same community can adopt a child, for example,

---

[27] *Mississippi Band of Choctaw Indians* v. *Holyfield*, 490 US 30 (1989) (U.S. Supreme Court).

[28] In subsequent years, the U.S. Supreme Court has narrowed the reading of *Holyfield*, but it has never reversed the decision. For an overview of proposed amendments to the ICWA, see Yablon 2004. In cases involving the adoption of an Indian child, the ICWA requires that "[a] preference shall be given, in the absence of good cause to the contrary, to a placement with (1) a member of the child's extended family; (2) other members of the Indian child's tribe; or (3) other Indian families." In *Adoptive Parents* v. *Baby Girl*, 389 S.C. 625 (2013) (U.S. Supreme Court), the Court ruled that the provisions of the ICWA apply to situations of involuntary termination or removal of a child, which typically requires the intervention of a state or child service agency, but will not apply to situations where an Indian parent (the father, in this legal dispute) has never had custody of the Indian child at the time when the adoption proceedings were voluntarily and lawfully initiated by the non-Indian parent (the mother, in this case) with sole custodian rights. In Canada, in adoption cases involving placement decisions concerning aboriginal children in need of protection, the courts are instructed by legislation to take into account "the uniqueness of Indian and native culture, heritage and traditions," and the child's best interests assessment must recognize the goal of "preserving the child's cultural identity." See, e.g., *Algonquins of Pikakanagan First Nation* v. *Children Aid Society of Toronto* [2004], Ontario Superior Court of Justice, Docket: 04-FA-12584. Note that these cases are not private as between individuals; they typically involve a government child welfare agency and the tribal band as the main parties to the litigation.

[29] For illuminating explorations of the tensions "between framing adoption policy to reflect the child's status as a freestanding individual or as a person to whom these biological and social

then the culture-override becomes *absolute*. The problem, in other words, is that no matter how fitting the prospective parent is, and no matter how urgent the need to find a secure and loving home for the child is, no person whose religion or ethnicity is different from that of the child can adopt him or her by virtue of *that* consideration alone.

Culture-Demystified

The culture-demystifying approach avoids the twin pitfalls of absolute *rejection* or total *endorsement* of identity-based claims, as respectively encoded in the culture-blindness or culture-override alternatives. Instead, it seeks to break up this dichotomy and change the terms of the debate: this approach permits the admission of culture or religion into the equation as a *relevant* consideration, but avoids granting it an overriding weight. It rests on the idea that ascent to citizenship, especially for those who have long been excluded from such full membership, does *not* require or presuppose the denial of sub-national and group-based culture or identity. This line of argument, which emphasizes substantive over formal equality, permitting individualized judgments about exemption or accommodation is familiar (though not always successful) in the rich jurisprudence dealing with questions of constitutional law, conscientious objection, employment, education, and the list goes on. It has recently received attention in the criminal law context as well. But our focus here is on situations where "culture" might be raised by individual parties in the context of a dispute over certain legal aspects of sharing, or dividing, responsibility over their children (as between separated or divorced parties). As we saw earlier, unlike constitutional or criminal cases, where a public entity is central to the legal process, the typical *civil* action in family law is between private parties, such as parents struggling over child custody. Here, the litigants are not raising a legal claim against the state (or its agencies).[30] Instead, they turn to the courthouse to find a peaceful and binding resolution to *their* dispute (Scott 1975). Once these "private" claims enter the justice system, however, the public as lawmaker is inevitably, if indirectly, present, setting the background rules and conditions that deeply shape the scope of freedom and obligation we shoulder in our various roles as family members and citizens.

In such a context, is it permissible and just to bring forward arguments from culture or religion to bear on the legal dispute, especially when the parties are already engaged in a family law battle? Courts and legislatures have long

---

relationships [as well as cultural and identity ties] are of continuing significance," see Shanley 2003; Sanger 2003. On historical injustice claims, see Spinner-Halev 2012.

[30] State agencies will become involved, however, if there are concerns about abuse or harm and they may lead to termination of parental rights proceedings.

maintained a great (public) interest in defining and regulating the behavior of married couples as they enter or exit a marriage, civil union, or domestic partnership relationship, even though such relationships are simultaneously understood (unless there is evidence to prove differently) as the product of volitional, individual choice. In the same vein, parents are given great latitude in defining the environment in which a child will be raised, including core decisions respecting a child's place of residence, education, religious affiliation, medical treatment, and a great many other decisions, so long as they do not violate a state-defined standard of care. If a parent or guardian fails to comply with such a standard of care, however, a host of state officials (including but not limited to child welfare or social workers, police investigators, judges and enforcement agents) are given a mandate, indeed, are entrusted with a *duty* to intervene in the family's affairs. The regulation of domestic relations thus sits at a delicate juncture between the intact family and the intervening state (Olsen 1983; Cohen 2002). While fully acknowledging this bleeding of private/public categories and the potential for state intervention in the family, my analysis focuses more narrowly on claims of culture as they operate in civil disputes between individuals, where the state and its agencies do not function as intervening parties. In these cases, the justice system permits alienated spouses or separated and divorced parents (or other relevant custodians and guardians) to litigate their most intimate disagreements, fitting them into the mold of an adversarial dispute.

So, we are back to our initial question: can, and should, culture be treated as *a* consideration, one among many, in resolving such disputes? Contrary to the culture-blindness and culture-override approaches, an empirical analysis of the pertinent jurisprudence reveals that courts are well equipped to treat culture as a *relevant* consideration, yet without falling into the trap of making it the *sole* consideration that guides their decision. Importantly, identity-based considerations can be raised by the parent, guardian, or even the child herself, if she is deemed mature enough.[31] Given that these family law decisions are highly individualized, they invite a comprehensive exploration of the life circumstances of the involved parties, of which religion or tradition may play a role. This contextual analysis rejects the predefined and binary options of granting either 0 percent or 100 percent weight to the claims of culture. Rather than a blanket prohibition (culture-blindness) or a full endorsement (culture-override), the courts, at least in Canada, have mostly provided ad hoc, case-by-case answers, without forcing them into a binding matrix or balancing formula. This last observation is not just impressionist. It results from a comprehensive review of the reported case law in Canada in regards to family law

---

[31] If the child is too young to express her own view, an independent legal representative may be appointed to represent her interests.

disputes over in-family adoption, custody, and access over the last twenty-five years (1980–2005).

CULTURE AS "BUT ONE FACTOR": LESSONS FROM THE CASE LAW

It is useful to begin this section with a statistical overview. The claims of culture have been raised in approximately 1 percent of electronically reported adoption cases, and were considered to be relevant in twenty-two cases out of a total of 2048 cases in the period under study. The percentage of custody and access decisions in which culture and/or religion was raised as a legal claim by one of the litigants was higher, representing approximately 2.5 percent of the total number of cases.

Within the quantitative and qualitative parameters of this study, the claims of culture were raised in a relatively small number of cases. This is an unexpected result. The "best interests of the child" test is among the most open-ended legal standards in the family law arena. In theory, if there was a place to raise the claims of culture, it would have been here. In most instances where the parties' or children's "identity" was raised as an issue in contention, the courts have considered the cultural/religious claims on the *merits* (rather than dismissing them categorically as inadmissible), but they balanced these claims against other relevant considerations. This balancing act has meant that in the vast majority of cases the claim of culture by itself has little success in shaping the result of a given dispute. It becomes a determinative factor only when the court assesses that *both* parents can *equally* provide for the best interests of the child. Judging from the case law in these family disputes, it appears that the claim of culture often becomes a last-ditch effort by the "losing" parent who wishes to overcome his or her diminished probability of winning the legal dispute. I will refer to this use of culture as a "sword" in an adversarial battle.

This study reveals yet another significant finding: the *absence* of a legal accusation (on trial or appeal) that by looking at culture or religion, the court has breached its commitment to equal treatment. In this respect, the inclusion of culture as *a* consideration, rather than *the* consideration has had a *demystifying* effect: judges refer to it as a factor that is no more and no less relevant than considerations such as the child's physical, mental, and emotional needs, her level of development, her views and wishes, the positive relationship that she has with the parent, or the security and stability of her place as a member of the family. Just like these other context-specific factors, the court considers the significance of the child's cultural background/heritage or the religion in which she is raised, as part of an overall assessment. This fits within the broader framework of interpreting the child's best interests imperative as demanding a highly individualized, almost microscopic scrutiny of the lives of the separated or divorced parents (and their children) before a decision can be reached by the court. This method of decision-making can be seen as overly intrusive, violating any conceivable protection of the parties' privacy and intimacy. Conversely, it might be defended as the only way to treat each child with respect and dignity, assessing her best interests by taking a holistic look at the universe of her life, revealing its complexity in the process. Whatever stance one takes on this normative debate, it suffices to say here that as a matter of legal practice, judges are indeed asked to cast the widest net possible in assessing the best interests of a child in the case before them.

In tracing the development of the use of culture in these family law disputes, it soon becomes clear that in Canada not all provincial and federal legislative frameworks have expressly directed the courts to consider culture and religion in their best interest of the child analysis. However, courts have recognized a common-law imperative to include these factors in the analysis. This was affirmed by the Supreme Court of Canada in 1999 in its landmark *Van de Perre* v. *Edwards* decision,[32] which I discuss below. Even prior to this precedent-setting decision, the factors or lists enumerated by the legislature (in various family law acts that govern child custody and access matters) were interpreted by judges as non-exhaustive. That is, these lists were understood as open (rather than closed and conclusive), meaning that all the relevant factors raised by the parties in relation to the assessment of the best interests of *this* child had to be considered.

A final note is required before we turn to an analysis of the case law: the vast majority of family decisions that engage the claims of culture are resolved at the trial level, and so they do not bear a precedential value. Very few custody, access, or adoption cases have reached the appellate court level, let alone the Supreme Court of Canada for determination of a principled question of law. On those rare occasions, the highest court of the land has *rejected* the culture-blindness approach *as well as* the culture-override approach, preferring a child-centered approach that treats culture and religion as valid factors to be weighted and balanced with other relevant factors. In so doing, the Supreme Court has effectively delegated the responsibility and discretion back to trial judges to find the right balance of factors, including culture/religion, in each particular case before them. This is not always an easy task. Consider the following examples, drawn from the docket of private family law litigation in Canada.

Culture as Sword

In the 2004 *Pejo* case, the Ontario Court of Justice heard an application by a custodian mother and her new spouse for dispensing with the biological

---

[32] *Van de Perre* v. *Edwards* [2001] S.C.R. 1014 (Supreme Court of Canada).

father's consent to a step-parent adoption. The case revealed the sad story of a history of violence by the biological father against the mother of Mia Isabella C.-B., the little girl whose best interests were at the heart of the legal drama that unfolded. Mia's mother and father married in 1998; the girl was born in 2000. The parents separated soon thereafter, when Mia was only four months old. The separation was precipitated by verbal and physical abuse of the mother by the father. Following the separation, the father was charged with assault, as well as making verbal threats. The charges were dropped in exchange for him agreeing to enter a peace bond for one year: this held that the father was not to have any contact with the mother, except through counsel for the purposes of arranging access to the child. The father strictly fulfilled the terms of the peace bond: he made no contact at all whatsoever with the mother, and this included seeking to arrange access. On consent, the mother was awarded sole custody of the child in 2000; the father was ordered to pay support to the sum of $96 per month. He did not pay the support, nor did he attempt to make arrangements for establishing access to the child. The parties divorced officially in late 2000, and less than a year later the mother married a new spouse, with whom she applied in 2003 for the adoption of Mia Isabella.

The governing legislation, the Child and Family Services Act,[33] holds that no adoption order can be made unless the consent of every parent is given in writing.[34] The biological father, who had not been involved in any way in his daughter's life, nevertheless refused to grant his consent for the family adoption. Mia's mother and stepfather then petitioned the court, requesting that the consent of the biological father be dispensed with in order to permit the adoption to proceed. The Act permits such an option if and only if the court is satisfied that dispensing the recalcitrant parent's consent is (a) in the child's best interests and (b) that the person whose consent is required has received proper notice of the proposed adoption.[35] In this case, there was no dispute that the condition of proper notification to the biological father was fulfilled. The decision thus hinged on the assessment of the child's best interest. The onus of proof lies on the applicant (here the mother and her new spouse), and it sets a significant burden: courts are generally *reluctant* to dispense with the consent of a birth parent.[36]

---

[33] Child and Family Services Act, R.S.O. 1990, c. C.11.
[34] Child and Family Services Act, s. 137(2).
[35] Child and Family Services Act, s. 138.
[36] This is also the approach of civil law jurisdictions. In Germany, for example, step-parent adoptions, which are always subject to the child's best interests standard, are rarely permitted so long as the non-custodian biological parent is alive. The exception to this rule of thumb is that step-parent adoption may be interpreted as serving the child's best interests in cases in which a "personal relationship with the other parent has never existed, or no longer [exists]" (Dethloff 2005).

The Child and Family Services Act, which governed this dispute, specified nine factors that a judge must consider in conducting the child's best interest assessment: eight of these clearly pointed to the fact that Mia was a happy little girl, whose interests were better served by the mother and stepfather, and not the defendant, her biological father. But Paulo Cesar C.-G., the father, did have one important factor working to his advantage. The Act explicitly asked the judge to consider the "child's cultural background" in assessing his or her best interests. However, the Act did not determine how much weight ought to be given to this factor in relation to others. This gave the father "his strongest case."[37] The mother and her new spouse were of Croatian background. The father was of Mexican descent. He argued that if the adoption were allowed, his daughter would not be exposed to her Mexican heritage and culture. He further argued that only through *his* future involvement with the child would she be properly exposed to Mexican culture.

How should the court address this claim of culture in the midst of a civil dispute in the family law arena? Does it matter that the claim is raised by a biological father whose past actions demonstrate a total lack of interest in his daughter, or, for that matter, in inculcating her with the claimed Mexican cultural heritage? In addressing the cultural claim, the trial judge in *Pejo* relied on the precedent set by the Supreme Court of Canada in the 1999 *Van de Perre v. Edwards* case. A brief detour is required here to explain the ruling in that case and its bearing on Mia's future.

Van de Perre was a high profile case: it involved a custody and access dispute between Kimberly Van de Perre, a single Caucasian Canadian woman of twenty-four years of age at the time of the trial, and Theodore Edwards, an African-American professional basketball player who normally resided in the US with his wife, Valerie Cooper Edwards, the mother of his twin daughters. Kimberly and Theodore met in 1996, when he was a member of Vancouver Grizzlies NBA team. They commenced a relationship that lasted approximately eighteen months. Of that relationship, Elijah Theodore Van de Perre was born in Vancouver in 1997; at this time, Theodore (his father), was spending the off-season period in the United States with his wife and twin daughters. Theodore then returned to Vancouver for the new basketball season, and continued his relationship with Kimberly. Upon learning this news, his wife, Valerie, a stay-at-home mother, decided to move with the twin daughters to British Columbia. At this point, the relationship between Kimberly and Theodore went sour, and Kimberly commenced proceedings against him for custody of their son Elijah, as well as for child support. Theodore responded by seeking sole custody over Elijah. The trial was rather lengthy, lasting twenty-six days. In testimony, the parenting abilities of each of Elijah's birth parents were

---

[37] *Pejo C. (Applicant) and Paulo Cesar C.-G. (Respondent)*, para. 15.

assessed, revealing the unflattering attributes of both: the trial judge heard evidence that Kimberly was "doing her best to minimize the extent of the conflicts between the demands of her social life and the demands of her parental responsibility." Theodore's ability to parent Elijah alone did not impress the court either: he was involved in a weak and unstable marriage, had had several extramarital affairs, and left all the day-to-day childcare activities (with regard to his twin daughters) to his wife, Valerie.

After hearing the evidence, the trial judge awarded sole custody to Kimberly and granted generous access to Theodore. The father appealed the trial decision. On appeal, the decision was reversed. In an unusual step, the Court of Appeal invited Theodore's wife, Valerie, to apply for admission as a party to the dispute. She did so and requested joint custody with Theodore over Elijah. The Court of Appeal assessed that she (Valerie) was a good mother, and therefore granted custody over Elijah to Theodore and Valerie, leaving Kimberly with unspecified access rights. The dispute then reached the Supreme Court of Canada. The main question raised by the parties was whether the trial judge or appeal court erred in the consideration, or lack thereof, of the child's biracial heritage. It was undisputed that the governing Act instructed the court to grant "paramount consideration" to the best interests of the child in making the custody decision. The issue in dispute, then, was *how much* weight ought to be given to racial and cultural factors in determining the best interests of the child.

The Supreme Court was well aware of the sensitivity of the case: it granted intervener status in the proceeding to the African Canadian Legal Clinic, the Association of Black Social Workers, and the Jamaican Canadian Association. The interveners submitted "that race is a *critical* issue in custody and access cases," arguing further that race *must* be addressed by the court, even if the parties themselves did not submit it as a factor for the court's consideration. This was a significant issue in this particular case, where counsels for *both* parties downplayed the significance of race and heritage in determining whether the white mother or black father would get custody over their biracial baby son. As one of the lawyers stated: "neither of the parties wanted to touch it, because it's so politically incorrect to say that race has any bearing."[38] The pertinent legislation in British Columbia (the Family Relations Act) did not provide a conclusive answer: its "child's best interest test" was silent on matters of racial, ethnic, or religious identity. These factors did not appear as enumerated considerations, although their inclusion was permitted as part of an assessment of the child's "health and emotional well-being."[39] Taking these considerations into account, the Court of Appeal held that "if it is correct that Elijah will be seen by the world at large as 'being black', it would obviously be in his

---

[38] *Van de Perre v. Edwards*, para. 43.   [39] *Van de Perre v. Edwards*, paras. 9, 41–43.

interests to live with a parent or family who can nurture his identity." That family, it held, is to be found in the home of Valerie and Theodore Edwards in North Carolina, rather than with Kimberly Van de Perre in British Columbia.

The *Van de Perre* decision by the Supreme Court reversed the Court of Appeal ruling and reinstated the original decision by the trial judge. As often happens when judges are faced with "uneasy" topics such as this one, the *Van de Perre* decision is written as a primarily procedural, almost technical, decision. Of its fifty-two paragraphs, only eight directly engage with "the importance of race in the custody determination of a child of mixed racial heritage," as the court's subheading puts it. The rest of the decision focuses on the appropriate standard of review that an appellate court ought to exercise over a trial court. In these eight paragraphs, the Court rejects the idea that race is, by definition, always a crucial factor. Instead, it holds that "the importance of this factor will depend greatly on many factual considerations."[40] It further stated that the question of which parents will best be able to contribute to a healthy racial socialization and overall healthy development of the child is but one of several factors to be determined by the courts "on a case-by-case basis and weighed by the trial judge with other relevant factors."[41]

At the end, then, the Court decided to bite the bullet, but in a typically Canadian fashion, it distributed the "chips" in such a way as to ensure that each side received a small share of its ultimate claim. This was achieved by rejecting the "culture-blind" alternative: the Court unambiguously guided the lower courts that "race *can be a factor* in determining the best interest of the child because it is connected to the culture, identity and emotional well-being of the child."[42] However, it refrained from endorsing the "override" alternative, stating instead that "racial identity *is but one factor* that may be considered in determining personal identity; the relevance of this factor depends of the context." Specifically, the Court instructs that "[a]ll factors must be considered pragmatically. Different situations and different philosophies require an individual analysis on the basis of reliable evidence."[43] This is a casebook manifestation of the culture-demystifying approach in action: identity matters, but it is "but one factor" in shaping the result of a legal dispute in which these factors are treated as relevant for the disposition of the case at bar.

Returning to the 2004 *Pejo* case, recall that the father's strongest case was his cultural claim. Paulo Cesar argued that only he could properly introduce the girl to her Mexican heritage and identity. Following the precedent set by the Supreme Court, the trial judge in *Pejo* addressed the father's cultural claim on its merits but without allowing it to override the decision, stating that "the court ought not to exaggerate the importance of race and culture in a

---

[40] *Van de Perre v. Edwards*, para. 37.
[41] *Van de Perre v. Edwards*, para. 42.
[42] *Van de Perre v. Edwards*, para. 40.
[43] *Van de Perre v. Edwards*, para. 38.

particular case."[44] The evidence brought by the parties revealed that the father and his family "have never attempted to provide Mia Isabella C.-B. with exposure to her Mexican culture in the past." Although the father's motivation may have been sincere in arguing that he wanted his daughter to develop an appreciation of her Mexican heritage, the trial judge ruled that "although culture was important, it should not be given paramountcy over other factors." In this case, allowing culture to override the child's best interest determination would have been its ultimate *ab*use as a "sword" by the biological father, who literally had no relationship with the little girl and had never bothered to establish one.

True, lawyers in an adversarial process will always continue to use whatever arguments they can find in the arsenal of admissible legal claims in order to strengthen the case of their clients; here, culture served as just such a "strong claim." But that should not cloud our judgment: if culture mattered in shaping this little girl's spectrum of choice and agency, so did other core factors. For Mia Isabella, those factors were found in the continuing, reliable care that she received from her mother and stepfather; they—not her biological father—established for her a secure, loving, and welcoming home—after, it should be recalled, a very rocky start.

The *Pejo* case illustrates how *individualized* the claims of culture turn out to be in practice in the adversarial family law dispute. Significantly, the father's identity-based argument did not present the civil court with a challenge that is fully analogous to the "cultural defense" in criminal law. That is, at no stage did the biological father argue that his history of violence or failure to provide support was itself, in some way, explained or informed by his cultural heritage. Even if such a claim had been raised, this would probably have been a moot line of argument. As the trial judge in *Pejo* observed, almost in anticipation of such a potential claim in "defense" of the biological father's action: "[i]t may be trite to say it, but the test is best interests of the child, not the interests or rights of the parents or the applicant [the biological father]."[45]

---

[44] *Pejo C. (Applicant) and Paulo Cesar C.-G. (Respondent)*, para. 16.

[45] *Pejo C. (Applicant) and Paulo Cesar C.-G. (Respondent)*, para. 11. In *Pejo*, the sword was used to boost the litigant's claim (his refusal to endorse the step-parent adoption) and designed to grant Mia Isabella's father "credit" in the best interests of the child assessment. Alternatively, it could be used as a sword to *dis*credit the other parent's claim for custody if he or she adhered to religious practices that diverge from those endorsed by the wider society. An example from the American experience is instructive here. Consider the case of Jennifer Sanderson and Robert Tyron (*Sanderson v. Tryon*, 739 P.2d 623 (Utah 1987), a Utah couple that engaged in a polygamous relationship for seven years. Of that relationship, three children were born. When the parents separated, the children remained with the mother. Jennifer then filed an application seeking custody of the children and increased child support from Robert. The father counterclaimed, arguing that he should be awarded custody on the ground that his former wife (the children's mother) continued the practice of plural marriage as a member of a church sect that endorsed such relationships, whereas he abandoned polygamy after they separated. There were no findings to support the conclusion that the father's custody would best serve the children's interest *except* for the mother's practice of polygamy; however, that fact alone was treated as dispositive by the

As if these cases are not complex and contentious enough, what is a judge to do when *both* parents belong to the same minority community and can raise the claim of culture? Under these circumstances, should the court give greater weight to the claims of a party that argues that his or her ways of life are more "authentic" to the tradition? Add a same-sex relationship to the mix, and this will land us squarely in the convoluted tale of the legal dispute between J.S.B. (the father) and D.L.S. (the mother), whose full names are concealed for the protection of identities.[46] J.S.B. and D.L.S. had lived together since 1990. They married in 1996 and separated in 2003. Four children were born of this relationship. Following the separation in 2003, a court ordered joint custody, but in practice, the mother, who had been the primary caregiver since the children's birth, continued to play this role after the break-up of the marriage. Both parents are Mohawk; their children were brought up in the Longhouse ways. The legal dispute revolved around disagreements that erupted after the initial joint-custody decision. The father argued that it would be in the children's best interests to reside primarily with him. He therefore petitioned the court to grant him sole custody. The mother countered by seeking sole custody herself.

The main argument that the father put forward in support of his claim was that "he has the stronger ties to the Longhouse ways. He is strongly committed to passing on his culture to his children." The mother was also a Mohawk who cared greatly about her cultural and native identity, passing it on to the children through traditional stories, songs, and by speaking to them in Mohawk. She also regularly attended the Longhouse with the children. Unlike the father,

---

trial judge. As a result, the mother lost custody of the children. On appeal, the Supreme Court of Utah reversed the decision, holding that a parent's practice of polygamy, by itself, is insufficient to make a conclusive determination about a children's best interest. Instead, the judges held that "a determination of the children's best interests turns on numerous factors, each of which may vary in importance according to the facts in the particular cases... [The mother's] polygamous practice should only be considered as one among many other factors regarding the children's best interests" (*Sanderson v. Tryon*, 626–627). The father's attempt to discredit the mother due to a non-mainstream religious practice—a practice that, it must be noted, remains criminally prohibited—failed to persuade in the private civil action between the parties; this result occurred not by endorsing or ignoring the controversial polygamy factor, but rather by taking the culture-demystifying step of considering it as part of the overall assessment of the best interests of the children. In the same vein, a Texan appellate court ruled in 2008 that a termination of parental rights and removal of children from their families cannot merely rely on the fact that the parents engaged in polygamous relationships sanctioned by the tenets of their religious beliefs; instead, supporting evidence of immediate danger to the children needs to be established. This case, unlike the "private" family disputes I review in this chapter, engages the state directly as a side to the proceedings. It thus raises core constitutional issues of religious freedom as well as important questions about the adequacy of Texas' standard of demanding proof of *immediate* danger of sexual or physical abuse as a basis for intervention, rather than following a more protective standard to children as vulnerable parties.

[46] *J.S.B. v. D.L.S.* [2004] O.J. No. 16, Court File No. 03-66 (Ontario Superior Court of Justice, Docket: Cornwall).

however, she no longer lived on the reserve. Even more crucially, she was not as "traditional" as the father in her "Mohawk" life-style. The father thus emphasized his relative advantage in his court submission, arguing that "he has stronger ties to the Longhouse ways and is better able to maintain and foster the children's identity as Mohawks."[47] Specifically, the father disapproved of the same-sex relationship that the mother had entered into (with a non-native woman) after the marriage break-up. In their adversarial dispute, the father raised before the court the possibility that the mother might be ousted from the Longhouse because of her same-sex relationship—just as a woman might face ousting if she had an extramarital relationship with a non-native man. This, however, was just a possibility: in the event, no such ousting had taken place, and if it were to occur, it would not have affected the status of the children as full members of the Mohawk nation.

The extensive evidence collected in this case included many testimonials from family members and tribal elders. Crucial among these testimonies was the one given by the children's paternal grandmother—a respected Clan mother—who described D.L.S. as a "beautiful mother." The father, on the other hand, had a serious alcohol problem and the potential for violence. Although he was deeply devoted to his children, he had never served as their primary caregiver. The bulk of the evidence in assessing the children's best interests pointed towards granting sole custody to the mother with access rights to the father. But the sticking point remained her same-sex relationship. The paternal grandmother summarized the issue well: the disagreement was, as she put it, "with D.L.S. living with that lady [against the tradition]. It is the only reason I want J.S.B. [the father] to have the children."[48]

What is a judge to do? A culture-blind approach would have guided the court to pay little, if any, attention to the father's claim that he had a more traditional life-style as a native parent or the fact that he provided spiritual leadership for his children. The mother, as established by the evidence, was the person on whom the children relied for comfort, security, stability, and guidance. Thus she would have had the upper hand in establishing that the children's interests were best served by permitting her to continue to serve as their primary caregiver, legally validating this position by granting her sole custody. (Joint custody was no longer a viable alternative in this case.) The culture-override, on the other hand, would have led to the opposite conclusion: the father's cultural claim would have won over the mother's established parental skills and continued care for the children. He would have received sole custody.

The culture-demystifying approach, for its part, provides no ready-made answer. Instead, it helps identify the main questions to be asked in this

---

[47] *J.S.B.* v. *D.L.S.*, para. 131.   [48] *J.S.B.* v. *D.L.S.*, para. 135.

case: how determinative ought culture, race, or religion be in deciding the best interests of *these* specific children? Can the court ensure that they do not become pawns in their parents' cultural/sexual wars? And what precisely is the adequate balance here between equality and diversity? As we saw earlier in *Van de Perre*, the Supreme Court refused to allow collective identity-based factors such as race to gain a predeterminative status, offering instead assurances to the trial judge that "custody and access decisions are inherently exercises in discretion. Case-by-case consideration of the unique circumstances of each child is the hallmark of the process." The discretion vested in the trial judge, continues the Supreme Court, "enables a balanced evaluation of the best interests of the child and permits courts to respond to the spectrum of factors which can both positively and negatively affect a child."

This open-endedness is significant in allowing an individualized decision-making process that is sensitive to the facts and legal arguments raised by both parties. At the same time, it places a heavy burden on the trial judge. In custody decisions like this one, there is no option, as Kent Greenawalt rightly notes, "of 'staying out'; a court must decide in favor of one parent or the other" (Greenawalt 2005: 970). After considering all the evidence presented in this case, the judge ruled that the father's cultural claim could *not* gain determinative status because the mother too was a Mohawk. This is correct, but it misses the crux of the argument: in accordance with the traditional norms of the specific community to which both parents belonged, the father clearly held a stronger cultural claim. His objection to the same-sex relationship was genuine and, at least according to evidence presented before the court, squarely grounded in the tribal tradition. On the relevance of the mother's same-sex relationship, the court ruled that it, too, is "merely one of the factors, which a court should consider in determining the best interests of children."[49] As such, the mother's sexual orientation could not block a decision in her favor as the sole custodian, especially in light of the equality issues involved.[50] And so it was held. The problem with this decision is not so much the bottom-line conclusion, which is quite sensible. It lies in the reasoning process: by focusing on the details, the court managed to dilute the larger picture. It simply avoided the lurking challenge of addressing head-on the potentially competing claims of culture and equality.

Culture as Shield

In this final section, I wish to focus on the use of the claims of culture as a "shield" in court-centered resolution of family disputes. This latter manifestation

---

[49] *J.S.B.* v. *D.L.S.*, para. 136.
[50] Any other ruling could have led to a constitutional challenge, which was not an issue raised in the trial proceedings.

proves crucial for allowing women, especially those in non-dominant positions, to claim their rights as equals and to enjoy the full protection of the law, often in the face of recalcitrant spouses or partners who seek to cherry pick their obligations. In this set of cases, the weaker party in a relationship is seeking to establish an entitlement to a remedy that is defined and codified in the general law of the land. However, the other spouse claims to have no such legal obligation (for instance, to pay support) because the parties never fully complied with the requirements of "marriage" as defined in the civil legislation of the country of residence. This scenario can occur if the parties followed their respective religious personal law for solemnization, or where immigrants entered a marriage contract according to the legislation of the country of origin. In such circumstances, failure to attend to culture and religion by dismissing them as "too different" may cause harm to the weaker party in the relationship. For instance, if the parties lived as "husband and wife," why should a wife not receive equal entitlement to whatever rights the general law has attached to this marital status? I now turn to examine the different options on offer.

A culture-blindness approach will not provide an attractive option. In fact, it will permit stronger parties to argue, unfairly, that once the parties did not comply with state law in entering their marriage, no subsequent rights and remedies can be established in favor of the weaker party after separation or divorce, on the basis of that universal law. A culture-override approach will instruct the judge to pay attention *only* to the religious personal law or the foreign family code that governed the solemnization of the relationship in the first place, again potentially chipping off some of the hard-won rights of women in the civil arena of family law in their new home country.

Ideally, a culture-demystifying approach will permit the court the flexibility to explore whether the parties themselves, or their relevant cultural/religious communities, treated the relationship as a valid marriage bond for all practical purposes. If the answer is affirmative, then culture can serve as a *shield*: instead of allowing the stronger party to "invalidate" the relationship (whenever such a maneuver helps *avoid* a legal obligation to a former spouse or the couple's children), paying attention to the cultural context will allow a civil court to provide remedies to the parties according to actual need. Here, the admission of culture to the courtroom serves to protect the rights of the vulnerable. An example may help illustrate this last point.

In *Hassan* v. *Hassan*,[51] the Ontario court had to determine whether Camelia Hassan, the wife, could apply for matrimonial relief by her husband, as specified by the provisions of the then-governing Canadian law (the Deserted Wives and Children's Maintenance Act). The legal problem that Camelia faced was as

---

[51] *Hassan* v. *Hassan* [1976] CarswellOnt, 189, 28 R.F.L. 121 (Ontario High Court of Justice, Docket: Toronto).

follows: her husband argued that he owed no support to her or their children, because she was not a "wife" in the meaning of this term as defined in s. 2(1) of the Deserted Wives and Children's Maintenance Act. The husband based his argument on the fact that the parties' marriage was potentially polygamous, according to the family law governing the marriage in the country of origin (Egypt). As such, the Ontario court could not recognize the marriage as legally valid. The main facts were undisputed: the couple was married in Egypt in a Muslim marriage ceremony in 1962. Three children were born of this marriage. The family left Egypt in 1971. They settled in Canada, where they established their permanent residence and domicile. Three years later, in 1974, the husband obtained a Muslim divorce decree from the Egyptian Consul in Montreal. The wife, now deserted, turned to the Ontario court seeking to establish matrimonial relief (in the form of support) to which, under Canadian legislation at the time, she was entitled as a former wife. The husband swiftly replied: he argued that he was under no obligation to pay support or any other remedy according to Canadian law because the Muslim marriage ceremony entered in the country of origin, although *de facto* monogamous, was *potentially* polygamous. The fact that the marriage was potentially polygamous, argued the husband's legal counsel, must lead the Ontario court to conclude that it was *no marriage at all*.

The question before the court, then, was whether the husband's "culture-override" claim should prevail. Formally, he had a strong case: according to the precedent set in the governing English authority in *Hyde* v. *Hyde and Woodmansee*,[52] courts following the common-law tradition should not agree to entertain jurisdiction over polygamous or potentially polygamous marriages. Without jurisdiction, the wife was technically barred from even bringing forward her legal claim for relief. This procedural barrier meant that no discussion on the merits could occur. The Ontario Supreme Court saw this jurisdictional barrier as causing a great injustice. Using untypically strong language, it rebelled against the "tragic and inequitable results that follow from the application of the principle in *Hyde* v. *Hyde*."[53] Instead of accepting the legal definition of the marriage as defined by the *lex loci celebrationis* (Egyptian family law), the Ontario court ruled that once the parties settled in Canada, their domicile had changed. As such, the marriage was governed by Canadian law; it no longer held the potential to become polygamous, and thus was no longer subject to the precedent set in *Hyde* v. *Hyde*. To understand why the concern about polygamy figures so prominently in that case in the first place, a quick review of the history of *Hyde* v. *Hyde* (itself a culturally loaded decision) is required. This was a landmark nineteenth-century decision in which the House of Lords ruled that polygamy was prohibited: it did not fit with what was then termed as a "Christian marriage," namely, monogamy. In this

---

[52] *Hyde* v. *Hyde and Woodmansee* (1866), L.R. 1 P.&D. 130.
[53] *Hassan* v. *Hassan*, para. 18.

decision, the court stated that "marriage, as understood in Christendom, may for this purpose be defined as the voluntary union for life of one man and one woman to the exclusion of all others" (*Hyde* v. *Hyde and Woodmansee* 1866: 133).[54] This definition of marriage was accepted in Canada through reception of the common law. It was never replaced by legislation. To move forward in time, the *Hyde* v. *Hyde* precedent was at the heart of the landmark *Halpern* same-sex marriage ruling in Canada, in which the Ontario Court of Appeal ruled that the "one man and one woman" component of the marriage definition (as inherited from the judicial formulation in *Hyde* v. *Hyde*) was unconstitutional because it violated the equality provision set out in s. 15, the equality provision, of the Charter of Rights and Freedoms, in a manner that was not justified in a free and democratic society under s. 1 of the Charter.[55]

In the case of Camelia Hassan, the legal dispute had no constitutional overtones. It was merely a request by a wife to have access to matrimonial relief. The Ontario court rejected the husband's claim that the parties' marriage should *not* be recognized as such, thus blocking his attempt to avoid payment of matrimonial relief. Instead, the court ruled that *notwithstanding* the fact that the spouse entered into a potentially polygamous marriage in the country of origin, what matters is that once they had settled in Canada, they changed their domicile; this provided sufficient basis for the court in Ontario to establish jurisdiction over the case and to treat it as a marriage for the purposes of enforcing a statutory remedy in favor of the wife.

Once the full civil status of the wife was recognized (by virtue of her domicile in Canada), she was in a position to claim an entitlement in this country, just like any other similarly situated former wife. Here, the court's willingness to go beyond the formal black-letter analysis proposed by the husband—exploring instead the real "cultural" context of the relationship—granted the wife not only her day in court but also her requested remedy. Instead of endorsing the override approach, which is essentially what the husband was seeking (by asking that the definition of "marriage" follow the law of the country of origin), the Ontario court concluded that although the fact that the marriage took place in Egypt had some weight, it was not determinative. As the court concluded: "I see no reason why Camelia Hassan should not be considered a 'wife' pursuant to the provisions of the Deserted Wives and Children's Maintenance Act."[56]

Another example of the use of the culture-demystifying approach as a shield is found in the case of *Basi* v. *Dhaliwal*.[57] In this complex tale, Parsini

---

[54] *Hyde* v. *Hyde and Woodmansee*, 133.
[55] *Halpern* v. *Canada* [2003] O.J. No. 2268 (Ontario Court of Appeals); *Reference re Same-Sex Marriage* [2004] 3 S.C.R. 698 (Supreme Court of Canada).
[56] *Hassan* v. *Hassan*, para. 19. In the United States, the "putative spouse" doctrine can lead to similar results.
[57] *Basi* v. *Dhaliwal* [1992] B.C.J. No. 1814 (Vancouver Registry No. 91-2065).

Is There Room for "Culture" in the Courtroom?

Basi, the applicant, was seeking maintenance for herself and her two children, from Gurmail Dhaliwal, the respondent. Mr. Dhaliwal objected. His argument was simple: he told the court that Ms. Basi was not his "spouse" within the meaning of the governing Family Relations Act. To address this charge, the provisional court had to make a factual determination of whether or not the parties lived together as husband and wife. This investigation revealed the following facts: Gurmail was the father of Parsini's two children, born in Canada. Parsini herself had been born and raised in India, where she lived with her parents and siblings. In 1980, she left India with them, arriving in Canada with the intention of staying in this country. After she entered on a visitor's visa, unmarried and uneducated, it became clear that Parsini could not be sponsored (for immigration purposes) by her relatives in Canada. She then moved to live with Mr. Dhaliwal and his wife (Parsini's sister). Instead of returning alone to India, the trial judge found that at some point, the following plan unraveled:

> [T]hings [were] arranged so she could stay... if she were to have a child, fathered by a Canadian, immigration might look more favorably on her. Mr. Dhaliwal stepped in to perform this "duty." The arrangement worked quite well for the Dhaliwals. Both of them worked outside the home. Ms. Basi was available to look after the house, performing chores such as cleaning and cooking and caring for the Dhaliwal children as well as her own two.

Faced with this unusual family arrangement, the court had to decide whether Ms. Basi could claim maintenance as a former "spouse." Instead of dismissing the case, a move which would have penalized Ms. Basi, the judge found a creative way to ensure that her rights as a spouse, under Canadian law, would be enforced. The court ruled that the fact the Mr. Dhaliwal already had a legal spouse (Ms. Basi's sister), did not prevent him from also having a common-law spouse. Importantly, the judge did not legitimate or "authorize" polygamy—an act which is prohibited by criminal law in Canada. All that was required here, in order to provide remedy to Parsini, was a proof that she and Gurmail established such a common-law relationship, as evidenced, for example, by the fact that they had an ongoing sexual relationship, shared a principal residence, and coordinated their homemaking and breadwinning responsibilities, during a continued relationship that had lasted for over ten years. Based on this evidence, the judge ordered Mr. Dhaliwal to pay maintenance to Ms. Basi, rejecting his claim that he could not have legally entered a "spousal" relationship with the Ms. Basi, because he was already married to her sister. Instead of culture-blindness, this court was willing to consider how culture and immigration played a role in shaping the family relations as between these specific parties. It granted a remedy to the weaker party, treating the culture-demystifying approach as a *shield* to ensure that Ms. Basi was not deprived of what the general law defined as a universal entitlement that anyone falling into the category of a "spouse" can claim after the break-up of a relationship.

CONCLUSION

The culture-demystifying approach identified and defended in this chapter is attractive because it permits judges to be attuned to the complex identity-factors that are part and parcel of the life of the parties entering their courtroom and seeking remedy. In rejecting the prohibition against admitting the claims of culture into the courtroom (as advocated by the culture-blind alternative), this approach better responds to the diverse society in which the general law's provisions apply in practice. It also provides a more sensible solution than the culture-override alternative, by rejecting the idea that the rights of the adversarial parties in civil disputes will be determined by a predefined "identity" box into which they are compartmentalized by virtue of ascriptive identity. Instead, as we have seen, the culture-demystifying approach offers a more cautious, case-by-case, and contextual treatment of the claims of culture, fitting them within a broader factual and legal assessment of the circumstances of this case. This flexibility, while operating as a major strength of this approach, can also be seen as its main weakness: it relies heavily on the exercise of discretion. In the two cases just discussed, *Hassan* and *Basi*, the trial judges were willing to focus on the *actual* relationship and the requested remedy, rather than being bogged down by formalism or mainstream conceptions of the "family." But other judges may not feel equally comfortable in assessing non-mainstream relationships and their legal consequences. Another charge that might be raised against the culture-demystifying approach is that it ultimately waters down or "de-radicalizes" the claims of culture, by including them as but one factor in the legal analysis. This is a fair, but unconvincing rebuttal. It simply pushes the question back one step: namely, unless it is first established that members of a pluralistic society have an innate right to expect that their family's or community's claims of culture will bear an absolutist weight in an individualized, adversarial process, the observation that the legal system does not provide such an override does not by itself establish its injustice.

The actual body of jurisprudence reveals that the claims of culture are not often used in adversarial family law disputes. When these claims have been raised by litigants, the courts have used discretion in these already highly individualized cases, deciding in ad hoc fashion how much weight to grant to "culture" in relation to a host of other relevant factors. In this respect, adding culture to the mix of considerations in the child's best interests' assessment, for example, does not risk the erosion of a general principle of equal treatment. If anything, it permits its substantive application.

Is There Room for "Culture" in the Courtroom? 149

Importantly, the claims of culture raised by the parties in these adversarial disputes do *not* challenge public policy at large, unlike group-based demands raised at the societal level. A telling example of the latter is found in demands raised by some of the more conservative branches of the Muslim community in Canada, with their proposal to establish in Ontario *binding* private, non-state tribunals to conduct family arbitration over consenting parties according to faith-based principles, potentially at the expense of women's hard-earned equality rights. This proposal provoked a major public debate and was rejected by the government after consultation with the core stakeholders. Ultimately, it led to a legislative ban prohibiting any reliance on religious principles (or any other non-state sources of law) in family arbitration (Shachar 2008).[58] This saga represented a *political* renegotiation of the place and role of religion and sub-state authorities in regulating a significant aspect of their members' affairs—in this particular instance, the terms of entry into and exit from a marriage relationship—*in lieu* of the exercise of this authority by the secular state itself.

In the family law cases that I have examined here, *Pejo, Van de Perre, J.S.B., Hassan,* and *Basi,* the litigants made no similar attempt to reshape the balance of power between state and religion; they did not argue that *anyone* who belonged to their identity group must be treated in an X or Y fashion by virtue of belonging to that minority community. Their claims were "private," shaping their own specific life circumstances. This is most visible in the shield cases: here the court's willingness to use its discretion in understanding the place and weight of culture in generating the factual situation that is the basis of the legal claim proved crucial for the women involved. In the sword cases, we saw a more strategic use of culture by the litigants, stripping it from any epistemological stance of "difference." It was transformed instead into a mere *legal* argument, just like any other in the arsenal of a diligent lawyer seeking to advance a client's adversarial claim.

In the end, it is precisely by including—rather than blocking or privileging—individualized claims of culture in the legal process, that the goal of "neutralizing" culture and religion may best be fulfilled. This is achieved, perhaps paradoxically, not by ignoring the value of identity and heritage, but by carefully and judiciously embracing it. In *Pejo*, for example, where it was clear that the biological father's objection to the family adoption on cultural grounds was *not* in the child's best interest, the judge nevertheless ordered that Mia Isabella's mother and stepfather ensure that the girl be raised with an awareness of her Mexican heritage and culture. Similar attention to Elijah's racial identity was emphasized by the court in *Van de Perre*, shaping, at least in part, the generous access provisions given to Elijah's father, Theodore, who served

---

[58] Arbitration Act, R.S.O. 2006, c. C. 1.

as a strong and positive role model for the child in fostering his racial identity and belonging. In *J.S.B.*, both parents were committed to continuing to raise their children as active participants in Longhouse ways, a fact that figured prominently in the consideration of whether or not to permit the off-reserve parent (the mother) to gain custody over the children.

Under the culture-demystifying approach (which the courts exercised in practice without giving it this name), the claims of culture have therefore not gone unnoticed. Even where they failed to sway the judgment on behalf of the claimant party, they left their mark on the life of the parents and children whose identity interests were at stake. The culture-demystifying approach creates an opening for members of minority communites and marginalized parties who have turned to the state's institutions in search of enforceable remedies to hold on to what they defined as significant sources of the self and to retell their life stories in coherent narratives, even if they defied the official strict separation of law from religion, immigration from gendered power relations, identity from parity. This is no small feat in a world in which diversity and equality are rapidally shaping up as the core causes of our times.

REFERENCES

Alston, Philip. 1994. "The Best Interests Principle: Toward a Reconciliation of Culture and Human Rights," *International Journal of Law and the Family* 8/1: 1–25.

Banks, R. Richard. 1998. "The Color of Desire: Fulfilling Adoptive Parents' Racial Preferences through Discriminatory State Action," *Yale Law Journal* 107/4: 875–964.

Barry, Brian. 2001. *Culture and Equality: An Egalitarian Critique of Multiculturalism* (Cambridge, MA: Harvard University Press).

Bartholet, Elizabeth. 1991. "Where do Black Children Belong? The Politics of Race Matching in Adoption," *University of Pennsylvania Law Review* 139/5: 1163–1256.

Beiner, Ronald. 2003. *Liberalism, Nationalism, Citizenship: Essays on the Problem of Political Community* (Vancouver: UBC Press).

Chayes, Abram. 1979. "The Role of the Judge in Public Law Litigation," *Harvard Law Review* 89: 1281–1316.

Cohen, Jean L. 2002. *Regulating Intimacy: A New Legal Paradigm* (Princeton: Princeton University Press).

Cott, Nancy F. 2000. *Public Vows: A History of Marriage and the Nation* (Cambridge, MA: Harvard University Press).

Dethloff, Nina. 2005. "Parental Rights and Responsibility in Germany," *Family Law Quarterly* 39: 315–337.

Foblets, Marie-Claire and Adriaan Overbeeke. 2004. "Islam in Belgium: The Search for a Legal Status of a New Religious Minority," in *Islam and the European Union*, ed. Richard Potz and Wolfgang Wieshaider (Leuven: Peeters), 1–39.

Fodden, Simon R. 1999. *Family Law* (Toronto: Irwin Law).

Fogg-Davis, Hawley. 2001. *The Ethics of Transracial Adoption: Public Policy and Parental Choice* (Ithaca: Cornell University Press).

Greenawalt, Kent. 2005. "Child Custody, Religious Practices, and Conscience," *University of Colorado Law Review* 76: 965–1057.
Grossberg, Michael. 1983. "Who Gets the Child? Custody, Guardianship, and the Rise of a Judicial Patriarchy in Nineteenth-Century America," *Feminist Studies* 9/2: 235–260.
Halev-Spinner, Jeff. 2012. *Enduring Injustice* (Cambridge: Cambridge University Press).
Holmes, Stephen and Cass R. Sunstein. 1999. *The Cost of Rights: Why Liberty Depends on Taxes* (New York: W. W. Norton).
Joppke, Christan. 2008. "Comparative Citizenship: A Restrictive Turn in Europe?," *Law and Ethics of Human Rights* 2/1: 1–41.
Kymlicka, Will. 1995. *Multicultural Citizenship: A Liberal Theory of Minority Rights* (Oxford: Clarendon Press).
Kymlicka, Will. 2002. *Contemporary Political Philosophy: An Introduction*, 2nd edition (Oxford: Oxford University Press).
Lacey, Linda J. 2000. "Liberal Thought and Religion in Custody and Visitation Cases," in *Law and Religion: A Critical Analysis*, ed. Stephen M. Feldman (New York: New York University Press), 411–424.
Laquer-Estin, Ann. 2004. "Toward a Multicultural Family Law," *Family Law Quarterly* 38: 501–527.
Lawrence, Sonia N. 2001. "Cultural (in)Sensitivity: The Dangers of a Simplistic Approach to Culture in the Courtroom," *Canadian Journal of Women and the Law* 13: 107–136.
Minow, Martha L. and Mary Lyndon Shanley. 1996. "Relational Rights and Responsibilities: Revisioning the Family in Liberal Political Theory and Law," *Hypatia* 11/1: 4–29.
Neef, Marian and Stuart Nagel. 1974–75. "The Adversary Nature of the American Legal System from a Historical Perspective," *New York Law Forum* 20: 123–164.
Olsen, Frances E. 1983. "The Family and the Market: A Study of Ideology and Legal Reform," *Harvard Law Review* 96: 1497–1587.
Orgad, Liav. 2010. "Illiberal Liberalism: Cultural Restrictions on Migration and Access to Citizenship," *American Journal of Comparative Law* 58: 53–105.
Perry, Twila L. 1994. "The Transracial Adoption Controversy: An Analysis of Discourse and Subordination," *NYU Review of Law and Social Change* 21/1: 33–108.
Phillips, Anne. 2003. "When Culture Means Gender: Issues of Cultural Defense in English Courts," *Modern Law Review* 66/4: 510–531.
Renteln, Alison Dundes. 2004. *The Cultural Defense* (New York: Oxford University Press).
Roach, Kent. 2004. *Criminal Law*, 3rd edition (Toronto: Irwin Law).
Sandel, Michael J. 1982. *Liberalism and the Limits of Justice* (Cambridge: Cambridge University Press).
Sanger, Carol. 2003. "Placing the Adoptive Self," in *NOMOS: Child, Family, and State*, ed. Stephen Macedo and Iris Marion Young (New York: New York University Press), 58–97.

Scott, Kenneth E. 1975. "Two Models of Civil Process," *Stanford Law Review* 27: 937–950.
Shachar, Ayelet. 2001. *Multicultural Jurisdictions: Cultural Differences and Women's Rights* (Cambridge: Cambridge University Press).
Shachar, Ayelet. 2005. "Religion, State, and the Problem of Gender: New Modes of Citizenship and Governance in Diverse Societies," *McGill Law Journal* 50: 49–88.
Shachar, Ayelet. 2008. "Privatizing Diversity: A Cautionary Tale from Religious Arbitration in Family Law," *Theoretical Inquiries in Law* 9/2: 573–607.
Shachar, Ayelet. 2011. "Earned Citizenship: Property Lessons for Immigration Reform," *Yale Journal of Law & the Humanities* 23: 110–158.
Shanley, Mary Lyndon. 2003. "Toward New Understandings of Adoption: Individuals and Relationships in Transracial and Open Adoptions," in *NOMOS: Child, Family, and State*, ed. Stephen Macedo and Iris Marion Young (New York: New York University Press), 15–57.
Taylor, Charles. 1992. *Sources of the Self: The Making of Modern Identities* (Cambridge, MA: Harvard University Press).
Volpp, Leti. 1994. "(Mis)Identifying Culture: Asian Women and the 'Cultural Defense,'" *Harvard Women's Law Journal* 17: 57–101.
Waldron, Jeremy. 2002. "One Law for All? The Logic of Cultural Accommodation," *Washington and Lee Law Review* 59/1: 3–34.
Yablon, Marcia. 2004. "The Indian Child Welfare Act Amendments of 2003," *Family Law Quarterly* 38: 689–710.
Young, Iris Marion. 1989. "Polity and Group Difference: A Critique of the Ideal of Universal Citizenship," *Ethics* 99/2: 250–274.

8

The Cultural Defense: Reflections in Light of the Model Penal Code and the Religious Freedom Restoration Act

Kent Greenawalt

INTRODUCTION

The phrase "a cultural defense" suggests an either/or choice that any legal system might make. That matters are much more complex than this is part of the burden of this essay, and indeed of many of the other essays in this volume. A "cultural defense" in its most general sense refers to a wide range of ways in which evidence about a defendant's cultural upbringing or practices could influence legal judgment about his guilt or responsibility. So understood, the phrase could refer not only to a general, separate defense labeled a "cultural defense," but also claims about culture that either are relevant under standard defenses in the criminal law, such as duress and provocation, or could be relevant were those traditional defenses expanded in some way.

Much of this essay is an inquiry into just how cultural factors might figure in claims about elements of offenses, justifications, excuses, and mitigations under the Model Penal Code—still the most comprehensive and systematic code of criminal law in the United States. That exploration gives us a sense of how culture may matter for criminal liability absent a specifically labeled "cultural defense"; it also provides an idea of how much could be accomplished by expansions of the standard defenses.

In the latter part of the essay, I think about cultural practices as a potential justification or generalized exemption in advance, comparing such a defense with an analogous defense based on religious belief and practice that now exists in many American jurisdictions.

DRAWING SOME IMPORTANT DISTINCTIONS

If one understands a "cultural defense" as a general defense labeled as such and that reaches beyond more traditional, standard defenses as they now are formulated, or as they could comfortably be revised, one needs to situate a cultural defense among a range of possibilities and approaches. Whether having a specific cultural defense makes good sense depends greatly on whether other responses to cultural traditions and assumptions meet whatever needs there may be for accommodation and fairness.

A Cultural Defense in Criminal Law versus Other Forms of Accommodation Outside the Criminal Law: A cultural defense concerns the criminal law. There are many other ways in which cultural traditions and practices may be accommodated. Allowing for the use of a cultural defense in the criminal law is sometimes described as an example of "multiculturalism," and it is often assumed that people's positions on the cultural defense follow from their more general attitudes towards accommodating cultural diversity outside the criminal law. However, we should not conflate debates about the cultural defense with broader debates about multicultural accommodations, since the criminal law is unique in many ways.

On the one hand, there may be reasons why people who support multiculturalism in general would not support the cultural defense. One might think that society has an obligation to accommodate the cultural practices of minorities even when these impose some cost or inconvenience on society, but no corresponding obligation to accommodate practices when they impose harm. On this view, there might be an obligation to adapt the workplace to accommodate a minority's group holidays, traditional dress, or cuisine, or to publicly fund a minority group's cultural activities, but no obligation to allow defendants to invoke culture as a defense for conduct that has harmed other people.

On the other hand, there might be reasons why people who oppose multiculturalism in general might nonetheless support greater scope for evidence of cultural norms in criminal cases. Given that the criminal law has the potential to deprive individuals of their life and liberty, one might think that the perspectives of defendants should matter to a degree that they do not even for civil damages, as to which the fair expectations of those who are injured should control. Perhaps criminal defendants should be allowed every opportunity to demonstrate that they are not appropriately held blameworthy or responsible, even if one does not agree that the state generally has any duty to fund or accommodate cultural practices in, say, the schools or public media. The cultural defense in criminal law must be assessed on its own terms.

A Cultural Defense versus Choices Not to Criminalize Behavior: If a person's behavior is not covered by the law of crimes in the first place, he obviously does not need a defense. Suppose that a small ethnic minority in a country engages in a traditional practice that would violate a law that legislators are considering: Sikh men cannot wear motorcycle helmets because their cultural practice requires that they wear turbans; the traditional life of the Inuit depends upon killing a limited number of a protected species of whales. Legislators may respond by declining to adopt the general restriction, for example allowing everyone to ride motorcycles without helmets, or by exempting members of a particular cultural group from a mandate that applies to everyone else, what we may call the exemption strategy. As I shall explore in more detail in the last part of this chapter, I assume that the exemption strategy is sometimes justified. Any need for a general cultural defense depends partly on the legislature not having achieved all the desirable accommodations to cultural practices through specific exemptions.

A Cultural Defense versus Jurisdictional Allocation: One way in which the legal system can accommodate minority cultures is to grant them jurisdiction to regulate their own affairs in certain respects. Some countries assign matters of marriage and divorce to various religious groups. This is not done in the United States, although general principles allowing private arbitration permit members of religious and cultural groups to choose arbitrators for civil disputes from their own traditions. Native American tribes are given jurisdiction over minor criminal matters within their reservations. That assignment rests on a legal notion that the tribes are semi-sovereign; but the strategy of jurisdictional autonomy could be followed with respect to other cultural minorities.[1] That is a very different approach from creating defenses within the ordinary criminal law, and it is not a promising approach for serious crimes like murder and rape.

Substantive Liability versus Sentencing: Many factors count for sentencing that are not relevant for underlying criminal liability. One might think that the right place to consider diverse cultural influences is in sentencing, not the substantive criminal law. The plausibility of this position rests significantly on how much sentencing discretion judges enjoy. If their choices are tightly circumscribed according to a range of considerations that omit cultural influences, then judges imposing sentences will be unable to give much weight to cultural factors. Even if judges have broad discretion, there are two strong reasons not to remit everything to sentencing. The first is that even a light sentence is misguided if the proper response to someone's behavior is that he committed no wrong. The second is that *if* judges have wide sentencing discretion (and there is not extensive review of sentences by appellate courts), different judges may reach radically different conclusions about the relevance of cultural traditions. (The concern about differential treatment will follow us in the rest of this essay.)

---

[1] However, any such scheme faces arguments by victims about their constitutional rights.

Alleviation in the Application of the Substantive Law versus Nullification: Juries (and judges) can refuse to apply the applicable law. Jury nullification occupies a paradoxical position in American law. Judges do not tell juries they can nullify, and lawyers have no general right to present facts and arguments that might lead juries to do so. But the practice of jury nullification is praised as a safeguard of justice and is protected by constitutional doctrines regarding jury verdicts (see Greenawalt 1987: 360–367). One question about cultural influences is whether defendants should have an opportunity to present such factors if they might lead a jury (or judge) to refuse to follow legal requirements. I disregard this possibility in what follows and concentrate on how cultural influences might affect applications of the law, not nullifications of it.

Minority Cultures versus Majority Culture: What counts as culture in the inquiry whether to create a general cultural defense? Suppose a member of the dominant culture claims that his perspective was strongly supported by aspects of that culture. Nicola Lacey provides the example of a young man who believes, according to traditional assumptions (among men) that a woman who says "no" to sexual intercourse in certain circumstances really means "yes."[2] Is he to have some kind of defense? Insofar as "culture" figures in the application of standard defenses, a defendant could rely on how he was affected by the majority culture, but I am assuming in this essay that a general cultural defense, labeled as such, would refer to minority cultures. This definitional gambit leaves us with the questions: even taking into account that the substantive criminal law will mainly reflect majority values, *why* should minority cultures get a defense that members of the majority do not enjoy?; and how should one determine exactly which minority cultures may benefit from such a defense?

A Cultural Defense versus Aggravation: The assumption underlying the phrase "a cultural defense" is that the connection to culture will count in favor of a defendant if it counts at all. It became clear at the "Columbia workshop where draft chapters for this volume were first presented" that cultural factors could be introduced against a defendant. This is evident in relation to ordinary standards of liability. Suppose a defendant claims that he acted on a momentary impulse. Evidence that according to his cultural traditions, a person in his position—he is, say, the brother of a woman his victim seduced a month ago—has a responsibility to kill the victim, could support the prosecution's argument that he killed after deliberation.

The second way in which cultural factors might work against the defendant is less obvious and more debatable. A participant at the "Columbia workshop where draft chapters for this volume were first presented" suggested that evidence that someone was raised in a Nazi culture and retained its perspectives might make him seem a worse person than he would otherwise. I am doubtful about the persuasiveness of this illustration. That someone is a Nazi might

---

[2] See Nicola Lacey's chapter in this volume.

well make him seem worse, but a person raised in the general culture who freely chooses Nazism may seem worse to us than someone raised in a Nazi culture. Thus, the particular claim of continuing connection to a culture might even here seem to mitigate blameworthiness. In any event, it is at least possible that cultural influence might make a person seem more, rather than less, blameworthy. This raises the question whether, were some general reference to culture to be included in the criminal law, judges and juries should be able to count culture *against* defendants as well as for them.

A General Defense versus Evidence That is Relevant to Components of Liability: The idea of a "cultural defense" sounds like a general defense, something on which a defendant might rely independent of evidence that would be relevant to ordinary matters of *mens rea*, excuse, and justification. Whether a general defense is needed depends heavily on the adequacy of evidence of cultural factors as parts of ordinary assessments of criminal wrongdoing.

To investigate that adequacy, we may take the standards of a legal system as they now exist, as they now exist (or might exist) if debatable open-ended issues are resolved in favor admitting cultural factors, or as they would exist with discrete reforms that fall short of a general defense. My inquiry below proceeds along these lines in respect to the Model Penal Code.

Were a legal system to employ some general requirement of personal blameworthiness in addition to all particular requisites of criminal behavior, the difference between admitting into evidence relevant cultural factors and having a specific cultural defense would recede in significance.[3] In either event, a defendant could claim that her having acted in accord with her cultural traditions rendered her not liable or less liable than she would otherwise be. For purposes of this essay, I will adhere to the assumption of common-law jurisdictions that there is no general defense of lack of blameworthiness if the prosecution establishes all the specific elements necessary for a criminal conviction.[4]

Cultural Factors versus Other Potentially Relevant Factors: A crucial question about *both* a general cultural defense *and* evidence of cultural factors as part of the ordinary criminal process is how cultural factors figure in relation to other possible factors. If one cannot come up with some reasonably persuasive distinctions between the kind of cultural factors that would make a difference and other factors, one must conclude that culture should not count, to put it crudely, or that other factors should also count.

If we think of cultural tradition as a basis for excuse or mitigation, comparison with factors such as abusive parents, brain damage, deprived

---

[3] One might reach the same conclusion if one thought that the system's ordinary more particular standards of criminality included all the bases of personal blameworthiness that might be affected by cultural factors.

[4] The closest approximation of such a general defense is the defense of diminished responsibility that reduces murder to manslaughter in some jurisdictions.

neighborhoods, and violent "subcultures" (such as gang life) may seem relevant. If we suppose that cultural tradition might actually supply a justification for behavior that would otherwise violate the criminal law, we can compare it with standard practices within the majority culture, such as physical aggression in sports like boxing and ice hockey. We can also compare the norms of cultural traditions with religious practices and claims of conscience (religious and non-religious). Of course, religious practice and cultural tradition overlap to a considerable degree, but a legal protection of religious practices does not embrace all cultural practices, and many religious claims do not attach to minority cultures. The final section of my essay engages the comparison of cultural tradition with religion and conscience.

Whether one is focusing on excuse or justification, one must decide what constitutes a relevant culture. I am assuming in this essay that the protection of a "cultural defense" would go to minority cultures of an "ethnic" or "national" sort, not to the subculture of sadists and masochists or gangs within the dominant culture or the "culture" of particular households or neighborhoods. Were a defense to be cast along these lines, one would need reasons to favor the kinds of "minority" cultures that would be included over those that would be excluded.

CULTURAL FACTORS AND THE MODEL PENAL CODE: IS A GENERAL DEFENSE NEEDED AS A SUPPLEMENT?

As we have already explored in a preliminary way, whether a special cultural defense is needed in American criminal law depends substantially on how cultural factors might figure in ordinary standards of criminal liability. It is time now to make this inquiry about one coherent set of standards, the Model Penal Code.[5]

Some initial words of explanation are needed for those who are not familiar with the place of the Model Penal Code in American law, and a few further words are needed about my degree of involvement with its commentary. Within the United States, principles of criminal law are left to individual states, so we have no criminal law of the entire country. There is, instead, the criminal law of fifty-three jurisdictions—the fifty states, the District of Columbia, Puerto Rico, and the federal jurisdiction. Up through the 1950s, basic principles of criminal law were developed by occasional judicial decisions and by piecemeal legislation that amounted to much less than comprehensive codes.

---

[5] American Law Institute, *Model Penal Code and Commentaries* (1985).

The Model Penal Code and the Religious Freedom Restoration Act

The Model Penal Code project of the American Law Institute was an effort to rectify this situation, to provide a model for states that was cohesive and comprehensive, that would clarify some aspects of the law and improve upon aspects that were irrational or unwise. The bulk of the project was completed in the 1950s under the leadership of Herbert Wechsler, widely regarded as our country's greatest criminal law theorist and reformer. The Code became official in 1962, with the approval of the membership of the Institute. At that point, the major sections we shall examine had extensive comments that explained their texts and rationales. The Comments for many individual crimes and for sentencing and jurisdictional provisions were much less fully developed.

In the late 1970s, the Institute received a federal grant to complete the Commentaries. I was brought into that project as Chief Reporter, but in actuality under the very active supervision of Professor Wechsler. The aim was to finish explanatory Comments and to trace the influence of the Code up to that time in actual jurisdictions. Those of us who were working at that stage had no authority to alter the Code's text (except to change an occasional "which" to "that" and to correct mispunctuation), and the Comments were (for the most part) to continue to explain and defend what the Code did, not to provide a critical perspective after two decades. We *were* free to consider how the Code might apply to phenomena not dealt with in the original Comments. Most of the sections I shall be discussing are in the General Part, for which I was responsible at that point in the revision. On rereading the Comments, I have been struck by their inattention to cultural factors. No doubt, a substantial part of the explanation was the focus of the drafters on individual psychological characteristics that could affect culpability, rather than attachments to groups with traditions and norms that varied from those in the dominant culture. What the Comments say needs to be understood as the thoughtful work of Wechsler and his collaborators roughly fifty years ago, but the failure to comprehend and consider some nuances in ways defendants might introduce cultural influences is partially mine.

Why consider the Model Penal Code, now more than forty years old? It is still by far the most systematic and comprehensive approach to a criminal code in the United States, and although not *the law* in any jurisdiction, it has been drawn upon heavily by many states in their revisions of their own penal codes. Its commentaries are often relied upon when state courts interpret provisions that are worded similarly to those of the Code, and even courts in jurisdictions without revised codes sometimes rely on Code approaches to develop their own law. The Code figures prominently in many of the casebooks used to teach criminal law to American students. Very importantly, the Model Penal Code adopts statutory formulations for general principles of liability as well as for specific crimes; one need not search patterns of judicial decisions to try to discern just what counts as duress or necessity. Thus, it is much easier to say what defendants can or cannot claim.

Were one to carry out the exercise I shall perform for any actual jurisdiction, one would need to see how far its approaches deviate from those of the Code. In my own more limited endeavor, I will comment on some aspects of the Code that have not been widely followed. If one can summarize the overall effect of these differences, it is that most actual jurisdictions are somewhat less hospitable to the introduction of cultural factors than is the Model Code itself.

Basic Standards of Culpability

Although the Model Penal Code requires an *actus reus*, i.e., a voluntary act or omission, and it is conceivable that a defendant might rely on a cultural practice to claim that he did not meet even the minimal standard of voluntariness, we can move beyond this possibility and focus on the Code's four standards of culpability—purpose, knowledge, recklessness, and negligence. In contrast with vague ideas of "intention" characteristic of much preceding law, Section 2.02(2)(a) treats purpose as a "conscious object to engage in conduct" of a defined kind or "to cause a result." *A* has a purpose to kill *B* only if that is his conscious object.

In a case that other essays in this volume mention, Kargar kissed his baby son's penis.[6] If the crime is defined solely as requiring contact between a person's mouth and a child's genitals, Kargar had that purpose. If sexual arousal is an element of the crime, Kargar lacked that purpose. He could establish his absence of purpose by pointing to the cultural tradition in Afghanistan, his country of origin, that fathers kiss the penises of their baby sons.

We can see that cultural practice could count *against* a defendant. In an illustration I have already used, if a defendant claims that his killing of a victim was an accident, evidence that according to his culture he had a duty to kill that person could help establish a purpose to kill.

Under the Model Code, a person acts knowingly with regard to a result if he is "aware that it is practically certain" his conduct will cause it.[7] Thus, a person who plants a bomb in a car with the purpose of killing one of its occupants knows that it will with practical certainty kill others who he realizes will also be in the car. Cultural factors could be introduced by a defendant to show he was ignorant of causal consequences other people would take as practically certain, or to show that he was practically certain of consequences others might take as unlikely.

The standards for both purpose and knowledge are rigorously subjective;[8] they depend on what an actual defendant aimed to do and understood. Thus,

---

[6] *State v. Kargar*, 679 A.2d 81 (Me. 1996).
[7] Model Penal Code, § 2.02(b)(iii).
[8] Knowledge does have an objective element as well. Suppose *A* believes that he has magical powers and that if he slaps *B* in the face, *B* will die. He does not want *B* to die and regrets that

any evidence bearing on a defendant's state of mind in regard to these elements of a crime could be relevant. No need arises for any special consideration of cultural factors, since they could be introduced like anything else.

However, we can see that if a crime is defined so that the crucial purpose depends only upon aiming to perform a certain physical act, one *might* need a general defense to exonerate the person whose tradition gives him an unusual, unthreatening reason to perform that physical act.

Whether a general defense *would* be needed to exonerate defendants like Kargar could depend on whether a jurisdiction has a provision covering *de minimis* infractions. In Section 2.12, not widely followed by states, which mainly leave judgments about unharmful behavior to prosecutorial discretion and to sentencing, the Model Code authorizes a court to dismiss a prosecution if a defendant's conduct did not cause the harm the law aimed to prevent or involved some other extenuation such that one cannot think the legislature envisaged it.[9] The way this language is formulated, it could help a defendant like Kargar, who relied on cultural tradition to show he did no real harm. It would not help a defendant who caused *some harm* (from the standpoint of the majority's culture) but argued that his cultural tradition shows that the harm was less than in the more ordinary context or that he was much less blameworthy than the typical defendant.

When we turn to recklessness and negligence, matters become more complicated. Recklessness involves conscious risk creation. According to § 2.02(2)(c), a person must "consciously disregard a substantial and unjustifiable risk.... The risk must be of such a nature and degree that, considering the nature and purpose of the actor's conduct... its disregard involves a gross deviation from the standard of conduct that a law-abiding person would observe in the actor's situation." Insofar as the issue is what risks a person actually perceives, analysis is the same as with respect to purpose and knowledge.

Cultural factors could be introduced to show that a parent did or did not perceive the risk of failing to take a child with a high fever to the doctor. Although this is not quite so clear, the actor's perception of the degree of risk is what should count, not an objective appraisal. If the actor perceives one chance in ten thousand whereas the actual risk is one in ten, his sense should control evaluation of whether the risk was substantial.

The determination of what degree of risk is substantial is not left to the actor; that is decided by the jury. The crucial question about recklessness is what makes a risk unjustifiable. One asks whether there is a "gross deviation" from how "a law-abiding person" would perform "in the actor's situation."[10]

---

his slapping B will have that consequence. A slaps B and causes B to have a heart attack; B dies. If that outcome was from an objective point of view highly unlikely, B could not have been "aware that it (was) practically certain."

[9] Model Penal Code, § 2.12(2)–(3).
[10] Model Penal Code, § 2.02 (2)(c).

Consider the following hypothetical case. According to the traditions of a cultural group, boys of fourteen should be exposed to a seriously dangerous situation—say confronting a wild animal or being exposed to the elements in a remote location—as part of the process of developing into manhood. The parents who put their sons in these situations realize that the danger they will die is real, and of the last one hundred boys in similar situations, two have in fact died.[11] If a boy now dies, have the parents committed reckless homicide?

Let us assume that in the majority culture, everyone would agree that short of authorizing medical treatment needed to preserve life or health, exposing a child to a 2 percent chance of death would be a substantial risk and that it would be clearly unjustified, a gross deviation from the standard a law-abiding person would observe. But from the perspective of the minority culture, this rite of initiation is so important, it justifies the risk. Does "the actor's situation" include his being embedded in the culture? And are the parents less than "law-abiding person[s]" because they are willing to take this particular risk? We can see quickly that the Code's standard might be understood to address this question "objectively" in terms of the values of the majority culture *or* to take into account the special perspectives of the minority culture.

The commentary gives us some guidance, but it is of a peculiar sort: "the point is that the jury must evaluate the actor's conduct and determine whether it should be condemned."[12] The Model Code, in other words, does not tell us whether the jury should treat the parents whose exposed son dies according to the standards of the general culture or to give weight to the standards of the parents' minority culture. The Code's language and the commentary do strongly suggest, however, that the parents should be able to present evidence about their cultural traditions and to argue that that is part of their situation and that they are not less than law-abiding persons.

The issues about negligence are similar to those concerning recklessness. Negligence does not depend on awareness of risk; it is enough that the actor should have been aware of a risk. For negligence under the Model Penal Code, the actor's failure must involve "a gross deviation from the standard of care that a reasonable person would observe in the actor's situation."[13] Again we have a reference to the actor's situation, which might or might not include his cultural practices. Again, the commentary tells us that the jury is to determine if the defendant's failure justifies condemnation,[14] and adds that "There is an inevitable ambiguity in 'situation.'"[15]

Certainly it would matter, it says, if a defendant were blind or had just suffered a heart attack, but "heredity, intelligence or temperament" would not be

---

[11] To shift to the mythical, in Mozart's opera *The Magic Flute*, part of the significance of the trials of fire and water is that Tamino and Pamina might actually die.
[12] Model Penal Code, § § 2.02 cmt at 237.
[13] Model Penal Code, § 2.02 (2)(d).
[14] Model Penal Code, § 2.02 cmt at 241.
[15] Model Penal Code, § 2.02 cmt at 242.

material and "could not be without depriving the criterion of all its objectivity."[16] The issue about such discriminations is left "to the courts."[17] If we put these various passages together, the court is to decide that some claims cannot be offered in respect to negligence—the standard is not the reasonable angry person—but that for others the jury is to determine their significance. For me, the language of the negligence subsection and its commentary sound slightly less promising for evidence of cultural factors than the analogous passages on recklessness, but I would nevertheless conclude that defendants typically should be able to argue that cultural traditions are part of the situation against which negligence should be determined.

Justifications

I turn now to two justifications for behavior that would otherwise be criminal—self-defense and general justification (or necessity). The Model Penal Code treats mistakes about justifying circumstances as matters of justification, not excuse.[18] Contrary to the law of most jurisdictions, it correlates culpability about justifying circumstances to the culpability level of the underlying offense. The culpability level for one form of aggravated assault is purposely or knowingly causing bodily injury with a deadly weapon.[19] If A intends to scare B by shooting near him, but the bullet creases the flesh of B's leg,[20] A has not committed this form of assault, even if his assumption that he would not hit B was unreasonable (negligence), and even if he was aware of a risk he might hit B (recklessness). Now, suppose A, acting under an unreasonable belief that B is about to shoot him, intends to hit B with his shot but without injuring him seriously, and he does inflict minor injury. In a jurisdiction in which a belief in justifying circumstances must be reasonable to provide a defense, A would be guilty of this form of aggravated assault. Under the Model Code he would not, because his culpability about his possible justification (negligence, or perhaps recklessness) is less than the culpability level for the underlying offense.[21] A negligent belief in justifying facts will, under the Model Code, provide a

---

[16] Model Penal Code, § 2.02 cmt at 242.

[17] Model Penal Code, § 2.02 cmt at 242.

[18] There is disagreement among theorists whether mistakes about justifying circumstances give rise to justifications or excuses. I have claimed that when a person has made the best judgment possible in the situation, but it turns out to be mistaken, he should definitely be viewed as justified. And I have also defended the Model Code's approach as one among appropriate options. See Greenawalt 1984.

[19] Model Penal Code, § 211.1(2)(b).

[20] I have put B's injury so that it is "bodily injury" under the Code but not "serious bodily injury." See American Law Institute 1985: § 210.0.

[21] Model Penal Code, § 3.09(2).

defense to a crime of purpose or recklessness, but in most jurisdictions it will provide no defense at all.

Section 3.04 of the Model Code allows the use of force for self-protection "when the actor believes that such force is immediately necessary" to protect himself against the use of unlawful force.[22] Deadly force is justifiable if "the actor believes (it) is necessary to protect against death, serious bodily injury, kidnapping," or forcible sexual intercourse.[23] Section 3.05 contains similar standards for the use of force to protect third persons.

Consider this fanciful variation on the Congolese case discussed by Claes Lernestedt.[24] Members of an African tribe that have moved to the United States believe that witches can cause people to die immediately by casting certain spells. B, believing he is a witch, begins casting a spell which both B and A believe will quickly kill A and her family. A shoots B dead. A has believed that deadly force was immediately necessary to protect herself and others against death.[25] A is not guilty of purposeful or knowing homicide under the Code, because she believes she has a justification. But is A guilty of reckless or negligent homicide? She is not guilty of reckless homicide unless she was aware of a risk that the facts did not justify her action. Apart from that problem, we are left with the question whether her belief was reasonable.

The relevant sections and commentaries on justification[26] do not provide as full an account of recklessness and negligence as do the section and commentary on the basic standards of culpability.[27] The earlier account of what those standards mean is incorporated for claims of justification. Thus, to take negligence, we are referred to what a reasonable person would do "in the actor's situation,"[28] and to the commentary that tells us that the jury needs to decide if A's failure justifies condemnation.[29] Here, A's failure involves a gross mistake about the nature of reality (at least as that is understood in the majority culture). When a person has killed another based on such a serious mistake, one strongly doubts that a jury would be inclined to say that she does not deserve condemnation for the least grave form of homicide, negligent homicide. And I am inclined to think that a judge could fairly refuse to allow the defense to raise that claim.[30] If these judgments are correct, one might think that a special

---

[22] Model Penal Code, § 3.04(1).
[23] Model Penal Code, Section 3.04(2)(b).
[24] See Lernestedt's chapter in this volume.
[25] A minor hurdle is that B's spell must count as unlawful force if it would work.
[26] Model Penal Code, § § 3.04, 3.05, and 3.09 and commentaries.
[27] Model Penal Code, § 2.02(2)(c), (d) and commentary.
[28] Model Penal Code, § 2.02 cmt at 241.
[29] Model Penal Code, § 2.02 cmt at 237.
[30] Thus, I distinguish this case from the one in which parents risk their son's life in an effort to help him move towards manhood.

cultural defense would be needed here to exonerate A, but would one conclude that A *should* be relieved of liability for even negligent homicide? I doubt it.

Jurisdictions in which belief in justification must be reasonable to count at all would be much harsher on A's claim in these circumstances. If reasonableness were assessed according to the majority culture, A would definitely lack a reasonable belief in justifying facts, and she would be guilty of murder, since she killed purposefully. For such a jurisdiction, the argument for some special cultural defense (or mitigation) would seem much more powerful.

The Model Code's general justification defense, in Section 3.02, applies, subject to some exceptions, if the actor thinks his conduct is necessary to avoid a harm that is "greater than that sought to be prevented by the law defining the offense charged…" Although the section's language is not entirely clear on the point, the section does justify taking one life if that is necessary to save many.[31] Thus, A, in our witch hypothetical, might be able to claim that she believed she was avoiding a harm that was greater than the death of B. If, as Section 3.02 seems to provide, she succeeded in defending against a prosecution for murder,[32] the question would remain whether she would be guilty of reckless or negligent homicide.

New York's statute, which some other states have followed, gives a general justification only if "such conduct is necessary as an emergency measure to avoid an imminent public or private injury."[33] This standard is decisively objective; if A makes an unreasonable mistake about justifying circumstances, she has no justification defense to any crime, and reasonableness is to be determined according to the dominant perspective about reality.

Duress and Mitigation from Murder to Manslaughter

Under the Model Code, duress, set out in Section 2.09, is an excuse. We need to be clear initially about how duress fits with the general justification defense. Some courts have used duress for all situations in which one responds to human threats by committing a criminal act, reserving the necessity defense for natural circumstances, such as a snowstorm that causes a mountaineer seeking shelter to break into someone else's cabin. Under the Model Code, the general justification defense reaches both natural emergencies and human threats. If I steal a watch in response to a credible threat that I will be shot to death if I do not, I have a defense of general justification.

---

[31] Model Penal Code, § 3.02.
[32] One wonders whether a court would really entertain this defense for purposeful murder if a person said he was complying with God's orders and that killing his victim was immediately necessary to save multiple lives.
[33] N.Y. Penal Law, § 35.05 (2008).

What is left for duress are circumstances in which a person is not actually justified in responding to a threat but cannot fairly be blamed for yielding. The formulation covers coercion by force or threatened force "that a person of reasonable firmness in his situation would have been unable to resist."[34] What of a wife who belongs to a minority culture in which women are expected to do what their husbands tell them, and who carries heroin on an airplane in response to her husband's threat that he will beat her if she does not? In the majority culture, a wife of reasonable firmness would not submit.[35] But most wives in the minority culture would submit. The question is whether membership in that culture is part of "her situation." The commentary refers back to the standards for recklessness and negligence; it tells us that factors like size, strength, age, and health are relevant, but temperament is not.[36] The commentary also indicates that the defense could be available to someone who was "brainwashed,"[37] and the wife might argue that being involved in a minority culture is analogous to being "brainwashed." As with many of the other sections we have looked at, this section leaves it to the jury to decide if the threat of force exculpates, and that judgment is inextricable from how the actor's "situation" is understood.

Something similar is true about the section that authorizes mitigation of murder to manslaughter. The Model Code greatly broadened the traditional rule that certain provocations could warrant reducing intentional killing from murder to manslaughter. According to Section 210.3(1)(b), a homicide that would otherwise be murder is reduced to manslaughter if it is "committed under the influence of extreme mental or emotional disturbance for which there is a reasonable explanation or excuse." That is to be determined "from the viewpoint of a person in the actor's situation under the circumstances as he believes them to be."[38] The commentary explains that the trier of fact must take the circumstances as the actor perceives them.[39] (However, the commentary does not focus on the circumstance when the actor's basic view about physical reality is fundamentally distorted, as in the belief about deadly magic, from the standpoint of the majority culture.)

Assessing the basic facts accurately, a Japanese woman kills her two children and tries to kill herself because she has been deeply shamed by her husband's infidelity. Let us assume that that would not provide a sufficient emotional disturbance for which there is a reasonable explanation or excuse in the majority culture. Might it nevertheless be such an excuse for a woman raised in a

[34] N.Y. Penal Law, § 2.09(1).
[35] However, one might argue that being a battered woman is part of one's situation and that the standard for a woman whose husband beats her should not be wives in general.
[36] Model Penal Code, § 2.09 cmt at 375.
[37] Model Penal Code, § 2.09 cmt at 376–377.
[38] Model Penal Code, § 210.3(1)(b).
[39] Model Penal Code, § 210.3 cmt at 68.

culture in which the humiliation she suffered would be horrible and would include her children?

The comment provides the familiar line that "situation" is ambiguous.[40] Blindness, shock from traumatic injury, and extreme grief would be included in one's situation, idiosyncratic moral values would not. The language aims for "flexibility," allowing argument about what is a reasonable explanation or excuse.[41] "In the end, the question is whether the actor's loss of self-control can be understood in terms that arouse sympathy in the ordinary citizen."[42] Given these portions of the commentary, the Japanese defendant clearly should be able to argue that she was acting under the influence of an emotional disturbance that would qualify.

Although the Model Code greatly broadens the circumstances that could allow a "provocation" mitigation to manslaughter and renders the relevant inquiry significantly more subjective than it had previously been, the Code lacks any general diminished responsibility mitigation. A defendant must be able to make an argument under the sections I have mentioned or other sections of a similar sort.

Ignorance of the Law

One kind of argument that a defendant might offer is that his cultural traditions left him unaware that his behavior was criminal. Kargar, for example, would not have assumed that kissing the penis of his son was actually a criminal act in the state of Maine.[43]

The common law's traditional harshness about ignorance of the law is captured by the phrase, "Ignorance of the law is no excuse." What is meant in this respect is ignorance about the law defining an offense, not every mistake about what the law provides. Suppose a woman breaks off an engagement, removing her engagement ring and placing it on a table in her apartment. Her fiancé mistakenly thinks he then becomes the legal owner of the ring he gave her months earlier. His taking of the ring is not theft. Given his mistake about the law of property, he has not knowingly taken the property of another.

The Model Code continues the tradition of not excusing ignorance of the relevant penal law, but it creates two exceptions. Section 2.04(3)(b) concerns people who rely on reasonable official statements about the law's content—not likely to be much help for recent immigrants from diverse cultural traditions.

---

[40] Model Penal Code, § 210.3 cmt at 62.
[41] Model Penal Code, § 210.3 cmt at 63.
[42] Model Penal Code, § 210.3 cmt at 63. The commentary does not make clear when a judge may refuse to allow a defendant's claim that he qualifies under this section to be put to the jury.
[43] *State v. Kargar*, 679 A.2d 81.

Section 2.04(3)(a) covers situations in which the law is "not known to the actor and has not been published or reasonably been made available." The language about "published" or "made available" focuses on general availability, not on whether people in subgroups of society had an adequate opportunity to be aware of the law.

The Comment does say, "There can be no point in punishing someone who neither knows his behavior is criminal nor has that information reasonably available to him."[44] But the Comment acknowledges that the Code's language does not protect defendants who had no reason to suppose that a mere failure to register might be criminal, a situation in which the Supreme Court had discerned a constitutional defense.[45] Before suggesting that a broadened defense might lead to spurious claims and reduce incentives to learn the law, the Comment remarks, "A legislative broadening of the defense to excuse all those who could not reasonably be expected to be aware of a law's existence would bar conviction in some cases that are not reached by the Code's language but in which liability may seem unjust."[46] (Except for a few provisions as to which prevailing sentiment had radically altered, this is about as close as the Comments get to criticizing formulations in the Code.) Such a broadening would give a foothold for claims of recent immigrants that they could not be expected to be aware of laws, but the commentary is clear that Section 2.04 as it stands does not provide a defense in these cases.

A GENERAL CULTURAL DEFENSE—EXCUSE OR MITIGATION

Is there any need for a general cultural defense that would allow the introduction of cultural traditions to excuse defendants or mitigate their liability? The argument for such a defense is much weaker for the Model Code than for jurisdictions with more objective standards of recklessness and negligence, with requirements that all justifications be reasonable, and with narrower standards for duress and provocation. We saw in connection with *Kargar* that the definitions of specific crimes are also important. If definitions are exclusively in terms of physical acts that may have vastly different significance among different cultural groups (and if a jurisdiction lacks a *de minimis* provision), there may be more need for a special cultural defense than if crimes are defined more flexibly in terms of anti-social purposes.

---

[44] Model Penal Code, § 2.04 cmt at 276.
[45] The Supreme Court had held that such a defendant had a due process right not to be convicted in *Lambert v. California*, 355 U.S. 225 (1957).
[46] Model Penal Code, § 2.04 cmt at 276.

The Model Penal Code and the Religious Freedom Restoration Act 169

In the most extensive treatment of a cultural defense, Alison Dundes Renteln has suggested that defendants should be able to introduce cultural traditions to be considered by judges and juries when that might lead someone to believe their actions are excused or less culpable (Renteln 2004). As it stands, this proposal suffers two serious flaws: a lack of clarity about just how the defense is supposed to work and inattention to how this proposed defense might relate to other proposed defenses.

The first point is fairly easy to understand now that we have run through some major provisions of the Model Code. A penal code has general principles, definitions of specific crimes, and provisions for sentencing. Sentencing in the United States is (with the exception of capital punishment) left to judges. I am assuming, without examining precise schemes of sentencing, that cultural traditions could be relevant at sentencing, whether they suggest lower or higher penalties for a defendant.

But how is the general cultural defense to work at trial? Juries rendering verdicts decide whether defendants are guilty of crimes with which they are charged. Sometimes juries may determine that defendants are guilty of lesser included offenses—a man charged with murder may be guilty only of manslaughter, a woman charged with grand larceny may be guilty only of petit larceny.[47] A jury may excuse a defendant who acted under duress. It may choose to nullify the law by acquitting someone who it believes is guilty of the crime charged.

But, and here is the point, criminal codes confer no power on juries or judges simply to reduce the level of offenses based on a sense that the defendant is less culpable then the typical defendant charged with that species of crime. For homicide, the provocation defense and its expanded Model Code counterpart do allow a reduction in the category of crime from murder to manslaughter; so also does the yet more general "diminished responsibility" defense for jurisdictions that recognize that defense. But the law contains no similar defenses for crimes of larceny, rape, and selling proscribed drugs. If cultural evidence does not show that a defendant lacked the basic culpability as prescribed in the offense, or that he acted under duress, or that his crime was *de minimis*, *what* is the jury to do if the evidence leads it to conclude that the defendant was less culpable than the typical offender? It is called upon to render a verdict of guilty or not guilty for the crime charged. Of course, it is free to acquit in the face of convincing evidence of guilt, but Professor Renteln seems to have in mind something more subtle than cultural evidence producing jury nullification (see generally Renteln 2004).

A jury *might* use cultural evidence to reduce the level of offense in a way not authorized by the criminal code—what we might consider a qualified form of

---

[47] The prosecution may fail to prove that jewelry she stole was worth the amount required for grand larceny.

nullification. Thus, assume that a woman has stolen $100,000 worth of diamonds. The jury, after hearing cultural evidence that makes her appear relatively sympathetic, convicts her only of petit larceny.

A simple proposal to allow evidence and argument about why cultural practice should reduce liability, even if it does not bear on the elements of a crime, founders on the problem of its relevance for what a jury must actually decide. I see only two ways out of this bind. One is to provide that for specific defenses with which we are familiar, cultural factors could relieve a defendant of liability, with the reference to cultural factors supplementing the more general formulation of the defenses. Thus, a criminal code could make reasonable ignorance of the law an excuse for a recent immigrant with a cultural background that differs significantly from that of the majority culture. That would then be a special added ignorance of law defense, limited only to cultural claims.

The second strategy would be to adopt a more general provision for cultural factors along the lines of:

(1) When a defendant's conduct is grounded in minority cultural traditions in such a way that his behavior is excusable, though not covered by any specific excuses, he shall not be guilty.

(2) When a defendant's conduct is grounded in minority cultural traditions in such a way that his behavior is less culpable than is typical for an offense, he shall be guilty of a lesser offense (to whatever degree the jury deems appropriate), whether or not the definitions of specific offenses make such factors relevant.

Either of these two approaches raises the question why cultural traditions should be treated differently from other factors that might reduce culpability, but do not connect to the basic elements of offenses in their general formulations, such as violently abusive parents, dire poverty, growing up as a member of a neighborhood gang, brain damage, or a genetic predisposition to violent action. Someone with any of these disadvantages might claim that he is less culpable than the typical offender.

One might answer that recognizing cultural factors would be less threatening to the overall deterrent objectives of the penal law or would be less subject to spurious claims than allowing these other factors to reduce culpability. Perhaps it matters that minority cultures form kinds of communities with their own norms and sanctions, ones that, unlike the norms and sanctions within gangs, may not *in general* be opposed to the basic norms of the dominant culture. I shall not try to engage the inquiry comparing cultural and other factors in detail here, but I do want to stress that a component of any plausible argument for a general cultural defense, conceived mainly as involving excuse and mitigation, must be an explanation of why a connection to an ethnic or national minority culture is going to be treated differently from other bases for arguments that a defendant's culpability is reduced. Of course, one might instead build from these cultural factors to conclude that other factors should be similarly treated, but then one would end up recommending reforms that would be much broader than introducing a general cultural defense or an explicit cultural defense supplement to existing defenses.

In concentrating on how the structure of defenses in the Model Penal Code relates to the possibility of a general cultural defense, I have slighted important aspects of the problem that deserve mention, however brief. The need for a specific defense (or specific additions to existing defenses) may seem greater if the sentencing discretion of judges is constrained. Adopted in a different era, the Model Code embodied highly discretionary, flexible, sentencing; that approach has been rejected in the United States in favor of a model in which guidelines sharply reduce discretion, and, therefore, variations among sentences. The need to recognize relevant factors in the substantive criminal law is more pressing if they cannot be given due weight in sentencing.

A serious difficulty with creating a specific cultural defense is the burden it would place on judicial administration. Judges would need to determine exactly what kinds of factors could be "cultural" in the right sense and which of these might plausibly bear on culpability. (Otherwise, a judge should not allow such evidence to go to a jury.) The judge would then have to decide how much evidence to allow about cultural traditions and practices *and* about whether a defendant was himself or herself connected to those traditions and practices in the necessary way.

A member of an ethnic minority, even one who engages in particular practices of that culture, may not regard those practices as including norms he should follow if he has reasons to act otherwise (Scheffler 2007).[48] If a defendant was a member of a minority with distinctive practices, but had lived in the United States for more than a decade and had developed an attitude of indifference to those practices, he should not be able to claim successfully that he was constrained by culture to engage in the particular practice that constituted the criminal act for which he was prosecuted; but a judge would be hard put to identify this attitude of indifference at the outset and to decide just how much evidence to allow about the defendant's degree of adherence to cultural norms. (A judge under the Model Penal Code already faces somewhat similar questions about what evidence to allow about a defendant's "situation" under the various provisions where that is relevant, but she need not worry about the specific boundary lines of (relevant) culture.)

Three more general concerns reach beyond these worries about practical implementation. People, especially people who emigrate to a country with a different culture, have a range of choices about what to accept and reject, and immigration itself often, though not always, signals rejection of aspects of the

---

[48] Samuel Scheffler points out that not all aspects of "cultures" carry normative authority for members.

culture from which the immigrant comes (see Scheffler 2007: 99–103). The "melting pot" tradition (or myth) in the United States assumes that immigrants of highly diverse traditions will be absorbed into the general culture. However benighted this tradition may be about broad cultural diversity, perhaps we should think of those who come to the country as free enough to conform with basic criminal standards. And often the victims of crimes for which there is a cultural explanation may be members of the minority culture who themselves have rejected the norms that guide the actor who harms them. Finally, decisions by judges or juries that an actor is less culpable because he was behaving in accord with cultural practices of his minority may be regarded as regrettable stereotyping by other members of the same minority who disagree about what cultural practices and norms have been or who have come to reject as long outmoded the practices on which the defendant has relied.

A GENERAL CULTURAL DEFENSE OR EXEMPTION: A CONCEPT OF JUSTIFIED ACTION

In some circumstances, the claim about cultural tradition is that members of the majority culture should recognize that people have a right to act according to their cultural practices, even if this contravenes ordinary legal standards. One might think of this as one form of a claimed right to one's culture. Thus, Kargar argued on appeal that he had a constitutional right to kiss his son's penis (although he later did not claim he should be allowed to continue the practice) (Renteln 2004: 245nn.53, 55).[49] I have already discussed the possibility of specific exemptions for conduct that is required or encouraged by cultural traditions. Undoubtedly, such exemptions are sometimes warranted. The question here is the possibility of a general exemption—that is, an exemption cast in terms of a general formula to be applied by administrators, judges, or juries on a case-by-case basis.

One inquiry along these lines is to ask how cultural traditions relate to religious traditions. That inquiry is not the only analogy one might choose in thinking about justified behavior,[50] but it has special interest because of the overlap of religions and cultures and because the law in many American jurisdictions does provide a general exemption—limited in scope as it may be—for religious practices.[51] Although the circle of religious practices intersects with

---

[49] No claim of constitutional right is addressed by the court's opinion.
[50] One might, for example, consider how justifications arising out of familiar contact sports might relate to cultural practices.
[51] I am particularly interested in this comparison because some of my recent work has focused on free exercise exemptions. See Greenawalt 2006, 2008.

The Model Penal Code and the Religious Freedom Restoration Act 173

the circle of cultural practices, some cultural practices are not religious (or not religious enough) and many religious practices do not attach to minority cultures. If a general exemption for religious practices is warranted, as much American law now assumes, should practices of minority cultures that members take as having normative force, but are not religious (enough), be treated similarly?

We can illustrate this issue in light of a recent Supreme Court decision upholding the right of a small Brazilian religious group to import a hallucinogenic tea used in worship.[52] Suppose a cultural group had a strong non-religious tradition that that tea should be used in family celebrations. Should members have a similar right, or at least have their claims to drink the tea assessed by standards similar to those used for the religious group?

In this brief discussion, I shall omit constitutional arguments that religion must be, or may be, given a special status. And by assuming that some cultural traditions are not religious (enough), I shall disregard the rich variety of connections between cultural practices and religion, which can present formidable difficulties in determining whether a particular practice should count as a form of religious exercise.[53]

A brief amount of legal history and explication is needed to set our inquiry in context. In 1963, the Supreme Court decided that a Seventh Day Adventist could not be denied unemployment compensation because she was unwilling to work on Saturday, her Sabbath.[54] It indicated more generally that, under the Free Exercise Clause, the government could not impinge on religious practices unless it had a compelling interest that could not be accomplished by less restrictive means.[55] Using that approach the Court later held that Amish families could withdraw children from school at the age of fourteen to undertake community vocational education, despite a state law requiring schooling until the age of sixteen.[56]

For these constitutional exemption cases, the language of "compelling interest" was always a bit misleading. That language was drawn from cases involving racial discrimination and legislative measures that curtailed freedom of speech. In *those cases*, it was very difficult for the government to establish a sufficient interest. By contrast, when religious claimants sought to be free of regulations that validly applied against everyone else, the showing of interest the government needed to make was less.

In 1990, the Supreme Court withdrew this protection as a matter of constitutional right for almost all areas.[57] If a law was neutral in respect to religion

---

[52] *Gonzales v. O Centro Espírita Beneficente União do Vegetal*, 546 U.S. 418 (2006) (applying the Religious Freedom Restoration Act).
[53] For my views about "defining religion," see Greenawalt 2006: Chap. 8.
[54] *Sherbert v. Verner*, 374 U.S. 398 (1963).
[55] *Sherbert v. Verner*, 406–408.
[56] *Wisconsin v. Yoder*, 406 U.S. 205 (1972).
[57] *Employment Division v. Smith*, 494 U.S. 872 (1990).

and of general application, that was essentially the end of the inquiry.[58] Thus, no matter how important peyote was for worship services of the Native American Church, members had no right to disregard a general ban on the use of peyote.[59] Congress responded by adopting a Religious Freedom Restoration Act (RFRA), explicitly incorporating a standard meant to track the constitutional test of the unemployment compensation and Amish schooling cases.[60] The Supreme Court next declared this law invalid as it applied to states and localities,[61] but RFRA still applies to actions of the federal government. Congress has since adopted a more limited law covering land use and prisons that does apply to states.[62] A number of states have adopted their own RFRAs, and some state courts continue to apply the compelling interest standard as interpretations of their own state free exercise clauses. In sum, a standard like that in RFRA applies to a significant range of situations in American jurisdictions.

The crucial language of RFRA is this: "Government may not substantially burden a person's exercise of religion even if the burden results from a rule of general applicability...(unless) it demonstrates that application of the burden to the person (1) is in furtherance of a compelling governmental interest; and (2) is the least restrictive means of furthering that...interest."[63] Among the circumstances to which this Act, and its state analogues, could apply are criminal prosecutions of people who use proscribed drugs in worship services, who withdraw their children from school, who violate humane slaughter laws, or who refuse to serve on juries. Obviously this language will not help people who commit intentional homicides or inflict serious physical harm; the government has a compelling interest in preventing that behavior.

RFRA and its analogues already protect those traditional practices of cultural minorities that are themselves religious. Should the Act be extended to reach non-religious minority cultural practices, so that the government may not "substantially burden a person's exercise of practices within a minority cultural tradition of which he is a part" unless it satisfies the (weak version of the) compelling interest test?

An argument in favor of this result is that such a right would go some distance towards recognizing equality among cultural traditions and would properly accommodate minority traditions when that could be done without serious cost to the general society. But there are some obvious difficulties. Exactly what would count as a minority culture? How attached would a person have to be to the minority culture in which he was raised? Insofar as the law

[58] *Employment Division* v. *Smith*, 879–882.
[59] *Employment Division* v. *Smith*, 890.
[60] Religious Freedom Restoration Act, 42 U.S.C. §2000bb.
[61] *City of Boerne v. Flores*, 521 U.S. 507 (1997).
[62] Religious Land Use and Institutional Person Act of 2000, 42 U.S.C. § §2000cc-§ §2000cc-5.
[63] Religious Freedom Restoration Act, 42 U.S.C. §2000bb-1 (a)–(b).

is trying to shift people away from cultural practices that do not fit well with the majority culture, should it have to rest on "a compelling interest," even a watered down compelling interest?

Another objection, often made as to *any* general cultural defense, could be raised here. The government should be protecting members of the minority culture, especially women, who are being treated unfairly *and* who may want protections they do not get within that culture. In response to this objection, it may be said that the government will have a compelling interest in protecting such victims. Thus whatever *excuses* their oppressors might have, a kind of RFRA extended to cultural practices would not give rights to oppress women and children. This response is adequate for most circumstances in which women and children might be victims, but it does not quite answer every situation. Most courts have supposed that religious organizations have a right to discriminate by gender in choosing their leaders. Would one wish to confer such a privilege on non-religious organizations of traditional cultural groups? That seems debatable.[64]

Extension of federal and state RFRAs to cover non-religious minority cultural practices would have relatively little practical effect in respect to criminal prohibitions. That is, it would not privilege many activities that are now made criminal. Its symbolic effect might be welcomed or not, depending on one's overall views about multiculturalism. And perhaps its main practical significance would be in areas of law other than criminal law.

My "on balance" view at this point is that such an extension would not be a good idea, but I believe the comparison with religious claims, and also with non-religious claims of conscience (protected by some laws), is one fruitful perspective for thought about justifying acts based on cultural practices.[65]

CONCLUSION

We have seen that how cultural traditions and practices should figure in criminal law defenses is a complex inquiry. One can make an argument for creating a general privilege to rely on the norms of minority cultures if that does not impair significant state interests, an analogue to the treatment of religion in a number of American jurisdictions. And one can make an argument for a general defense that could eliminate or reduce liability for acts that are not actually privileged. Just how persuasive this latter argument is depends on a

---

[64] Under present First Amendment law regarding freedom of association, an expressive association would have a plausible constitutional argument that such discrimination is protected.

[65] For such thought, personality disorders and parental abuse are inapposite comparisons, since no one believes such factors should actually underlie privileges to act.

number of factors: how crimes are defined; ordinary standards of culpability, excuse, and justification; a feasible assignment of roles to judges and juries; and the potentiality to expand existing defenses by particular references to cultural practices.

My own assessment is that a general privilege for cultural practice along the lines of the Religious Freedom Restoration Act would not be desirable, and that, at least in jurisdictions whose criminal law resembles that of the Model Penal Code, clarification and expansion of existing defenses that allow culture to be taken into account is a more promising strategy than the creation of a general cultural defense. Unlike a general cultural defense, such a strategy does not encourage (to the same degree) defenses based on cultural traditions sharply opposed to the values of the dominant society; it does not require judges to draw somewhat arbitrary lines between cultural factors that count and those that do not; and it does not entail all the problems of evidence and stereotyping involved in establishing what is an accurate portrayal of minority cultural practices and a defendant's attachment to those practices.[66]

REFERENCES

Greenawalt, Kent. 1984. "The Perplexing Borders of Justification and Excuse," *Columbia Law Review* 84/8: 1897–1927.

Greenawalt, Kent. 1987. *Conflicts of Law and Morality* (New York: Oxford University Press).

Greenawalt, Kent. 2006. *Religion and the Constitution: Volume 1: Fairness and Free Exercise* (Princeton: Princeton University Press).

Greenawalt, Kent. 2008. *Religion and the Constitution: Volume 2: Establishment and Fairness* (Princeton: Princeton University Press).

Renteln, Alison Dundes. 2004. *The Cultural Defense* (New York: Oxford University Press).

Scheffler, Samuel. 2007. "Immigration and the Significance of Culture," *Philosophy and Public Affairs* 35/2: 93–125.

---

[66] Of course, these drawbacks *are* present if the addition to a specific existing defense, such as ignorance of law, itself makes reference to minority cultural traditions. But then the drawbacks are contained to limited defenses as opposed to the sweeping coverage of a general cultural defense.

9

What Do We Have to Fear from the Cultural Defense?

Alison Dundes Renteln

INTRODUCTION: SCOPE OF THE CULTURAL DEFENSE

When individuals move across borders, they sometimes discover that established traditions from their countries of origin are not accepted in their new homeland. When charged with criminal offenses, defendants may seek to raise a cultural defense to explain what motivated their conduct. The cultural defense is a defense employed by individuals who claim that their cultural background predisposed them to commit certain actions, actions which apparently violate the law of the new country. It ensures that cultural evidence is considered in a case; it does not guarantee that the evidence influences its disposition. The defense can serve as a partial or complete excuse, or it can be rejected altogether. Judges often allow the consideration of cultural factors, either openly or surreptitiously, even though no legal system has adopted the cultural defense as an official policy.[1]

Although the phrase "cultural defense" is usually taken to refer to the role of culture in criminal proceedings, I construe the term much more broadly to encompass civil litigation as well (Renteln 2004a: 7). Courts have considered cultural factors in such matters as unauthorized autopsies, employment discrimination lawsuits challenging dress codes, civil rights suits stemming from illegal police searches, and constitutional litigation alleging ineffective assistance of counsel (Renteln 2001, 2004b). In these varied circumstances, the use of cultural evidence can result in granting an individual or group an exemption from a statute or it can be introduced to help courts assess the proper

---

[1] For consideration of the cultural defense in various countries, see, e.g., Bronitt and Amirthalaingam 1996; Foblets and Renteln 2009; Tomer-Fishman 2010.

size of damage awards (Renteln 2010). By the term "cultural defense" I have in mind every place that culture intersects the legal system; this includes legislative responses to cultural practices as well.[2] Although the primary emphasis of this analysis is on the role of culture in the courtroom, some discussion of its broader scope in public policy is also given.

As scholars and policy-makers have become aware of these phenomena, they have increasingly questioned the legitimacy of the cultural defense and the admissibility of cultural evidence in legal proceedings. To respond to some of these concerns, I begin by presenting the main principles supporting the adoption of the cultural defense. After a brief consideration of the principles, which I have treated at length elsewhere, I discuss the various objections raised by opponents of the cultural defense. For the most part I focus on the most commonly mentioned rationale for rejecting the cultural defense, which is the anarchy argument: if individuals can decide for themselves with which laws they will comply, this will lead to the demise of social order. Because many critics fear that the defense will have adverse consequences, in this essay I concentrate on their assertion that the cultural defense will have deleterious social effects. I discuss the impact of some of the most highly publicized culture conflicts that led to court cases and other requests for legal accommodation to see whether the worries of critics are justified to any degree. I consider cases falling under three categories of harm: minimal, contested or indeterminate, and irreparable harm. After scrutinizing the social effects of specific cases, I show why the rejection of the cultural defense policy on the basis of consequentialist arguments is unwarranted, given existing empirical data. Finally, I conclude with a normative argument: even if one were to concede that the defense will have some negative effects, fundamental principles of justice necessitate the use of the cultural defense.

ARGUMENTS FOR AND AGAINST THE CULTURAL DEFENSE

Justifications for the cultural defense include general principles of law, international human rights standards, and retributivist theory. Fundamental due process guarantees certainly support the policy. Foremost among these is the basic right to a fair trial (Robinson 2009). If defendants are prevented from presenting evidence that explains the motivation for their actions, the court

---

[2] Legislatures may decide to exempt customs from general statutes or to forbid a tradition. In this book contributors have tended to separate the question of criminalization of customs from the issue of whether those prosecuted for following traditions that violate the law may invoke cultural defenses in court. As this essay shows, I see these two matters as interconnected.

will be unable to reach a just verdict in their cases. Whereas the facts in ordinary trials will be relatively clear to a judge and jury, if the facts involve an unknown or bizarre custom, the court will not comprehend what transpired in a given case without the benefit of cultural evidence. Sometimes the question is whether the conduct is consistent with the reasonable person standard, and the case requires that the court recognize an alternate notion of reasonableness. In such cases, the exclusion of information as irrelevant arguably violates the principle of equal protection of the laws.

One aspect of due process is fair notice, i.e., that a person has been informed in advance of what actions constitute violations of the law, so that he has a chance to make his behavior conform to the law. In many cases, for example, dog eating and coining, individuals are entirely unaware that their conduct is deemed criminal. To punish them under these circumstances violates the fair notice requirement of due process.

Criminal defendants are also entitled to the right to counsel which is designed to ensure that they have a fair trial. In cultural defense cases this may mean that attorneys must present cultural evidence so that the defendants' actions will not be misunderstood. There is some basis in the United States for arguing that the failure of defense counsel to present cultural evidence constitutes a violation of the Sixth Amendment right to effective assistance of counsel.[3] Furthermore, it may be incumbent upon the government to pay for expert witnesses who can assist with the presentation of a cultural defense, if courts extend the precedent requiring subsidizing experts for defendants raising the insanity defense.[4]

The right to religious liberty, protected in both domestic and international law, should also authorize defendants to explain their religious customs to courts. Although the right to the free exercise of religion has been interpreted in US constitutional law to protect beliefs absolutely but not, for the most part, religiously motivated actions, it should be construed to allow a defendant to raise a religious defense. Courts have, indeed, ruled that it is a reversible error to exclude information relevant to such a defense.[5]

The jurisprudence of international human rights tribunals and committees requires state recognition of religious claims in some circumstances. Article 18 of the International Covenant on Civil and Political Rights (ICCPR) guarantees the right to religious liberty, including both beliefs and manifestations of belief. International human rights law also expressly protects cultural rights. The right to culture is explicitly guaranteed in Article 27 of the ICCPR, a treaty ratified by virtually all countries. Article 27 has no restrictions clause

---

[3] *Kwai Fan Mak* v. *Blodgett*, 754 F.Supp. 1490 (W.D.Wash. 1991); 970 F.2d 614 (1992). cert. denied 507 U.S. 951 (1993).
[4] *Ake* v. *Oklahoma*, 470 U.S. 68 (1985).
[5] *U.S.* v. *Bauer*, 84 F.3d 1549 (9th Cir. 1996).

subjecting the exercise of the right to limitations, and only one state entered a reservation to it. It is my view that the right to culture should, at the very least, be construed to allow individuals to present information concerning their cultural background in a court of law (Renteln 2002). The international community considers the right to culture a powerful norm that clearly imposes duties on states. In an interpretation of the scope of state obligations to guarantee the right to culture, the Human Rights Committee concluded that states have an affirmative duty to take steps ensuring the protection of this right (Human Rights Committee 1994). Despite assertions to the contrary, it is not simply an obligation of non-interference.

As I have argued elsewhere (Renteln 1993), the philosophical justification for the cultural defense is derived from the retributivist notion of proportional justice. In short, a defendant should be punished as much as he or she deserves, which may depend upon the particular context. Cultural evidence sheds light on relevant factors that may influence a judgment about culpability. Hence where individualized justice is a goal of a criminal justice system, the cultural defense is compatible with and furthers that objective. The cultural defense helps judges impose condign punishment.

Even though all of the above arguments support the adoption of a cultural defense and there is no particular reason why one should have to choose among them, one might, nevertheless, ask which one provides the strongest basis for justifying the use of the cultural defense. As the notion of the right to a fair trial is more widely known than the right to culture as a human right, it is possible that this due process argument will appear to be the more compelling rationale for the official adoption of a cultural defense policy. During the sentencing phase of trials, there is an expectation that attorneys will present mitigating factors of all sorts, which could easily include cultural motivations. Allowing for the consideration of contextual information for the purposes of arriving at an appropriate sentence may strike theorists as more intuitively appealing than invoking an abstract right to culture guaranteed in international human rights law.

Although the due process approach may be more familiar in some quarters, the right to culture is arguably a powerful principle that reinforces the contention that context matters for the evaluation of particular acts. Insofar as states take seriously their obligation to fulfill the right to culture required by Article 27 of the ICCPR, there is a compelling argument for the judicial consideration of cultural evidence necessary for the foundation of cultural defense claims in the courtroom.

Moreover, as I construe the cultural defense more broadly to include legislative in addition to judicial accommodation, the right to culture serves to remind states of their obligations to the international community. The fundamental question is whether the state can legitimately deny an ethnic minority group the right to follow traditions central to their way of life or whether the prohibition infringes upon their right to culture. The existence of such a right can help ensure that the rights of immigrants and ethnic minorities are respected.

Still, when defendants follow traditions that were either not anticipated by legislatures or were forbidden by statute, they will raise cultural defenses. It is inevitable that judges will have to evaluate cultural practices in courts. To ensure that officers of the court have all the information necessary to meet the requirements of the right to fair trial, principles of due process as well as religious and cultural rights arguments provide compelling justifications for cultural accommodation in the courtroom. While the right to a fair trial is much narrower in scope than the more all-encompassing right to culture, both apply to the case of the newly arrived who find themselves in trouble with the law when they follow their cultural traditions in their new homeland.

Objections

Those opposed to the cultural defense usually put forward a few main objections. They claim that the defense "essentializes" culture by treating "culture" as if it were static and monolithic. Another criticism is that the defense reinforces negative stereotypes of ethnic groups that may encourage prejudice and discrimination. In addition, there is concern that defendants and their attorneys will concoct false claims, and that the fraud will go undetected. Critics also worry that the successful use of the cultural defense will undermine the rights of women, children, and members of other vulnerable groups.[6] Yet another objection is that courts should leave policy-making to legislative bodies because democratic theory deems them more legitimate in this role. The strongest objection of all is that the cultural defense will lead to anarchy. Opponents maintain that there should be one law applicable to all (*E pluribus unum*), and immigrants must make their behavior conform to that law (this is in accordance with the adage "When in Rome, do as the Romans do"). If each person can decide which laws he will follow, this will undermine social order. This criticism relies on a logic that I have called "the monocultural paradigm" (Renteln 2010). After responding briefly to the various objections, I will focus on the anarchy argument, as it is the most commonly articulated reason given for rejecting the cultural defense.

Let us begin with the claim that in cultural defense cases litigants will present a tradition as though it never changes and is followed by all members of a group.[7] Although it is possible that lawyers or even expert witnesses may

---

[6] See the chapter by Lacey for discussion of this argument. For an analytic essay about the tensions between rights, see Evans-Pritchard and Renteln 1994.

[7] Critics also insist that the cultural defense be justified with an abstract definition of "culture." This is unfair and unnecessary. One can easily answer the question of whether a particular culinary dish was historically eaten or whether Sikhs traditionally wore kirpans without having

misrepresent customs in these ways, this type of cultural claim clearly involves distortion. And while one should guard against false representations of traditions, this is not a reason for rejecting the defense altogether, but rather one for establishing proper safeguards.

Likewise, it is obviously undesirable if highly publicized cultural defense cases reinforce pernicious stereotypes, and this should be avoided as much as possible. Rather than limiting the use of a legal strategy in court, however, it would be preferable to encourage lawyers and journalists to behave responsibly, adhering to standards of professional ethics. One must also recognize that stereotypes persist irrespective of litigation and media coverage of it.

There is also the worry that defendants will use deception to avail themselves of a cultural defense by masquerading as a member of a group, fabricating a custom, or pretending that their action was motivated by an actual custom when it was not. These are legitimate concerns, which can be addressed by means of the cultural defense test I have proposed. According to the cultural defense test, judges should ask:

1. Is the litigant a member of the ethnic group?
2. Does the group have such a tradition?
3. Was the litigant influenced by the tradition when he or she acted?

(Renteln 2004: 207)

If courts apply this test carefully, it should prevent much of the sort of abuse about which critics are concerned (Renteln 2006).

The argument that allowing cultural defenses will violate the rights of women and children presumes that the presentation of cultural evidence in the courtroom will necessarily affect the disposition of cases. One should recall that the defense only ensures that the evidence is treated as admissible but does not guarantee that it will influence the outcome in any case. However, it is possible that the information might lead to the imposition of a lighter sentence. The question then is whether this mitigation constitutes a violation of the human rights of women[8] and children in cultural communities by denying them equal justice. The claim seems to assume that all defendants who commit the same crimes should receive the same punishment, and if they do not, that this violates the rights of victims. This is a fallacy insofar as a legal system strives to mete out punishment compatible with the notion of individualized justice. As a result of this aspiration to take contextual factors into account, the sentences of defendants whose offenses are similar are likely to differ. Unless

---

a grand theory of culture. While scholars may enjoy a spirited debate about parameters of "a culture," resolving this matter is unnecessary for those raising a cultural defense tied to one specific custom in the context of a court case.

[8] It is also worth noting that women benefit the cultural defense in some cases, e.g., Fumiko Kimura and Helen Wu.

judges are required to impose exact penalties based on a mandatory sentencing scheme, sentences will vary in ordinary cases as well as in cases involving cultural defenses. As mentioned above, this outcome is consistent with the goal of achieving individualized justice. The fact that some defendants may experience mitigation of their sentences does not violate the rights of victims because most criminal justice systems do not guarantee particular results in specific criminal cases. Even under statutory schemes that stipulate mandatory minimum sentences, sentencing varies somewhat depending on the circumstances. The claim that the consideration of culture is incompatible with the notion of legal equality because defendants receive differing punishments is misconceived.

The notion that the cultural defense is less justifiable in cases involving irreparable harm has merit but should not defeat the claim that individuals are entitled to raise a cultural defense.[9] In my view, societies should certainly strive to abolish traditions like honor killings that cause irreparable harm.[10] If, despite these efforts, individuals kill someone and claim to have been motivated by honor or other cultural considerations, I would still allow the defendants to present evidence related to their cultural background, even though I believe defendants should receive full punishment in these cases. To reiterate, the cultural defense opens the door to the consideration of cultural evidence, but it does not require that the information affect the verdict. How much weight, if any, cultural factors should be given, is a separate question, which must be decided on a case-by-case basis.

One might think that this sort of case-by-case analysis is best carried out by legislatures. Why not let them decide which customs involve irreparable harm, enact legislation prohibiting those, and thereby deter future misconduct? The legislative question is an intricate one. According to democratic theory, it is preferable for legislatures to set policy because legislators represent the will of the majority. Moreover, legislatures can solve a problem for the entire community whereas a court generally settles the matter only for the immediate parties (unless the decision has precedential effect). When legislatures preemptively review customs likely to clash with state law in order to criminalize those deemed unacceptably harmful, this theoretically should avoid unnecessary litigation and obviate the need for prosecutions involving

---

[9] Lacey notes that the harm principle is subject to differing interpretations and may well be incapable of resolving all of the questions as to when traditions should be allowed. Of course, judging what counts as a harm is itself culturally biased.

[10] I agree with Michelle Moody-Adams (in oral comments at the Workshop on Criminal Law and Cultural Diversity) when she argues that members of one culture should criticize practices in another culture, particularly customs like honor killing that are based on a worldview tied to the maintenance of the honor of the family or group. Irreparable harm obviously includes the loss of life. For an argument that a relativistic perspective does not preclude moral criticism, see Renteln 1988.

the cultural defense. Consequently, those advocating culturally sensitive policies sometimes contend that we should defer to legislatures to draw the line between acceptable and unacceptable traditions. Although it is true that, in the best of all possible worlds, all laws would be equally fair, this is not, in fact, the case. Even though legislatures may prove capable of settling some cultural conflicts, it is not feasible to delegate decision-making about all cultural traditions to legislative bodies.

There are several reasons why we ought to be concerned about delegating this sort of judgment to legislative processes. Legislators who seek reelection may be disinclined to pass laws that protect the rights of minorities, if the policies risk antagonizing the majority of constituents in their districts.[11] Judges, at least those with life tenure, who need not be concerned about the electoral consequences of their decisions, are in a position to do what justice requires. Given the degree to which judges are insulated (at least theoretically) from majoritarian political pressures, it is simply more likely that the judiciary will act to protect the rights of ethnic minorities. Second, legislators are known to enact laws in the midst of controversy, and acting under such circumstances is frequently a recipe for disaster. As a result, the policies adopted may not be based on sufficient empirical investigation. They may simply represent a form of symbolic politics designed to appease enraged citizens. Third, there will always be new types of customs that were not anticipated, and this may occur more frequently as travel across the globe becomes easier and more economical. For these reasons and others, it makes sense to have decisions about the scope of the right to follow cultural traditions made in courts.[12] Fourth, even if legislators successfully enact legislation targeting a custom, its enforcement may be problematic. For example, when France passed a law forbidding conspicuous religious symbols, it was primarily applied to Muslim girls wearing headscarves. There can be selective enforcement of well-crafted legislation that arguably constitutes discrimination.

To sum up, with respect to this objection, in many cases legislatures can enact laws correcting existing biases, but oftentimes they are motivated for political reasons not to do so. In these circumstances the courts must be allowed to adjudicate contentious cultural claims.

We turn finally to the important question of whether a cultural defense policy will imperil the social order. To what extent, if at all, is the anarchy argument valid? The purpose of the rest of this essay is to respond to the contention that the cultural defense will perpetuate criminal activities. Philosophers often

---

[11] Jeremy Waldron, at the "Columbia workshop", alluded to this when he said the capitalist who fails to win the debate on welfare policy cannot expect to receive an exemption. The reality is the minority is unlikely ever to win a majoritarian debate on public policy.

[12] Ordinarily individuals can follow their traditions without difficulty. It is only when governments prevent them from doing so that they must invoke their right to culture.

argue this point in the abstract without considering whether their views are consonant with reality. In what follows I take up various customs that involve differing degrees of harm to see what transpired after the cultural conflict came to public attention. We will see examples in which legislatures have both succeeded and failed to protect the rights of cultural minorities. The central question is whether institutional mechanisms accommodated the cultural tradition, and if so, whether this led to social upheaval. Rather than presuming that legal regimes that entertain cultural defenses will endanger their citizenry and social order, we will investigate to see what actually occurred. After presenting evidence from actual cases, I return at the end to a discussion of the risks versus the benefits of a cultural defense.

CONSEQUENCES OF CULTURE CONFLICT CASES

Minimal Harm

Peking Duck

When a particular tradition seems to pose a risk, it is necessary to distinguish among the potential dangers it represents. It may not be obvious prima facie whether the custom is innocuous or harmful. In a number of cases the question was whether health inspectors were justified when they threatened to sanction restaurants for failure to comply with health and safety codes (Yi 2000). For instance, in the 1970s there was a public health concern about the traditional Chinese delicacy known as Peking duck (Berquist 1982). The ducks were often on display, hanging in the front windows of Chinese restaurants, where they were not kept at the temperatures (either high enough or low enough to avoid the growth of bacteria) required by California state law. Although enforcement of the provisions had been ignored for quite some time, at a certain juncture health inspectors inexplicably sought to close restaurants which refused to stop serving this dish. This occurred despite the fact that there had been no documented illnesses from consuming Peking style duck in the United States or China, even though it had been eaten for centuries.

As the controversy was raging, California State Senator Art Torres asked his legislative aide, Michael Woo, to drive a Peking duck to a laboratory in Northern California at the University of California, Davis for testing. The laboratory, after evaluating the duck, found no evidence whatsoever of any contamination or health hazard. Subsequently, Senator Torres decided to sponsor legislation to create an exemption in the health statute for the Peking duck.

The California legislature subsequently passed the bill, and then Governor Jerry Brown signed it (Erickson 1983). There have been no reported public health problems related to the Peking duck since that time.[13] Here, the legal accommodation of a cultural difference was accomplished without any dire social consequences.

Korean Rice Cakes

Another example of a culinary practice that led to conflict with the law was the consumption of traditional Korean rice cakes. Just as Peking style duck initially appeared risky, Korean rice cakes, if not refrigerated, were likewise presumed to endanger the health of those who consumed them (Kang 2001; Pierson and Tran 2006). When inspectors attempted to sanction Korean American bakeries, Assemblywoman Carol Liu sponsored legislation to create exemptions for these establishments from the pertinent health code provisions to protect them from onerous regulations. Instead of banning the sale of unrefrigerated rice cakes, the law required that they be stamped with a date and be sold within 24 hours, and that they should contain no animal products (Rizo 2001b). As there was no documented case of anyone ever becoming ill after eating the traditional rice cakes, the legislature acquiesced and the governor signed the law (Rizo 2001a; Morrison 2002).[14] Once again the consideration of empirical public health data influenced the decision not to act on what proved to be a false alarm.

These two examples of ethnic foodways that clashed with American health law demonstrate that the American political system is capable of assessing potential risks posed by diverse culinary dishes. In both instances the legislature easily accepted the notion that alternate ways of preparing food could be safe, and decided to authorize exceptions to policy in the form of statutory exemptions. Despite initial fears about food poisoning, empirical investigation confirmed that the culinary practices were, in fact, altogether safe.[15]

---

[13] Enforcement of the health code arguably still reflects cultural bias, and newspaper reports suggest ethnic minorities may disregard the inspectors' lower ratings (Pierson 2005). Another dispute involved the sale of freshly killed chickens because of the alleged odor and traffic congestion caused by the sales, especially during holidays (Knoll 2012).

[14] Letters supporting the law came from the President of the Korean Rice Cake Association and the President of the Korean Wrestling Association. Even the Consul General of the Republic of Korea, Jung-Kyung Sung wrote letter to Governor Gray Davis in support of Assemblywoman Liu's bill, explaining the importance of fresh Korean rice cakes. The only letter in opposition came from the California Association of Environmental Health Administrators, though the organization never officially went on record as being opposed.

[15] The success in obtaining exemptions for Peking duck and Korean rice cakes has inspired others to request additional exemptions. See Pierson and Tran 2006.

Dog Eating

Legally authorizing different ways of eating is not always accomplished with such ease, however. One notorious cultural defense case centered on the eating of a dog. In the city of Long Beach, two Cambodian immigrants, Sokheng Chea and Seng Ou, were arrested after they killed a German shepherd puppy that they had received as a gift in order to cook and eat it. Neighbors, disturbed by the yelping of the dog, called the police. After they were arrested, prosecutors discovered that it was impossible to prosecute the men for killing or eating a dog, as there were no laws on the books prohibiting either action. The district attorney decided instead to prosecute them for killing the dog in a cruel or inhumane manner (Haldane 1989a). However, the judge ultimately concluded that there was no evidence that the manner in which they killed their dog differed significantly from the manner in which slaughterhouses kill animals, and so he dismissed the case (Bishop 1989; Haldane 1989b).

In the aftermath of this controversy, many were distraught that there was no law that prohibited the eating of dogs, because Americans often consider them to be part of their families. Even though the Cambodians' actions violated no law, they were nonetheless perceived as outlaws. There was concern that because of this perception Americans would mistakenly draw the conclusion that many Cambodian or even Asian American immigrants were eating dogs. As a consequence, the Cambodian Association of America lobbied for the enactment of the "Pet Law" which prohibited the eating of pets which included dogs and cats.[16] The Association approached Assemblywomen Jackie Speier who agreed to sponsor the "Pet Law" bill, and the proposed law immediately became controversial (Abrams 1989). Evidently the Vietnamese American community thought the bill targeted their community and successfully lobbied their representatives to remove the reference to dogs and cats. Ultimately the bill passed and was signed into law by Governor Deukmejian. The new law clearly prohibited the eating of pets but did not define which animals constitute pets. To date there has been no litigation to clarify the scope of the legislation, and this matter remains unresolved. Despite the best efforts of the California legislature, litigation will be necessary to determine the proper interpretation of the law.

The perception of the dog as man's faithful companion apparently influenced legislation to ban the eating of an animal that was traditionally eaten elsewhere. The willingness of the legislature to authorize or ban particular dietary practices may hinge on the perceived effect of the consumption of that item on the dominant culture. That is, whether Chinese Americans eat Peking

---

[16] The Cambodian Association denied that Cambodians eat dogs perhaps because the defendants received death threats. Published scholarship suggests that the eating of dogs occurred in Cambodia but possibly because of necessity (Haldane 1989a). In addition, some members of the Vietnamese community also denied that the dietary custom ever existed (Lam 1989).

duck or Korean Americans consume rice cakes has little effect on the rest of the society. But the question of whether anyone might eat a dog, which is not considered food by the majority, was a highly sensitive question. Indeed, an urban legend was circulating that Asian Americans stole dogs to eat them.[17]

Let us consider how these examples relate to the general question of whether cultural defenses are justifiable. The argument hinges on whether or not the consumption of the delicacy can be considered an irreparable harm. But how can one decide whether the consumption of a particular food is a harm? If ingesting it leads to food poisoning, then that might well be a harm, a potentially fatal one. Even though health inspectors expressed concern about the dangers of eating Peking duck and rice cakes, it turned out there was, in fact, no cause for alarm. Because there was a willingness in these instances to evaluate empirical data, it was feasible to ascertain whether or not there was an actual risk, and there was none. Consequently legislatures were able to exempt these foods from the codes. If other types of dishes do pose an actual threat to the public health, one that can be empirically demonstrated, then there would be a basis for prohibiting the consumption of them.

The question of whether eating dogs counts as a harm is more difficult to determine. Although consuming dog flesh properly cooked would not be problematic from a physical standpoint as there is no evidence this results in food poisoning, consuming dogs for food is emotionally traumatic for many Americans; thus, it is a harm from a psychological perspective. It is conceivable that for someone unaccustomed to eating dogs, this would be so traumatic as to result in permanent psychic injury. However, the Cambodians in the Long Beach case were not insisting that everyone eat dogs; they were simply having their own supper. Whether Americans opposed to the eating of dogs would experience irreparable psychological harm simply from the knowledge that other people are eating dogs is unknown. Because canine Americans have a peculiar status as "pets" in American social life, a status it is worth noting that they do not hold in all other societies, the prospect of the Cambodians' eating dogs evoked an extraordinarily strong emotional response. This raises the question of whether legislatures should prevent people from eating particular animals only because other people are uncomfortable with the idea of it. There is a serious question as to whether it is justifiable to ban a food because it bothers the majority which is unfamiliar with that cuisine.[18]

---

[17] Evidently anti-Asian sentiment has sometimes manifested itself in the form of this urban legend (Cho 1991). According to interviews with police officers who had been in Long Beach for over fifteen years, there had not been another similar case (Sing 2008). This is mentioned in the documentary about the case—"Animal Appetites" by Michael Cho (1991).

[18] The controversy over shark fin soup illustrates this type of controversy. Conservationists allege that the killing of millions of sharks poses a serious threat to the ocean ecosystem; some Chinese Americans contend that this is a form of cultural discrimination (Ni 2011; Brown 2011; Barboza 2011). There was a division within the community over this issue and some, e.g., Paul Fong, openly rejected the tradition as "unhealthy" (Roosevelt 2011).

The passage of the Pet Law bill was obviously motivated by the controversy surrounding the prosecution of the two Cambodian immigrants. As has often been pointed out, it is unwise to pass a new law as a form of symbolic politics in the heat of the moment, without adequately considering the consequences of its adoption. Because the vagaries of the Pet Law, particularly the failure to include a definition of which animals constitute pets, left open questions such as whether individuals who keep chickens, rabbits, pigs, or calves as pets can eventually eat them, adjudication is likely to be necessary to answer them.[19]

Even if it were clear that the law definitely applies to dogs, since there is no text specifying that interpretation in the California law, there would be a further difficulty. It is possible that an immigrant, newly arrived in California, entirely unaware of the existence of the law, might decide to eat a dog and then to his surprise have to face the consequences. When prosecuted under the new law, would he be entitled to raise a cultural defense? Even though the legislature determined that the eating of pets is unacceptable, the logic of the cultural defense still requires that a defendant have the opportunity to explain to a court the motivation for his action. This means that even though legislatures may try to anticipate culture conflicts in order to solve them in advance, it is unreasonable to expect that a legislative prohibition will deter all future actions encompassed by the law. As a result, courts will have to sort out the complexities of facts to ascertain whether particular conduct is blameworthy. Although in an ideal world the legislature would solve culture conflicts and avoid unnecessary litigation, it is inevitable that some cases involving cultural clashes will wind up in court.

Kirpans

Another custom which generated a near panic is a religious symbol, the Sikh kirpan. After Sikh children have taken *amrit*, they are required by the tenets of their religion to wear the five ks one of which is the kirpan, a small ceremonial knife (Juss 1995; Bhachu 1996; Wayland 1996). Unfortunately, public schools often expel Sikh children for violating a campus policy prohibiting weapons on campus. This was the main issue in an unpublished case, *Cheema v. Thompson*,[20] litigated in Northern California on behalf of three children, and it attracted considerable media attention (Lal 1996). The American Civil Liberties Union (ACLU) of Northern California and cooperating attorney Stephen Bomse challenged the school board's interpretation on the grounds that no empirical evidence showed that a kirpan has ever been used in any act

---

[19] This is not an idle question as city dwellers are known to keep chickens and Vietnamese potbellied pigs as pets, for example (Tweti 2002).
[20] *Cheema v. Thompson* (1994) 1994 U.S. App. LEXIS 24160 (unpublished decision); *Cheema v. Thompson*, 67 F.3d 883 (1995); 1994 U.S. App. LEXIS 24160.

of violence (Bossert 1995; Deb 1996: 909). Thousands of Sikh children wear kirpans in Canada, the United States, and many countries in Europe, and not a single instance of violence had ever been reported involving a kirpan. By contrast, Bomse argued, pencils and scissors had caused numerous injuries in public schools, but no one had proposed banning those items! The Court of Appeals for the Ninth Circuit eventually ruled that the Sikh children had to be allowed to return to school wearing their kirpans, but they had to be rendered blunt or sewn or glued into the sheath. With respect to these students, the Court came up with a reasonable solution, a compromise that protected religious liberty and allayed the fears of non-Sikhs that the kirpan might be misused to harm children.

During the course of the litigation, the Sikh community approached then California State Senator President Bill Lockyer, who agreed to sponsor legislation exempting the kirpan from statutes regulating the carrying of weapons (Bjorhus 1994). Although the bill passed the Assembly and Senate unanimously, Governor Pete Wilson vetoed it. (It is possible that legislators endorsed the policy in order to appear sensitive to religious minorities because they knew that the governor would not sign the bill.) Despite California's reputation as a progressive state which formulates innovative public policies, Sikhs failed to secure uniform legal protection for an important religious symbol.

By contrast, other countries allow Sikhs to wear the kirpan. For instance, the Parliament in the United Kingdom successfully enacted a statutory exemption from relevant laws for carrying the kirpan.[21] Elsewhere the judiciary has ruled in favor of the Sikhs such as when the Canadian Supreme Court handed down the *Multani* decision (2006) vindicating the right of Sikh students to wear kirpans.[22] Despite the fact that there is worldwide understanding that the kirpan is a religious symbol that does not pose any danger, the California legislators failed to protect the religious liberty of Sikhs. Thus, it may inevitably fall to judges to entertain religious defenses when Sikhs are prosecuted for wearing required religious symbols.

In all of the cases discussed so far the cultural tradition caused no actual physical harm. Nevertheless, there were attempts to impose sanctions of various sorts on individuals. The legislatures made exceptions to health statutes for Peking duck and Korean rice cakes to protect the rights of ethnic minorities, but banned the eating of pets (by which they meant dogs). With respect to the wearing of the kirpan in California, it was a court which ultimately protected the rights of the students in a case. Although the California legislature could

---

[21] One commentator remarks: "England's experiences prove that a country concerned with public safety and the use of dangerous weapons can make a narrowly tailored exception to accommodate those who wear kirpans. Indeed, England is more safety-conscious than the United States, yet has been able to carve out an exception, without fretting over non-sensical concerns such as whether someone dressed up as a Sikh really is a Sikh" (Bhachu 1996: 218).

[22] *Multani v. Commission scolaire Marguerite-Bourgeoys*, 2006 SCC 6.

have protected the rights of the Sikhs as did the British Parliament, the failure to enact a statutory exemption underscores the need to allow courts to evaluate cultural traditions. Even with innocuous traditions, one cannot presume that members of the dominant culture will see fit to permit ethnic minority customs.

Contested or Indeterminate Harm

Khat

The practice of chewing khat is central to the social life of individuals, primarily men, in countries such as Kenya, Somalia, and Yemen (Renteln 2004: 74–76). They chew khat during conversation, as they discuss politics and other issues of importance. In societies in which khat is a significant part of their way of life, houses often have a special room designated for this purpose. Khat is chewed like tobacco, has an amphetamine-like effect sometimes compared to a double espresso, and causes a state of euphoria. Although overuse of khat can lead chewers to be in a kind of stupor, its medical effects do not appear to be well documented. If it is a dangerous substance, that is not entirely clear. It is difficult to reconcile competing interpretations of the degree of risk that khat poses that are reflected in the various policies (Anderson et al. 2007). In some countries the use of khat remains legal, even if there is some recognition of its possible negative effects. The President of Yemen, Ali Abdulah Saleh, noted its impact on worker productivity and depletion of family financial resources. He announced publicly that he would restrict his own khat chewing to the weekends and proposed lengthening the workday by an hour to discourage khat chewing.

For quite some time, the United Nations has classified khat as a dangerous substance.[23] In contrast to those countries where it is not proscribed, the United States DEA treats it as a felony offense equivalent to heroin, LSD, and other Class I Narcotics. A number of individuals are known to have been prosecuted in California, Georgia, Minnesota, and New York (Verhovek 2006; Shukovsky 2006). Immigrants are sometimes unaware that khat is considered illegal in the United States. Even when defendants are informed that khat is considered illicit in the US, some are incredulous that Americans would ban something they consider so important a part of their day-to-day existence and that, at least to them, has no clearly identifiable harm.

Although legislatures could hold hearings on the effects of khat, to my knowledge this has not occurred yet. Furthermore, even if the United States

---

[23] Although it was not widely prohibited in the early twenty-first century, European governments, in the past few years, began to consider criminalizing the use of khat.

Congress were to ban khat explicitly, it is likely that some individuals would choose to continue to chew it, as it is apparently such a significant aspect of their way of life. If these individuals were prosecuted under a law specifically forbidding khat, the defendants should, in my view, be entitled to raise cultural defenses. Without information about the social significance of khat, a court would be unable to understand its use, as Americans remain largely unfamiliar with it.[24]

As there is an expectation that the liberal democratic governments should not impose life-style choices on citizens, the case must be made for outlawing the chewing of khat.[25] For example, even though drinking alcohol certainly can cause harm, it has not been banned since Prohibition. Furthermore, if we compare the use of khat to caffeine, it becomes even more clear that a double standard is operating. Although some studies point to adverse health consequences associated with coffee, this beverage is still widely available. It is hard to imagine what would transpire were we to ban coffee in the United States, given the prevalence of coffee shops like Starbucks; sipping lattes has become a significant part of American popular culture.

Child Marriage

Another custom leading to conflict is child marriage. In Southern California it came to the attention of Orange County social workers that teenage Latina girls were living with much older men, sometimes twice their age (Lait 1996). Although this had been previously treated as statutory rape, social workers decided to encourage the girls involved to marry the men with whom they cohabited, provided their parents consented to the union. When this was reported in the *Los Angeles Times*, there was an enormous public outcry. The governor interceded (Ayres 1996), and the agency rescinded the policy (Renteln 2004: 118).

If men are prosecuted for statutory rape when they live with girls who are comparable to common-law wives and with whom they have children, it is not self-evident that prosecuting them and imprisoning them is the ideal solution. However, pressuring girls to marry may not be a suitable outcome either. Situations are likely to vary, and courts should be empowered to take cultural

---

[24] A Canadian court affirmed the absolute discharge of a woman who was caught taking 34 kilograms of khat into Canada. The attorney who argued the appeal, Mark Halfyard, noted: "This is an important ruling because it recognizes that while khat is illegal in Canada there is no empirical evidence that this drug is harmful to the individual or the community at large" (Powell 2012).

[25] At the Columbia workshop, Waldron discussed the possibility that with respect to victimless crimes, rather than enacting a statutory objection, the paternalistic law should be discarded. While this argument may have merit, until such time as the law is overturned, ethnic minorities will be forced to request statutory exemptions to enable them to follow customs which are required or important to their way of life.

considerations into account, where appropriate. If judges do consider cultural factors, it is doubtful in any event whether their decision-making will prevent future romantic relationships in their jurisdictions.

Folk Medicine

It has also been unclear to authorities how to proceed when parents use traditional forms of folk medicine to treat their ill children leaving marks that some interpret as child abuse (Chin 2005; Black 1986). This has been a difficult matter for some South Asian refugees who use a technique known as *cao gio*, or coining, to cure their children when they are afflicted with the flu, colds, and other physical ailments (Renteln 2004: 57–58; 1994). Parents put mentholated oil on the child, and then perform a massage with a coin that has a serrated edge like a quarter or a dime. This leaves a distinct pattern of bruises on the skin which is temporary and disappears in a few days. Although coining technically violates the law because child abuse is defined as the intentional infliction of physical harm (and parents have the requisite *mens rea* and commit the *actus reus*), most police officers and others familiar with the remedy realize that it really is not abuse. In essence, this is because the parents' motive is to heal their children, not to harm them.

After a publicized incident of parents being apprehended for the use of folk medicine, State Senator Pete Chacon of San Diego sponsored legislation to educate officials about cultural practices affecting children that might be misconstrued.[26] The law would have required those legally obligated to be trained to recognize certain folk remedies. The proposed bill was ultimately defeated because medical practitioners, particularly pediatricians, were afraid that faith healers would exploit the provision to escape punishment for failing to treat critically ill children (Griffin 1992). Christian Scientists use only spiritual prayer because they view illness as an illusion and a sign of sin. Using modern medicine means they do not believe in the efficacy of prayer; hence prayer and medicine are mutually exclusive. By contrast, families that use folk medicine often combine both traditional and modern techniques simultaneously. However, it is true that some parents might try the folk remedy before resorting to modern medicine. There may not be a problem if a child is not seriously ill. But if the folk medicine is not effective, trying "cosmopolitan" medicine subsequently could be too late. So, although coining is innocuous,

---

[26] The purpose of California Assembly bill 1687 "Cultural Awareness in Child Abuse Reporting" was: "…to make individuals responsible for reporting child abuse aware of cultural practices which create physical marks raising a reasonable suspicion of child abuse, but in fact are representative of non-abusive behavior." It proved to be controversial because of fear that it would lead to under-reporting of child abuse.

the proposed legislation failed because of the larger implications of carving out a statutory exemption.

Families have continued to employ folk remedies but try to avoid conflict with the law by employing techniques of circumvention. They have learned to rub the coin on the torso where the marks will not show. Fortunately for the families, police officers who are familiar with the custom generally do not apprehend parents who are genuinely trying to heal their children. Even if parents are seldom imprisoned for using folk medicine, they follow this tradition at their peril. The absence of the cultural defense leaves parents in a precarious position. As they are technically guilty of child abuse, they could be incarcerated for many years.

These examples raise the question of how to decide which customs should be treated as crimes in the legal system. If there is no obvious harm, what decision rule should be employed to determine what is a permissible practice? Whether in a legislative or judicial forum, the group rendering a decision about the cultural tradition should include representatives from the community to ensure cross-cultural understanding. Policies ought to be designed to retain some flexibility, as situations vary. Where the degree of harm associated with a custom is unclear, political institutions should proceed with caution to avoid the imposition of draconian punishments.

Irreparable Harm

We turn now to culture conflicts involving traditions that cause irreparable harm. When defendants present cultural evidence explaining the context in which they acted, the cultural defenses may generate a backlash of some sort. If so, what are their long-term societal effects?

One practice that arguably involves irreparable harm is female genital cutting. This custom, which has affected millions of girls, is defended on various cultural grounds (Crossette 1995; Obiora 1997). Although a few scholars contend that the surgery should not be construed as a harm, this argument has lost force as campaigns in many of the countries of origin have struggled to eradicate the tradition (Lane and Rubinstein 1996). From a Western perspective, the surgery is undeniably an irreparable harm for girls who, according to law, are too young to consent to the procedure. Because it is considered self-evident in North America and Europe that the tradition should be banned, it has been treated as a straightforward policy matter. Many countries have enacted laws forbidding the practice entirely (Renteln 2004: 51–53).

The problem with laws prohibiting the custom has largely been one of enforcement, i.e., persistent attempts to circumvent the policies. The statutes have effectively driven the practice underground. Families who have the means to do so are known to take their daughters back to countries where the surgery is performed and then return with them to North America or Europe. However, as government authorities have become aware of this subterfuge, they have enacted new laws criminalizing this conduct as well. A practical problem with these laws is that the girls who are the victims are often unwilling to testify against their female relatives. The degree of success of the original and supplementary laws remains to be seen. This example shows that even where there is widespread agreement as to the existence of irreparable harm, the challenge remains one of enforcement, due to ubiquitous circumvention of legislative bans.

When female relatives perform the surgery in the United States, the question is whether they should be entitled to raise a cultural defense. It is likely that many courts would be unable to understand why anyone would do such a thing unless they are provided with a cultural explanation. Yet some laws, for example, the U.S. Federal Female Genital Mutilation Prohibition Act of 1996, explicitly forbid the use of a cultural defense for defendants charged with violating the law (Renteln 2004: 53). But is it reasonable to allow a cultural defense only for those on a list of predetermined traditions? That would be like limiting the use of the insanity defense only to a limited subset of disorders. It is true that mental illnesses that are codified in the *Diagnostic and Statistical Manual* may be the basis of insanity defense. But here there is no question that FGM is a tradition; it is simply a tradition that many, both within and outside the communities, wish to eliminate.

I take the position that it is illegitimate to attempt to legislatively remove the use of a defense that is necessary to ensure fairness in the legal system. As no court has ruled on this matter, the question of whether a statute can deprive a defendant of the right to present cultural evidence in a case remains to be seen. Denying the use of the defense with respect to a custom may be deemed inconsistent with principles such as the right to a fair trial. It is important to remember that even if a defendant presents cultural evidence to explain what motivated her action, the court may decide not to mitigate the sentence. The defense simply ensures that the information concerning the cultural context is treated admissible in court.

What are the social effects of the FGM laws and prosecutions under the statutes? It stands to reason that if the laws forbidding FGM were entirely effective, there would not continue to be reports of families circumventing the laws. The deterrent effect of the statutes is uncertain (Obiora 1997: 357–360; Gunning 2002: 121–122). It is clear, however, that the question of whether or not a particular defendant is allowed to raise a cultural defense in a given case will not protect the child who was cut, as it is already too late for her. The question is whether allowing the cultural defense undermines the potential deterrent effect of the FGM laws in the future, and that is unknown at the present time. It is probable that more effective techniques exist to discourage the continuation of the practice than disallowing the use of the cultural defense in FGM trials. Educational campaigns promise to yield better results than the imposition of severe penalties.

Homicide

Other sensational cultural defense cases that involve irreparable harm are those in which jealous husbands kill their wives in response to some cultural offense. In these cases the defense attorney often advances a standard argument: as a consequence of the wife's infidelity which disgraced the family, the husband lost self-control and killed his wife. In most cases even though culture may have been taken into account, defendants usually receive full punishment. But in one case, *People* v. *Chen*, the punishment was minimal. In a bench (non-jury) trial, an expert witness presented evidence that Mr. Chen had "lost face," as infidelity is extremely shameful in Chinese culture, and that in China a social network would have intervened to prevent the husband from acting in a violent manner (Chen 2008; Coleman 2001). Influenced by the testimony, the judge imposed a sentence of only five years of probation.

The widely publicized *Chen* case generated a huge outcry. Asian American organizations described the ruling as flawed, based on outmoded stereotypes, and grossly unfair. Furthermore, there were public calls to remove the judge from the bench (Sherman 1989). Women's organizations, Asian American groups, and others condemned the decision (Bohlen 1989). They even went so far as to file a complaint with the State of New York Commission on Judicial Conduct asking for an investigation into the judge's decision. Eventually the coalition splintered because some groups disagreed with banning the consideration of cultural information in all cases (Jetter 1989).

Although by virtually all accounts the sentence was unjustifiably light, the decision did not have the drastic effect of precipitating a trend towards Chinese men killing their wives in Brooklyn or elsewhere.[27] Because of the enormous backlash against the judge's deplorable decision, it appears to have raised awareness of the plight of new immigrants, the challenges of cultural adaptation, and the reality of domestic violence in general. The *Chen* case also mobilized women's rights, civil rights, and other advocacy organizations to seek greater protection for women who are victims of domestic violence.

In another homicide case *People* v. *Wu*, Helen Wu strangled her son to death (Renteln 2004: 27). When Helen Wu realized that her boyfriend had abandoned her and had treated her son poorly, she went into a fugue state and tried to kill her son and commit suicide; she survived. When she was prosecuted for murder, she attempted to raise a cultural defense, but the judge excluded

---

[27] According to Mr. Ken Taub, head of the Homicide division of the District Attorney's office in Brooklyn, the county experienced a significant drop in the number of homicides in the 1990s (Taub 2008).

the cultural evidence as irrelevant.[28] When the California Court of Appeal reversed the lower court's ruling on the ground that it should have allowed the automatism defense, the court also said that on remand the trial court should take into consideration the evidence concerning her cultural background. When the California Supreme Court declined to review the case on appeal, it depublished the decision, which removed the appellate decision from the case reports, thereby stripping it of any precedential value.[29]

Shortly afterwards the California Center for Judicial Education and Research launched a course "Jurisprudence and Culture" as part of its Continuing Judicial Studies Program. The reaction to the decision to depublish inspired the leading judicial organization in California to create a course addressing the importance of culture in the courtroom. Throughout the 1990s this two and a half day course exposed judges to the cultural issues that arise in the courtroom.[30]

The question remains: should defendants benefit from the cultural defense if their acts involve irreparable harm? As explained above, my view is that defendants should be entitled to present evidence concerning their cultural background, even if it does not reduce the sentence. It is worth pointing out, however, that in these homicide cases some of these defendants invoked the provocation defense, a classic partial excuse which can reduce a murder charge to manslaughter. If defendants who are part of the dominant culture may benefit from the defense, why shouldn't ethnic minority defendants be able to do so as well? While it may be time to abolish the provocation defense for all criminal defendants, as long as this partial excuse is part of the criminal law, it should be available to all defendants, regardless of their cultural background. To allow provocation only on the basis of insults understood by the majority, but not those inflammatory to the minority, arguably violates equal protection.

The cultural defense simply ensures that defendants in criminal cases have the opportunity to present evidence concerning their cultural background. It is a separate question how much weight it will be given. Chai Vang, a Hmong defendant, received life in prison after he shot and killed several men in Wisconsin who allegedly shouted racial slurs at him. Clearly, juries may choose to reject the cultural defense (Baldas 2004). Despite widespread criticism of the possible use of cultural factors in the case, they ultimately did not have any effect on the disposition of the case at all.

In some of the cases we have discussed the cultural defense led to complete acquittal as in *Chen*, but in others it did not. Regardless of the outcome, there

---

[28] *People v. Wu* (1991). 235 Cal.App.3d 614, 286 Cal.Rptr 868.

[29] *People v. Wu* (Jan. 23, 1992). Order of depublication.

[30] I was the instructor for the course which I first taught with the late Alan Dundes, Professor of Anthropology and Folklore at the University of California, Berkeley, and subsequently with two judges: Philip Champlin, then Presiding Judge of Napa Superior Court and Ming Chin, Associate Justice of the California Supreme Court.

was no documented trend towards dog eating, wife-killing, or school violence. Following many of the cultural conflicts there were no reported repeated incidents at all. Although it is possible that some crimes went unreported, it suggests that the fear of critics that allowing the consideration of cultural factors in legal processes will increase the crime rate for that type of offense is not supported by the facts. We must ask how to proceed in the absence of clear empirical data. Should we permit the cultural defense or prohibit it under these circumstances?

Legitimacy

Even though there is no conclusive empirical evidence showing that specific cases allowing cultural defenses caused any harm in a given community, some argue against the cultural defense as a matter of principle. There is an underlying concern that distinguishing between individuals on the basis of the traditions they follow is somehow unfair, making the legal system appear illegitimate. The philosophical objections depend much less on specific negative consequences, and turn instead on concerns about equality under the law, legal pluralism, and fairness.

The basic idea is that taking cultural considerations into account for ethnic minority defendants constitutes unequal treatment violating the principle of equal protection. This way of interpreting equality assumes that equality means identical treatment, even though this not the only way of understanding this key principle. Recalling Ronald Dworkin's famous distinction between equal treatment and treatment as an equal, one can see that the actions of some ethnic minority defendants make no sense unless they are explained. The mental state, motivation, and conduct are in some cases incomprehensible in the absence of information about the cultural context. For instance, whereas provocation in an ordinary case of marital infidelity might be understandable to a jury, the idea that a gesture or verbal phrase could be sufficiently offensive to provoke violent action by defendants who come from another culture may not be. The testimony of an expert is needed to clarify the meaning of the particular insult in such a case. Thus, contrary to critics' claim that allowing cultural arguments violates equal protection, it is actually the failure to take cultural evidence into account that violates equal protection of the laws.

Yet another fear is the tacit assumption that acknowledging cultural differences in official courtrooms would jeopardize the foundation of the modern legal order by causing the national legal system to fracture into many separate legal systems. Critics presume that recognizing cultural factors in national institutions would necessarily result in the operation of multiple legal systems, i.e., legal pluralism. I do not address the relative merits of legal pluralism here except to say that legal pluralism is already a reality in many countries such as India and Israel.[31] Indeed,

---

[31] In the United States, for example, the American legal system includes state courts, federal courts, tribal courts, religious courts (Beth din), the courts of the Roma (the Gypsy *kris*),

a great many modern legal systems are comprised of multiple legal orders.[32] That many countries in the world operate under conditions of legal pluralism does not call into question the legitimacy of their judicial institutions.

The fear of decentralization seems to depend on the idea that multiple legal orders will undercut the authority of national institutions. Yet empirical evidence shows the falsity of that assumption. Philosophers must assess the validity of their eloquent theoretical claims in the light of factual information from the real world. While it is conceivable that the existence of legal pluralism could erode confidence in the national legal order, it is equally possible that citizens could embrace multiple legal orders simultaneously.

In the final analysis, the legitimacy of the legal system depends on its ability to safeguard the rights of citizens. Having the flexibility to provide individualized justice makes the system more legitimate and not less so. Tailoring the punishment to fit the crime in cases through use of the cultural defense may result in a reduction in punishment, but it does not necessarily lead to exoneration. Taking culture into account in a legal order is similar to considering whether a person is an adult or a minor, sane or insane, and so on. It is simply one of many attributes which may be relevant to the blameworthiness of an individual.

Legal systems have changed over time in the direction of less severity, and are, for the most part, not as repressive as they once were. For instance, the death penalty is no longer imposed for every minor infraction of the law. That the criminal law has become less punitive is a desirable change. To the extent that legal systems are capable of mitigating the full force of legal sanctions for individuals who were enculturated to follow traditions, this makes the criminal justice system more progressive and humane. By accommodating cultural traditions the system is more just, thereby achieving greater legitimacy. From the vantage-point of minorities, the system is more fair and inclusive. While the majority might object to differential treatment, there is no evidence that the capacity of legal systems to adjust punishment as appropriate renders the system less legitimate in the eyes of citizenry.

CONCLUSION

Although critics have frequently claimed that the sky would fall if the cultural defense were allowed, the examples show that despite the admission of cultural evidence in some cases, there have been no manifestly deleterious

---

and others. Moreover, state and federal courts are further subdivided by specialization, e.g., tax courts, family courts, traffic courts, and immigration courts.

[32] For a powerful analysis of legal pluralism, see Menski 2005.

societal consequences. The assertion that the defense would cause severe problems is not consistent with the evidence. Of course, as no country has officially adopted a cultural defense, it is impossible to settle this question in the abstract. Obviously society still exists despite frequent cultural conflicts. It is also impossible to measure the deterrent effect of not having a cultural defense.

In this essay I outlined the main justifications for adopting the cultural defense as an official policy and discussed the main objections to it as well. Through the consideration of selected highly publicized cases, I have argued that no apparent drastic consequences occurred following the use of a cultural defense in court. In fact, the cultural defense did not lead to the demise of civilization as we know it. Although many feared that the introduction of cultural evidence would lead to anarchy, based on our consideration of some of the most well-known cultural defense cases, there is no evidence that this has occurred. Had there been disasters caused by the cultural defense, they would have been evident.

There is a tendency among members of the dominant majority culture to fear both the ethnic minority traditions and a defense which allows their formal presentation in court. As we have seen, these fears appear to be largely irrational. Nevertheless, this anxiety about the potential societal effects has continued to influence intellectual debates. Although critics have advanced eloquent arguments suggesting possible risks associated with the cultural defense, they have not presented any evidence to substantiate their claims. As they are without the benefit of evidence indicating that widespread use of the cultural defense would affect deterrence, this surely weakens their position, i.e., arguing against the adoption of the cultural defense as public policy. Furthermore, if there are compelling principled grounds in favor of a cultural defense and no evidence indicating that cultural accommodation causes severe problems, then such accommodation should be allowed. If evidence eventually comes to light that the use of the cultural defense has a demonstrable effect on the behavior of individuals inside or outside the community following the tradition, then its validity should be reassessed at that time. If principles of law and human rights norms support the adoption of the cultural defense, it would indeed be unjust to abandon the defense on the basis of paranoid fears that lack any basis in reality.

REFERENCES

Abrams, Richard. 1989. "Ban on eating pets splits Asian-Americans," *Sacramento Bee*, November 6: A3.

Anderson, David, Susan Beckerleg, Degol Hailu, and Axel Klein. 2007. *The Khat Controversy: Stimulating the Debate on Drugs* (Oxford: Berg).

Ayres, B. Drummond Jr. 1996. "Marriage Advised in Some Youth Pregnancies," *New York Times*, September 9: A10.
Baldas, Tresa. 2004. "Culture Issues may be Raised in Killing of Six Hunters; Lawyers Debate Defense Strategy in Shootings," *National Law Journal* 26/61: 4.
Barboza, Tony. 2011. "Shark Fin Ban Clears Hurdle," *Los Angeles Times*, August 26: AA3.
Berquist, Louise M. 1982. "Peking Duck Legislation Attacked as Dangerous," *Los Angeles Times*, July 24.
Bhachu, Amarjeet S. 1996. "A Shield for Swords," *American Criminal Law Review* 34: 197–223.
Bishop, Katherine. 1989. "U.S.A.'s Culinary Rule: Hot Dogs, Yes, Dogs No," *New York Times*, October 5: A10.
Bjorhus, Jennifer. 1994. "School's Knife Ban Angers Sikhs," *San Francisco Chronicle*, August 1: A1, A12.
Black, J. A. 1986. "Misdiagnosis of Child Abuse in Ethnic Minorities," *Midwife Health Visitor & Community Nurse* 22: 48–53.
Bohlen, Celestine. 1989. "Holtzman May Appeal Probation in the Killing of a Chinese Woman," *New York Times*, April 5: B3.
Bossert, Rex. 1995. "Ceremonial Knife Is Allowed in School," *Daily Journal* 101/149: 1, 7.
Bronitt, Simon and Kumaralingam Amirthalaingam. 1996. "Cultural Blindness: Criminal Law in Multicultural Australia," *Alternative Law Journal* 21/2: 58–63.
Brown, Patricia Leigh. 2011. "Soup Without Fins? Some Californians Simmer," *New York Times*, March 6: 1, 23.
Carstens, Pieter. 2005. "The Cultural Defense in Criminal Law: South African Perspectives," *De Jure* 2: 312–330. Reprinted in Foblets and Renteln 2009.
Chen, Cher Weixia. 2008. "A Critique of 'Loss of Face' Arguments in Cultural Defense Cases," in *Multicultural Jurisprudence: Comparative Perspectives on the Cultural Defense*, ed. Marie-Claire Foblets and Alison Dundes Renteln (Oxford: Hart Publishing), 247–259.
Chin, William Y. 2005. "Blue Spots, Coining, and Cupping: How Ethnic Minority Parents can be Misreported as Child Abusers," *Journal of Law in Society* 7: 88–113.
Cho, Michael. 1991. *Animal Appetites* [documentary]. More information available at http://www.twn.org/catalog/pages/cpage.aspx?rec=790&card=price.
Coleman, Doriane Lambelet. 2001. "Culture Cloaked in Mens Rea," *South Atlantic Quarterly* 22: 981–1004.
Crossette, Barbara. 1995. "Female Genital Mutilation by Immigrants is Becoming Cause of Concern in U.S.," *New York Times*, December 10: 18.
Deb, Dipanwita. 1996. "Of Kirpans, Schools, and the Free Exercise Clause: *Cheema v. Thompson* Cuts Through RFRA's Inadequacies," *Hastings Constitutional Law Quarterly* 23: 877–919.
Erickson, Steve. 1983. "Ancient Art That's Edible," *PSA Magazine*: 90–1.
Evans-Pritchard, Deirdre and Alison Dundes Renteln. 1994. "The Interpretation and Distortion of Culture: A Hmong Marriage by Capture Case in Fresno, California," *Southern California Interdisciplinary Law Journal* 4: 1–48.

Foblets, Marie-Claire and Alison Dundes Renteln, eds. 2009. *Multicultural Jurisprudence: Comparative Perspectives on the Cultural Defense* (Oxford: Hart Publishing).

Griffin, Mary J. 1992. Letter of opposition to Assembly Member Chacon on behalf of the California Medical Association, June 9.

Gunning, Isabel. 2002. "Female Genital Surgeries: Eradication Measures at the Western Local Level-A Cautionary Tale," in *Genital Cutting and Transnational Sisterhood*, ed. Stanlie M. James and Claire C. Robertson (Urbana: University of Illinois Press).

Haldane, David. 1989a. "Culture Clash or Animal Cruelty? Two Cambodian Refugees Face Trial After Killing Dog for Food," *Los Angeles Times*, March 13: 1, 6.

Haldane, David. 1989b. "Judge Clears Cambodians Who Killed Dog for Food," *Los Angeles Times*, March 15: 1, 4.

Human Rights Committee (1994). General Comment No. 23(5). CCPR/C/21/Rev.1/Add5 (April 26).

Jetter, Alexis. 1989. "Fear is Legacy of Wife Killing in Chinatown," *Newsday*, November 26: 1.

Juss, Satvinder S. 1995. "The Constitution and Sikhs in Britain," *Brigham Young University Law Review*: 481–533.

Kang, K. Connie. 2001. "New Law is a Nod to Korean Tradition," *Los Angeles Times*, August 25: B3.

Knoll, Corina. 2012. "Poultry Plant to Remain in Rosemead," *Los Angeles, Times*, September 1: AA3.

Lait, Matt. 1996. "Agency's Role in Teen Weddings to be Reviewed," *Los Angeles Times*, September 2: A3, 18.

Lal, Vinay. 1996. "Sikh Kirpans in California Schools: The Social Construction of Symbols, Legal Pluralism, and the Politics of Diversity," *Amerasia Journal* 22: 57–89.

Lam, Andrew. 1989. "Cuisine of a Pragmatic Culture," *San Francisco Chronicle*, August 9: A17.

Lane, Sandra D. and Robert A. Rubinstein. 1996. "Judging the Other: Responding to Traditional Female Genital Surgeries," *Hasting Center Report* 26/3: 31–40.

Menski, Werner. 2005. *Comparative Law in a Global Context*, 2nd edition (Cambridge: Cambridge University Press).

Morrison, Patt. 2002. "Chef Gray Review Deli Dining, Rice Cakes," *Los Angeles Times*, November 4: B2.

Ni, Ching-Ching. 2011. "Scales of Law Tilting Against Shark Fin Soup," *Los Angeles Times*, April 2: AA7.

Obiora, L. Amede. 1997. "Bridges and Barricades: Rethinking Polemics and Intransigence in the Campaign Against Female Circumcision," *Case Western Reserve Law Review* 47: 275–378.

Pierson, David. 2005. "Where 'A' is Not on the Menu," *Los Angeles Times*, September 28: A2, 23.

Pierson, David and Mai Tran. 2006. "Can Not Too Hot, Not Too Cold Be Just Right? Legislators Want to See How Long Asian Pastries Can Safely Be Kept at Room Temperature," *Los Angeles Times*, September 1: A1, A24.

Powell, Betsy. 2012. "Woman Who Brought Khat to Canada Wins Appeal," *The Star*, April 12.

Renteln, Alison Dundes. 1988. "Relativism and the Search for Human Rights," *American Anthropologist* 90: 56–72.
Renteln, Alison Dundes. 1993. "A Justification of the Cultural Defense as Partial Excuse," *Southern California Review of Law and Women's Studies* 2: 437–526.
Renteln, Alison Dundes. 2001. "The Rights of the Dead: Autopsies and Corpse Mismanagement in Multicultural Societies," *South Atlantic Quarterly* 100/4: 1005–1027.
Renteln, Alison Dundes. 2002. "Cultural Rights," in *International Encyclopedia of Social and Behavioral Sciences*, ed. Paul Baltes and Neil Smelser (New York: Elsevier), 3116–3121.
Renteln, Alison Dundes. 2004a. *The Cultural Defense* (New York: Oxford University Press).
Renteln, Alison Dundes. 2004b. "Visual Religious Symbols and the Law," *American Behavioral Scientist* 47: 1573–1596.
Renteln, Alison Dundes. 2006. "The Use and Abuse of the Cultural Defense," *Canadian Journal of Law and Society* 20/1: 47–67.
Renteln, Alison Dundes. 2009. "The Influence of Culture on the Determination of Damages: How Cultural Relativism Affects the Analysis of Trauma," in *Legal Practice and Cultural Diversity*, ed. Ralph Grillo, Roger Ballard, Alessandro Ferrari, Andre J. Hoekema, Marcel Maussen, and Prakash Shah (Aldershot: Ashgate), 199–213.
Renteln, Alison Dundes. 2010. "The Cultural Defense: Challenging the Monocultural Paradigm," in *Cultural Diversity and Law State Responses From Around the World*, ed. Marie-Claire Foblets, Jean-François Gaudreault-Desbiens, and Alison Dundes Renteln (Brussels: Bruyant), 791–817.
Rizo, Chris. 2001a. "Culture Clash on Rice Cakes," *Daily News*, June 24: 1.
Rizo, Chris. 2001b. "Governor to Sign Bill to Protect Korean Rice Cake," *Pasadena Star News*, August 24: A1.
Robinson, Patrick Judge. 2009. "The Right to a Fair Trial in International Law, with Specific Reference to the Work of the ICTY," *Berkeley Journal of International Law Publicist* 3: 1–11.
Roosevelt, Margot. 2011. "Shark Fin Soup Debate Divides a Community," *Los Angeles Times*, June 20: AA1, AA4.
Sherman, Rorie. 1989. "Cultural Defenses Draw Fire," *The National Law Journal*, April 17: 3, 28.
Shukovsky, Paul. 2006. "14 Somalis Accused of Dealing Drug Khat, But Community Says It's a Cultural Issue," *Seattle Post-Intelligencer*, July 27.
Sing, Eric. 2008, "Personal Communication," Long Beach Police Department, Community Relations (February 17).
Taub, Ken. 2008. "Personal Communication," Chief of Homicide division, District Attorney's Office, Brooklyn, New York (February 19).
Tomer-Fishman, Tamar. 2010. " 'Cultural Defense,' 'Cultural Offense,' or No Culture At All? An Empirical Exmination of Israeli Judicial Decisions in Cultural Conflict Cirminal Cases and of the Factors Affecting Them," *Journal of Criminal Law & Criminology* 100/2: 475–522.
Tweti, Mira. 2002. "They're Pets, Not Lunch," *Los Angeles Times*, November 8: E32.

Verhovek, Sam Howe. 2006. "DEA's Khat Sting Stirs Up Somali 'Cultural Clash,'" *Los Angeles Times*, August 22: A10.

Wayland, Sarah V. 1997. "Religious Expression in Public Schools: *Kirpans* in Canada, *Hijab* in France," *Ethnic and Racial Studies* 20: 544–561.

Yi, Daniel. 2000. "Health Codes Often at Odds with Ethnic Tastes," *Los Angeles Times*, September 6: A3, A17.

Index

Abrams, Richard 187
absolute liability 56
absolutism 12
acceptable penal content 70
accidents 56
actus reus 123, 160, 193
adultery 105, 113, 196
adversarialism 124–5, 133, 148–9
affirmative action 21, 33, 35, 128 n21
Afghan culture 30, 110, 115, 160–1,
    167–8, 172
African Canadian Legal Clinic 138
age 52, 59, 65, 92
agency 3, 6, 13, 56, 58, 105, 108–11, 117, 140
aggravation 156
alcohol 84, 112, 142
Alston, Philip. 121
American Civil Liberties Union
    (ACLU) 189–90
American Indian Religious Freedom Act 2 n3
Amirthalaingam, Kumaralingam 177 n1
Amish community 173
Anderson, Benedict 44
Anderson, David 191
Anglo-American criminal law 9, 17 n1, 18,
    23, 26–8, 36, 42, 83, 125
animal protection 78 n2
    see also dog eating
answerability 11, 100–2
anthropology 4 n5, 15, 86–7
apostasy 105
Armenia 112
Ashworth, Andrew 1 n2
Asian American organisations 196
assault 17, 37, 60, 84, 94, 105, 136, 163
Association of Black Social Workers 138
attribution 54–8
attributive judgment 96
Ayres, B. Drummond Jr. 192

Baldas, Tresa 197
Banks, R. Richard. 119 n, 128
Barboza, Tony 188 n18
Barry, Brian 2, 99 n8, 127
Bartholet, Elizabeth 128
battered-woman syndrome 5
    see also domestic violence
Bayles, Michael J. 55
Beiner, Ronald 127 n15

Berger, Benjamin J. 60, 63
Berquist, Louise M. 185
Bhachu, Amarjeet S. 189, 190 n21
Bishop, Katherine 187
Bjorhus, Jennifer 190
Black, J. A. 193
Blackstone, William 62, 125
blameworthiness 2–11, 17–44, 68, 76, 82, 86,
    97, 111, 157, 199
blind justice 31
bodily harm 49, 54, 104–5, 110, 115
Bohlen, Celestine 196
Bossert, Rex 190
Braithwaite, John 23 n2
Brazilian culture 173
Brelvi, Farah Sultana 4 n6
British Columbia 138
Bronitt, Simon 177 n1
Brown, Patricia Leigh 188 n18
Buddhism 106
burden of proof 63, 123

Cambodian culture 187
Canadian legal system 114, 120–50
Cane, Peter 51
caogio (coining) 193
carelessness 28–9
casuistics 17
Catholicism 112
cause of action 124
Chacon, Pete 193
charity 42
Charter of Rights and Freedoms 146
Chayes, Abram 125
Chen, Cher Weixia 196–8
children 2, 28, 30, 32, 34, 38, 43, 82 n4, 97,
    114, 115, 116, 175, 182
    abuse 193–4
    access 123, 135–8
    adoption 123, 128 n23, 131, 135–6, 149
        transracial 128
    Child and Family Services Act
        136–7
    child-rearing practices 126
    custody 121–50
    marriage 192–3
Chin, William Y. 193
Chinese culture 30, 34, 110, 113, 196
    peking duck 185–6

Cho, Michael 188 n17
Choi, Carolyn 112
Christianity 104–5, 112, 117, 145–6
circumcision 83, 84 n6, 116
circumvention 194–5
citizenship 10–11, 68, 86, 127–8, 130
civil disobedience 79
civil rights 196
claims of culture 119–20, 1227
class perspectives 1 n1, 52, 65
coercive power 99
coffee culture 173, 191–2
Cohen, Jean L. 133
Coleman, Doriane Lambelet 4 n6, 96
collective rights 114
communism 38
communitarianism 5, 48, 50, 62, 69, 79, 87, 105
community 47–65
competition 24
Congolese case 15–18, 31, 34, 43, 164
Connolly, Anthony 4 n6
Connors, Catherine R. 4 n6
conscientious objection 8–9, 132
consequentialism 3 n4
constitutional law 69
cosmopolitanism 87
Cott, Nancy F. 127
courtroom procedures 4 n6, 119–50
crime
    definition 11
    seriousness of 11
criminal responsibility
        character conception of 55–7
Croatian culture 137
Crossette, Barbara 194
culpability principle 82
    basic standards 160–3
cultural accommodation 107–8
cultural conflict 75
cultural defense 1, 3–5
    arguments for/against 177–200
    criminal law and 104–17
    Model Penal Code and 153–76
cultural evidence 1–3, 6–12, 18, 21, 23, 33, 49, 53, 57, 63, 169–70, 177–83, 194–200
cultural identity 12
cultural imperatives 7–9
cultural information 18–21, 34, 39, 44
cultural relativism 5
cultural scripts 8–9
cultural sensitivity 68–73, 86–7
culture, definition of 3–4 n5, 181 n7
culture-blindness approach 10–12, 122, 126–9, 144
culture-demystifying approach 12, 122, 132–4, 144–8, 150

culture-override approach 12, 122, 126, 129–32, 144–5

Dan-Cohen, Meir 126
de minimis provision 38, 168
Deb, Dipanwita 190
defense
    definition 17 n1
degradation 70
deliberativeness 79
Dershowitz, Alan M. 21
desert 3–4, 6, 69
Deserted Wives and Children's Maintenance Act 144–6
deterrence 79–80, 99 n7
Dethloff, Nina 136 n36
dietary customs 185–9
diminished responsibility 157 n4, 169
doctrinal topology 81–6
dog eating 187–9
    see also animal protection
domestic violence 126 n14, 136, 166, 196
drowning 30
drugs 2, 30, 70 n1, 72, 111, 115, 169, 191–2
due diligence 56
due process 168 n45, 179
Duff, R. A. 2, 21–2, 47–8, 50–2, 55, 58, 61–3, 93–6, 100–1
duress 8–9, 82, 106, 113, 123, 165–7
Dustin, Moira 49, 63
Dutch legal system 130
duty-bound behavior 8

E pluribus unum 181
education 58, 173–4
Egyptian culture 144–5
embedded culture 7–9, 74, 89, 104, 106, 162
enculturation 9, 58, 89–95
Enlightenment era 68
equal protection principle 121, 179, 197–8
equal treatment 19, 21, 24–8, 32, 33–7, 41, 107, 112, 134, 148, 198
equality 5, 112, 128, 130
Erickson, Steve 186
Eser, Albin 38, 82
ethnicity 50
European Conference Report 116
European Court of Justice 114
Evans-Pritchard, Deirdre 181 n6
excusatory defenses 51
excuses 82–3, 168–72
exorcism 15–16

face scarring 30
fairness 53–5, 59–60, 63, 65, 198
    fair opportunity theory 54–6, 59–60, 63

family law 12, 119–50
Family Relations Act 138, 147
Farmer, Lindsay 62
Feinberg, Joel 1 n2, 22
feminism 128 n20
Finnish legal system 78n2, 83 n5, 84–5
Fish, Stanley 43
Fletcher, George 26–7, 83, 85
Foblets, Marie-Claire 4 n6, 81, 129–30, 177 n1
Fodden, Simon R. 121
Fogg-Davis, Hawley. 128
folk medicine 193–4
Fong, Paul 188 n18
foresight of relevant consequences 53
formalism 77, 148
Frazer, Elizabeth 62
Frischknecht, Tom 81–2
fundamental rights 71–2
    see also Charter of Rights and Freedoms; human rights

Gallin, Allice 112
gang culture 92, 158
Gardner, John 4 n6, 42, 55, 60n3
Garland, David 80 n3
Geertz, Clifford 3–4 n5
gender perspectives 1 n1, 32, 59, 65
    equality 2, 5 n7
    see also children; homosexuality; marriage; rape; women
genocide 108
German-inspired criminal law 18, 27–8, 42, 81, 84, 130, 136 n36
Golding, Martin P. 51
Goldstein, Taryn F. 112
Greece, classical 105
Greenawalt, Kent 12, 119 n, 128, 143, 156, 163 n18, 172 n51, 173 n53
grievous bodily harm 105, 115
Griffin, Mary J. 193
gross assault 17
Grossberg, Michael 121 n6
guilt 6 n8, 7, 17, 29, 153, 169
Gunning, Isabel 195
Günther, Klaus 76
Gusfield, Joseph A. 50

Habermas, Jürgen 10
Haitian culture 113 n7
Haldane, David. 187
Halev-Spinner, Jeff 132 n29
Hampton, Jean 23
harm principle 70, 183
    contested/indeterminate harm 191–4
    harmfulness 41–2, 91

harmlessness 41–2
irremediable harm 60
    see also bodily harm; grievous bodily harm; minimal harm
Hart, H. L. A. 54, 91 n1, 2
health policy 83
health programs 112
hermeneutics 86–7
Hirsch, Andrew von 2, 22, 70
Hmong culture 30, 33–4
Holmes, Stephen 125
Holocaust 112
homicide 54, 60, 162, 164–6, 169, 196–8
homosexuality 60, 104–5
honor killings 1 n1, 82–3, 105, 113, 116, 183
Honoré, Tony 56
Horder, Jeremy 1 n2, 35, 57, 63
Huigens, Kyron 55
human capacity 53
human rights 60, 63, 72–4, 107, 178–80, 182, 200
Human Rights Committee 180
humanity 87
humiliation 70, 108, 111, 166–7
hurtfulness 93–5
Husak, Douglas 2, 22, 62, 64, 99

ignorance of law 8–9, 167–8
immigration 20, 36, 42–3, 50, 114, 130, 147, 150, 167, 171–2, 181, 187
imperatives 29
    see also cultural imperatives
Indian Child Welfare Act (ICWA) 128 n23, 131
India
    cultural norms 147
    legal system 114, 198
individualism 67–9, 86
infidelity 30
integrity of law 73
intent 28, 82
intention 53, 160
Interethnic Placement Act (IEPA) 128n23
International Covenant on Civil and Political Rights (ICCPR) 179–80
interventionism 70–1, 84–5
intoxication 58, 123
intuition 54
Inuit culture 155
Iraqi culture 94–102
irreparable harm 194–9
Israeli legal system 198
Ivison, Duncan 70

Jacobs, James A. 86
Jakobs, Günther 23

Index

Jamaican Canadian Association 138
Japanese culture 30, 34–5, 43, 82 n4
Jareborg, Nils 84
Jetter, Alexis 196
Jewish community 78, 112
Joppke, Christan 130
Juss, Satvinder S. 189
justifications 2–3, 19, 21–2, 57, 120 n4, 153, 157, 163–5, 168, 172 n50, 176, 181

Kahan, Dan M. 55
Kang, K. Connie 186
Kant, Immanuel 18, 74
khat chewing 191–2
kidnap 30
Kimura-case 82 n4
kleptomania 90
Kluckhorn, Clyde 3 n5
Knoll, Corina 186 n13
knowledge 53, 58, 160 n8
Korean culture
   rice cakes 186
Kymlicka, Will 2, 15 n, 104 n, 119n, 50, 127 n16, 128 n20

Lacey, Linda J. 128–9
Lacey, Nicola 1 n1, 10–11, 44, 52, 55, 62, 156, 181 n6, 183 n9
laissez-faire ideology 125
   see also liberalism
Lait, Matt 192
Lal, Vinay 189
Lam, Andrew 187 n16
Lane, Sandra D. 194
Laquer-Estin, Ann. 129 n25
larceny 169–70
Lawrence, Sonia N. 119
learned behavior 4 n5
legal imputation 76
legal personhood 10, 68, 75
legal pluralism 10, 45, 53, 69, 84, 198–9
   see also moral pluralism
legal positivism 116
legitimacy 7, 11–12, 50, 53, 58–9, 61, 64, 71, 73, 75–6, 79–80, 86, 99–100, 115, 178, 198–9
Lenman, Bruce 44
Lernestedt, Claes 9–10, 21, 119 n, 127 n19, 164
lesser person argument 42–3
lex loci celebrationis 145
lex patriae 130
liberal democracy 10, 64
liberal individualism 67–9
liberalism 5, 87, 101
   see also laissez-faire ideology

luck egalitarianism 24
Lyman, John C. 4 n6

Macklem, Timothy 4 n6, 60 n3
Maguigan, Holly 4 n6
Maher, Gerry 28
majority culture 156
mala in se offenses 70–1, 81
mala prohibita offenses 70–1, 81
manslaughter 157 n4, 165–9, 197
marriage
   divorce and separation 126 n1, 128–9, 132–6
   forced 116
   marriage-by-capture 30, 33–4
   matrimonial rape 94–9, 105
   polygamy 140 n45, 145–6
   prenuptial agreements 126
   same-sex relationships 141–3, 146
   'spouse', meaning of 147–8
Marshall, S. E. 21
Matravers, Matt 11, 97 n5, 99 n7, 101
media ethics 85
medical ethics 83–5
medicine, *see* folk medicine
mens rea 51, 53–4, 59, 90, 110, 113, 123, 157, 193
Menski, Werner 199 n32
mental illness 16, 28, 58, 74, 90, 195
Mexican culture 110–11, 115, 137
Michaels, Alan C. 55
migration, *see* immigration
minimal harm 185–91
Minow, Martha L. 127
mistake of fact 8–9, 65, 123
mistake of law 83
mitigating circumstances 29
mitigation 51, 57, 59, 102, 165–72
Model Penal Code 12, 153–76
Mohawk culture 141–3
Mona, Martino 87
moral pluralism 53
moral reasons 93, 96, 98
moral values 167
morality 48, 70–1, 75, 80 n3, 82, 89–102
Morrison, Patt 186
Morse, Stephen J. 4, 92, 94
Mozart, Wolfgang A. 162 n11
Mugabe, President R. 100
multiculturalism 1, 4–5, 13, 19, 33, 70, 154, 175
   boutique 43–5
   challenges of 67–8
   multicultural theory 44
Multiethnic Placement Act (MEPA) 128 n23
murder 15–17, 85, 98, 105, 110, 124, 155, 157 n4, 165–9, 196–7

Index

Murphy, Jeffrie G. 23
Muslim culture 94–9, 105, 111, 113, 115, 117, 130, 145, 149, 184
mutual legal obligations 87
mutual recognition 76–7

Nagel, Stuart 125
Native Americans 72, 128 n23, 131, 155, 174
Nazism 101 n10, 156–7
necessity 15, 123
Neef, Marian 125
negligence 54, 82, 161–6
Netherlands, *see* Dutch legal system
neutrality 32, 44, 54, 59, 127–8
Ni, Ching-Ching 188 n18
Nigerian culture 109–10, 115, 116 n8
Nordic legal systems, *see* Finnish legal system; Swedish legal system
normal conditions of choice 58, 63
norms 49–50, 59, 64
Norrie, Alan 1 n1, 53, 60 n3, 69
Nourse, V. F. 55
nullification 156, 169–70
Nuotio, Kimmo 10–11, 28
Nuremburg trials 101 n10
Nussbaum, Martha C. 55

Obiora, L. Amede 194–5
objective requisites 28–9
objectivity 32, 54
Okin, Susan 4 n6, 5 n7
Olsen, Frances E. 133
oppression 108
ordre public 69
Orgad, Liav 130
ostracism 8
Ottoman Empire
  millet system 129
Overbeeke, Adriaan 130

Packer, Herbert 1 n2
Parekh, Bhikhu 2, 11, 22, 107 n1
Parker, Geoffrey 44
pedophilia 97, 115
penal value 24
penalty severity 11
Perry, Twila L. 128
Peršak, Nina 22
personal blameworthiness 23–9
personal particularity 40–1
personal responsibility 1 n2, 5, 12, 25, 41, 45
personal status 129–30
personhood *see* legal personhood
Pettit, Philip 23 n2
Phillips, Anne 4 n6, 49, 60, 119
Pierson, David 186
pluralism, *see* legal pluralism; moral pluralism

political philosophy 2, 13, 18, 37
polygamy, *see* marriage
polygyny 116
pornography 112
Potter, Kimberley 86
poverty 10, 52, 58–9, 61, 170
Powell, Betsy 192 n24
practical indifference 54
presuppositions 10–11, 25, 68, 75
professional ethics 182
property ownership 105
proportionality 16, 23, 85 n7
provocation 8–9, 34, 57, 60, 106, 113, 123, 167
psychological illness, *see* mental illness
public health and safety 2
putative justification 15–16

racial humiliation 108
racial identity 138–9
racism 70 n1, 86
rape 7, 30, 33–4, 48–50, 64, 94–9, 104–6, 156, 169, 192
  see also marriage: matrimonial rape
Rastafarianism 37
Rawls, John 10
reasonable person concept 27
reasonableness 16, 34, 54, 57–60, 83, 95–8, 124, 165, 179
reasons-responsiveness 91
Rechtsstaat 71
recklessness 28–9, 53, 160–6
refugees 94–102
Religious Freedom Restoration Act 12, 153–76
Renteln, Alison Dundes 4 n6, 12–13, 30, 47, 49, 60, 69, 81, 98, 99n9, 110 n2, 4, 112 n6, 116, 119n2, 169, 172, 177–8, 180, 182–3, 191–6
restorative justice 69
retribution 32
retributivism 3 n4, 23
richtiges Recht (law as Right) 83
Ricoeur, Paul 76
Ripstein, Arthur 50 n2
Rizo, Chris 186
Roach, Kent 124
Robinson, Patrick Judge 178
Rome, classical 105, 107, 181
Roosevelt, Margot 188 n18
Rubinstein, Robert A. 194

Sacks, Valerie L. 112
sado-masochism 158
Saleh, Ali Abdulah 191
Sandel, Michael J. 127 n17
Sanger, Carol 132 n29
Scanlon, T. M. 96–7

Index

Scheffler, Samuel 171–2
Schonsheck, Johathan 1 n2, 2, 70 n1
Schünemann, Bernd 79
Scott, Kenneth E. 132
Scottish culture 43
self-control, rational 8, 52, 57
self-defense 15, 34, 82, 105, 115, 123
sentencing 54, 85
Seventh Day Adventism 173
sex discrimination laws 112
sexual crime 38
　see also rape
sexual morality 48–9
Sexual Offences Act (2003) 64
Shachar, Ayelet 11–12, 127, 129–30, 149
Shanley, Mary Lyndon 127, 132 n29
Sherman, Rorie 196
Sheybani, Malek-Mithra 112
shoplifting 90
Shukovsky, Paul 191
Sikh kirpan 30, 36, 38, 113, 155, 181 n7, 189–91
Simester, A. P. 1 n2, 2, 22
Simons, Kenneth W. 55
Sing, Eric 188 n17
Sing, James J. 4 n6, 35
slavery 112
social adequateness. 37, 85
social exclusion 61
social injustice 53
social welfare rights 75
socialization 7–9, 28, 43, 123, 139
Spears, Britney 101
sport 37, 84–5, 158, 172 n50
standard-setting 25, 27–8, 42
state centrism 69
stereotypes 55–6
Strawson, P. F. 191 n2
strict liability 25
structural perspectives 1 n1, 31–3
subcultures 158
subjectivity 35, 54, 57–8, 75
substantive judgment 96
suicide 30, 196
Sullivan, G. R. 1 n2
Sunstein, Cass R. 125
Swedish legal system 15–17, 28–9, 33–4, 40, 84–5

Tadros, Victor 1 n2, 55–6, 63
Taub, Ken 196 n27
taxation 112
Taylor, Charles 10, 77, 86, 122 n10
Temkin, Jennifer 49
tender years doctrine 121–2
terrorism 160

theft 104–5, 167
Tomer-Fishman, Tamar 177 n1
torture 71, 82
'tough life' arguments 24
Tran, Mai 186
transport services 112
Tunick, M. 94
Tweti, Mira 189 n19

United Kingdom legal system 63, 99, 190–1
United Nations (UN) 191
United States legal system 64, 94–102, 105, 114, 128–9, 153–76, 179, 191–2, 198 n31
　Federal Female Genital Mutilation Prohibition Act 195
　Prohibition 112, 192
universalism 61, 99 n7
use of force 82
utilitarianism 79

value conflict 53
Verhovek, Sam Howe 191
viciousness of disclosed character 63
victim-offender mediation 86
Vietnamese culture 187, 189 n19
village mentality 44
violence 8, 10, 16, 50, 69, 82–3, 106, 136, 140, 142, 190, 196–8
　see also under various categories of violence
Volpp, Leti 4 n6, 49, 60, 119

Waldron, Jeremy 4 n6, 15n, 38, 84, 94 n3, 94 n4, 89 n11, 104 n, 119 n, 128, 184 n11, 192 n25
Wallace, R. J. 91, 93–6
Wanderer, Nancy A. 4 n6
Wayland, Sarah V. 189
weapons 190–1
Wechsler, Herbert 159
willful killing 82, 85
Wilson, James Q. 21, 190
Wolfenden Committee 48
women 32, 48, 64, 98, 106, 128 n20, 144, 149, 166, 175, 181–2, 187, 196
　see also domestic violence; marriage; rape
Wootton, Barbara 25, 90–91
World War II 130
wrongfulness 28–9, 37–9, 63, 70, 76, 79, 85, 98–111, 125

Yablon, Marcia 131 n28
Yemeni culture 191
Yi, Daniel 185
Young, Iris Marion 127 n15